TOP
10
LISTS

MUSIC

OVER 100 TOP 10 LISTS

TOP
10
LISTS

MUSIC
OVER 100 TOP 10 LISTS

BARNABY HARSENT

Bounty
Books

For Sarah, who not only tolerates, but encourages, my passion and has been so, so patient while I was putting this thing together; and my children, Nat and Alice – it's done now, I can come out and play!

Publisher: Samantha Warrington
Editorial & Design Manager: Emma Hill
Designer: Eoghan O'Brien
Senior Production Manager: Peter Hunt

First published in 2014 by Bounty Books,
a division of Octopus Publishing Group Ltd
Endeavour House,
189 Shaftesbury Avenue,
London WC2H 8JY
www.octopusbooks.co.uk

An Hachette UK Company
www.hachette.co.uk

ISBN: 978-0-753728-57-4

A CIP catalogue record for this book is available from the British Library

Printed and bound in China

CONTENTS

INTRODUCTION

The first music to make a real impact on my juvenile mind wasn't the sound of hushed lullabies singing me to sleep, or the strains of other peoples' music fighting to be heard in a small house. While The Jam (my brother), Kraftwerk (my sister) and Bob Dylan and Marley (my mum) all jostled for space in our semi-detached I, aged 5, had my own record collection and I was completely in its thrall. It consisted of a 7" single of the Beatles' *Sgt Peppers…* backed with 'A Day in the Life' and an album called *Spin a Magic Tune*. This was a record of surprisingly enduring funky soft-psych songs for children composed by a man called Mike McNaught and loosely based around Hannah Barbera cartoon characters of the day. My son now has this album and plays it as much as I ever did. (The Beatles 45 did not, sadly, fare so well. I sat on it and made an important childhood discovery about the maximum load-bearing capabilities of vinyl.)

Soon, *The Muppet Show LP* had been added to the collection (a special one, this – not only for its hilarious musical *tour de farce* but also, when you held it to the light, you could see quite clearly that the record was purple!) I was off – fascinated in equal measure by the transformative power of music and the joy that these peculiar objects that housed it could bring. As I grew older, I shuffled on the fringes of electro and hip-hop, was a teenage Talking Heads fanatic and became slightly too obsessed with the Cramps. Since then, I've been a fantastically unfaithful music lover, falling for grunge, indie, house, techno, folk, funk and more while holiday romances have seen me eyeing up far-flung foreign climes for increasingly exotic melodies.

Of course, the main problem with trying to rate any of this music lies in its subjective appeal – one person's sentimental schmaltz is another's wedding waltz, and who's to say which is right in their assessment? The following lists have not been arrived at using some complex algorithm to determine their absolute value, they're just an opinion, albeit one that I've taken every care to justify – at least to myself. Having said that, some could not have been compiled without the generosity of spirit shown by those willing to share their huge knowledge – both on internet forums and in person. With this in mind, I would like to thank Alan McKinnon, Andy Lewis, Kishan Patel, Paul Hillery, Merrick Gordon, Anthony Nyland and Tom Watt for their help with some of the lists herein.

Now, if you've made it this far down the introduction, well

done – you've either got way too much time on your hands or you're a *very* thorough browser. Either way, it shows commendable effort and it shall be rewarded with an Easter egg hiding in plain sight – an extra list. These are my Desert Island Discs – without which I would be a substantially different person (though to be fair, this list can be subject to near hourly change).

10 David Bowie – *Space Oddity*
9 Kraftwerk – *The Model*
8 Hashim – *Al Naafiysh (The Soul)*
7 Talking Heads – *Once In A Lifetime*
6 The Cramps – *Human Fly*
5 Dinosaur Jr – *Freak Scene*
4 Can – *Halleluhwah*
3 Ron Trent – *Altered States*
2 Glenn Underground – *Sound Struck*
1 Jean Claude Vannier – *L'Enfant Au Royaume Des Mouches*

In the spirit of sharing, I have put these up in a collaborative Spotify playlist that can be found at http://goo.gl/kxxwYK. If you are able (or indeed willing), feel free to have a listen and add your own.

BARNABY HARSENT

CHAPTER 1
ON THE STAGE

TOP 10

A vital focus point providing passion, excitement and a real sense of contact with the audience, or just an inflated ego whose delusions of grandeur get in the way of the lead guitarist and block a decent view of the drummer? Whatever your opinion, the role of a frontperson really can't be overstated. Here are 10 of the best to set foot on the stage.

FRONTMEN/WOMEN

10 IGGY POP
Rock icon Iggy – James Newell Osterberg to his parents – blurs the lines between artist and performer, or rather vaults them – he was famously the first performer to stage-dive into the crowd during a gig in Detroit, cementing his place in history, and on this list.

9 DEBBIE HARRY
Something of an anomaly on the judgmental New York punk scene, the drop-dead beauty of Blondie's singer was impossible to ignore. She was also blessed with one of the most defining voices in pop and an insouciant cool like no other.

8 JIM MORRISON
No frontman polarizes opinion quite like the Doors singer. To his fans, he was the poetic voice and spiritual figurehead of the Sixties' west-coast countercultural scene.

Good looks and a brooding stage persona helped to complete the self-proclaimed Lizard King's reputation.

7 JARVIS COCKER
In stark opposition to the classic rock stereotype, Jarvis has created a role of his own, one suspects, largely by being himself. His secret? Wit, style, charm and the ability to dance like no one's watching even when thousands are.

6 ROGER DALTREY
As one quarter of the High Numbers, Daltrey was poised to take the Mod scene by storm. As one quarter of the Who, the world was his stage, and he had the attitude, the look – and the voice – to become one of the best of all time.

5 FELA ANIKULAPO KUTI
Born in 1938, the Nigerian multi-instrumentalist and singer was an elemental

musical and political force, crucial in defining the afrobeat sound. His assured showmanship held audiences rapt – no mean feat when songs would regularly stretch to half an hour.

4 JAMES BROWN
It's one thing to have the audience in the palm of your hand, but your band as well? Dictating each note with the smallest of gestures, the Godfather of Soul was as much a conductor as frontman, in control of performance *and* reaction.

3 JANIS JOPLIN
Joplin's amazing voice and electrifying performances secure her a top 10 place despite her life being cruelly cut short at the age of 27. The Who's Pete Townshend put it best when he said, 'Even Janis on an off-night is incredible.'

2 MICK JAGGER

It was once said of the Stones frontman that he's 'forgotten more about stagecraft than most singers will ever know'. On recent evidence, it doesn't look like he's forgotten a thing however and is still able to hold his own at 70.

1 FREDDIE MERCURY

Songwriter, musician, singer... there wasn't much Freddie couldn't do, but it was in concert that he really shone. He brought a sense of theatre and drama that none has equaled. Need proof? No one bettered his 1985 Live Aid performance. No one.

	ARTIST	BAND	LISTEN TO...
10	Iggy Pop	The Stooges	The Stooges (album)
9	Debbie Harry	Blondie	Parallel Lines (album)
8	Jim Morrison	The Doors	The Doors (album)
7	Jarvis Cocker	Pulp	Different Class (album)
6	Roger Daltrey	The Who	Meaty, Beaty, Big and Bouncy (compilation)
5	Fela Anikulapo Kuti	Africa 70/Egypt 80	Expensive Shit (album)
4	James Brown	The JBs	Sex Machine (album)
3	Janis Joplin	Big Brother and the Holding Company	Cheap Thrills (album)
2	Mick Jagger	Rolling Stones	Exile on Main Street (album)
1	Freddie Mercury	Queen	A Night at the Opera (album)

TOP 10

Layering melody, texture and colour to incomplete song sketches, the best keyboard players are like accomplished painters. Quite how the analogy extends to the treatment some of the more excitable in the list mete out to their instrument of choice is unclear, but the musicians here hit all the right notes and, crucially, in the right order.

KEYBOARD WIZARDS

10 JON LORD
As part of proto-metal monsters Deep Purple, Lord could count on blues, jazz, rock and classical in his musical arsenal and used them all. Often at the same time. His unmistakable Hammond hooks are stunning, most notably on the wonderful *Hush*.

9 LONNIE LISTON SMITH
After playing alongside legends Pharoah Sanders and Miles Davis, jazz pianist Liston Smith formed his own band, The Cosmic Echoes, who delivered some of the best and most influential jazz-funk recordings ever made, including the outstanding *Expansions*.

8 BOOKER T
A child prodigy, Booker T Jones went from session player to bandleader with the MGs alongside Donald 'Duck' Dunn and Steve 'The Colonel' Cropper. The song Green Onions propelled them to fame, while his driving Hammond groove became a defining sound of the era.

7 RICHARD WRIGHT
With big personalities at the front of stage, Pink Floyd's keyboardist is easy to overlook. Never a showy player, it's his subtle touch that sets him apart. His textured, luxurious playing defined their sound just as much as Gilmour's guitar or Waters' lyrics.

6 BILLY PRESTON
One of only two musicians outside the Fab Four to be credited on a Beatles release, Billy Preston also played alongside artists including the Stones and Dylan. The influence of his light, rhythmic, gospel-infused touch on these artists' sound shouldn't be underestimated.

5 RAY MANZAREK
Devoid of a bassist for much of their career, the Doors looked to Manzarek to provide the insistent groove as well as killer hooks, something he managed with flair and elegance. Few keyboardists are so immediately identifiable, or as accomplished.

4 BERNIE WORRELL
Having written a concerto by the age of eight, it was perhaps clear that Bernie Worrell was destined for great things. Those 'things' include playing a pivotal role in the Parliament/Funkadelic line up and becoming one of the greatest funk musicians of all time.

3 STEVIE WONDER
Few keyboard players have the funk quite like Stevie. His career has been full of highlights, but if there's one reason he's here, it's the neck-snapping grooves that he created on the massive TONTO synthesizer over the course of *Innervisions* and *Talking Book*.

2 KEITH EMERSON

Tired of bandmates getting all the attention? Try stabbing your instrument! While the unorthodox use of knives supposedly given to him by Lemmy may have grabbed the headlines, you can't ignore the staggering virtuosity and versatility of the Emerson, Lake and Palmer star.

1 RICK WAKEMAN

Often dismissed for his fancy dress and gauche sense of prog-rock abandon, Rick Wakemen is, in fact, an extraordinary musician. He proved this to the world when he replaced Tony Kaye in Yes, finding fame, fortune and a fondness for fancy flourishes.

	ARTIST	BAND	LISTEN TO...
10	Jon Lord	Deep Purple	*In Rock (album)*
9	Lonnie Liston Smith	Cosmic Echoes	*Expansions (album)*
8	Booker T	The MGs	*Melting Pot (album)*
7	Richard Wright	Pink Floyd	*Meddle (album)*
6	Billy Preston	Various (The Beatles/The Rolling Stones)	*I Wrote a Simple Song (album)*
5	Ray Manzarek	The Doors	*The Doors (album)*
4	Bernie Worrell	Parliament/ Funkadelic	*Maggot Brain (album)*
3	Stevie Wonder	N/A	*Innervisions (album)*
2	Keith Emerson	Emerson, Lake & Palmer	*Brain Salad Surgery (album)*
1	Rick Wakeman	Yes	*Tales From Topographic Oceans (album)*

TOP
10

Diddly, Clapton, Hendrix... any list of the guitar greats inevitably ends up following a well-worn path. So, what about the lesser-known visionaries? People who invented a whole new sound or whose playing possesses unmistakable personality? The overlooked guitar heroes. This list celebrates the fretboard less travelled but, sadly, doesn't go to 11.

LESSER-KNOWN GUITAR GREATS

10 JONNY GREENWOOD
If he'd retired after the crunching release of Radiohead's *Creep*, he'd probably still make this list. That he didn't gives us the chance to look back on a career defined by a muscular musicality that few guitar players could ever match.

9 FREDDIE STONE
Finding room to shine between Sly Stone's psychedelic organ and Larry Graham's booming bass is a tall order. Sly and the Family Stone's Freddie Stone managed it with his choppy, scratchy style and, in doing so, has influenced a whole generation of guitarists.

8 JOEY SANTIAGO
With the Pixies' guitarist, it's all about the lead lines. His playing was as much a defining part of the Pixies' tour de force as Frank

Black's songwriting. Listen to any of their songs and it's his melodies that you end up humming.

7 PRINCE
OK so he's hardly lesser-known, but the pop legend's guitar playing is rarely mentioned and that's a crying shame. The showman's ability to effortlessly switch styles have led to comparisons with the best. Ignore them –

he's his own man. His name is Prince. And he is funky.

6 STEVE ALBINI
If Woody Guthrie's guitar could kill fascists, Steve Albini's would mow down anyone in its path. He manages to make a guitar sound like sheet metal and, while many have tried to replicate the Big Black and Shellac man's sound, none has come close.

5 J MASCIS
Take the emotive power of Neil Young, the pop nous of The Cure's Robert Smith and the noise of a hurricane jet flypast and you might be approaching the sonic assault of the Dinosaur Jr frontman. Teasing melody from chaos, his tone is achingly effortless.

4 AL MCKAY
So deep in the groove you wonder if he'll ever

climb out, the Earth Wind & Fire guitarist has a sense of rhythm and feel beyond compare. A truly progressive and underrated player who incorporates jazz, soul, pop, rock, psychedelia, blues and folk.

3 KEVIN SHIELDS

Phil Spector pioneered the wall of noise, but Kevin Shields, in his band, My Bloody Valentine, bulldozed it down with relentless, tremulous beauty. To invent a new sound is one thing, to make white noise sound so appealing is quite another.

2 RANDY CALIFORNIA

Having played wth Jimi Hendrix in Jimmy James and the Blue Flames, Randy later formed Spirit before he had turned 17. His prodigious talent didn't go unnoticed, particularly by Led Zep's Jimmy Page, who was accused of 'borrowing' heavily from the young maestro.

1 ROY BUCHANAN

A true pioneer and possibly the most influential guitarist on this list, Roy Buchanan achieved previously unheard, spine-tingling sounds using just his intuition and, on occasion, a razor blade. Years later, Jimi Hendrix had to rely on pedals to emulate his visionary style.

	ARTIST	BAND	LISTEN TO...
10	Jonny Greenwood	Radiohead	The Bends (album)
9	Freddie Stone	Sly & The Family Stone	There's a Riot Goin' On (album)
8	Joey Santiago	Pixies	Doolttle (album)
7	Prince	The Revolution/ New Power Generation/ 3rdeyegirl	Sign O' The Times (album)
6	Steve Albini	Big Black/ Rapeman	Songs About Fucking (album)
5	J Mascis	Dinosaur Jr	Bug (album)
4	Al McKay	Earth, Wind & Fire	All 'n' All (album)
3	Kevin Shields	My Bloody Valentine	Isn't Anything (album)
2	Randy California	Spirit	Twelve Dreams of Dr. Sardonicus (album)
1	Roy Buchanan	N/A	When a Guitar Plays the Blues (album)

TOP 10

The drummer is victim to a host of stereotypes. To some, they're little more than a sentient metronome – one that speeds up towards the end of songs and gets uncontrollably drunk after gigs. In most cases this isn't true – the best not only keep heads nodding, they possess a talent for the unpredictable that can cause jaws to drop.

DRUMMERS

10 TERRY COX
Pentangle drummer Terry Cox is often overlooked, perhaps because of the subtle shifts and deceptively unshowy style often displayed in folk-rock-jazz supergroup Pentangle. However, songs like *Rain and Snow, Travelling Song* and *I Saw an Angel* show a clever and adaptable mind.

9 DAVE GROHL
The Foo Fighters frontman was the pummeling force behind Nirvana. Technically brilliant, his hard-hitting style is key, yet listen again to the 'nicest man in rock'™ underpinning the riff on *Smells Like Teen Spirit* and marvel at his touch in driving the song.

8 JAKI LIEBEZEIT
NEU!'s Klaus Dinger gave Krautrock a propulsive, driving beat, but it took the genius of Can's Jaki Liebezeit to bring the swing into play, managing to meld the intellectual concerns of Can's musical manifesto with a phenomenal funk sensibility.

7 KEITH MOON
The Who's Keith Moon played like he lived – flamboyant, chaotic, exhilarating... True at times he looked like he was falling down stairs rather than keeping time, but the results were always staggering and his work on tracks like *Quadrophenia's The Real Me* still amazes.

6 CLYDE STUBBLEFIELD
You may not know the name, but you'll have heard him. Stubblefield's break on James Brown's *Funky Drummer* is one of the most sampled pieces of music ever. Quite simply, he set the standard for every funk drummer that followed.

5 JOHN BONHAM
Not many drummers could contain Page and Plant yet, no matter how heavy Led Zeppelin got (and that was, let's face it, pretty heavy), Bonham made sure they never strayed too far from the blues groove. And what a groove that was!

4 GINGER BAKER
Difficult, taciturn, aggressive... all adjectives used to describe the legendary drummer. Another is genius. The most influential drummer of his generation and possibly any other, Baker's instinctive gift has graced Graham Bond, Cream, Blind Faith and Fela Kuti among others.

3 TONY ALLEN

"Without Tony Allen there would be no afrobeat", said Fela Kuti, and he's not alone in his appreciation. Eno hailed The Africa 70 sticksman as the best ever and it's easy to see why as Allen continues to amaze with dexterity, skill and infectious grooves.

2 MAX ROACH

While wanting to avoid a top 10 populated entirely by technically amazing jazz drummers at the expense of their rock counterparts, Max Roach is a shoe in. A huge influence on Ginger Baker, there was melody and tone to his drumming like no other.

1 BUDDY RICH

Despite no formal training, jazz virtuoso Buddy Rich had it all - speed, technique, intelligence and power. Few could live up to being billed as the best in the world, but then few would have the ability to carry it off.

	ARTIST	BAND	LISTEN TO...
10	Terry Cox	Pentangle	*Basket of Light (album)*
9	Dave Grohl	Nirvana	*Nevermind (album)*
8	Jaki Liebezeit	Can	*Ege Bamyasi (album)*
7	Keith Moon	The Who	*Meaty Beaty Big and Bouncy (compilation)*
6	Clyde Stubblefield	The J.B.s	*Sex Machine (album)*
5	John Bonham	Led Zeppelin	*Led Zeppelin II (album)*
4	Ginger Baker	The Graham Bond Organisation/ Cream/Blind Faith/ Ginger Baker's Air Force	*Ginger Baker's Air Force (album)*
3	Tony Allen	Africa 70/Egypt 80/Afrobeat 2000	*Expensive Shit (album)*
2	Max Roach	N/A	*Members Don't Get Weary (album)*
1	Buddy Rich	N/A	*Buddy and Soul (album)*

TOP 10

'My spine is the bassline' sang post-punk pioneers Shriekback, and while it may sound like nonsense, they've actually got a point. The bassist provides the framework around which everything else sits and reign in the worst excesses of their bandmates with good grace and quiet authority, lest they be forced to use the two most feared words in the English language... bass solo.

BASS PLAYERS

10 ROBBIE SHAKESPEARE

With reggae's deep register, the bass takes on an added importance – particularly when you can feel it in your chest. Everyone who's anyone has called on Robbie Shakespeare for his trademark sound, but it's as part of Sly and Robbie that he's best known.

9 FLEA

Red Hot Chili Peppers bassist Flea has developed a sound uniquely his own, melding perfectly rock power and bouncing funk slap with the power and attitude of punk. He has often been emulated, but no one can capture his exhilarating tone.

8 PAUL MCCARTNEY

To many, McCartney's a songwriter first and foremost, but that is to do his bass playing a huge disservice. Always bringing melody to his perfect rhythms, it's hard to believe he only took the bass up following Stuart Sutcliffe's departure from a fledgling Beatles.

7 JOHN PAUL JONES

A well-regarded session bass player before stepping onto a stage with Led Zeppelin, John Paul Jones had played alongside Jimmy Page for years. Never flashy, he was the band's backbone and, along with Bonham, was part of arguably the best rock rhythm section ever.

6 DONALD 'DUCK' DUNN

As the bass-player of choice for the legendary Stax label, Booker T & The MGs' Dunn played on era-defining records including 'In the Midnight Hour', 'Soul Man' and 'Respect'. He knew what the song needed and nailed it every single time.

5 BERNARD EDWARDS

What can be said about the fluid, irresistible disco-funk of Chic's bassman that can't be conveyed infinitely more eloquently by simply listening to *I Want Your Love*, *Le Freak* or *Good Times*? Quite simply, he was the best disco bassist of all time.

4 BOOTSY COLLINS

As part of James Brown's backing band, it was clear Bootsy's larger-than-life personality and talent couldn't be kept in the shadows for long. Indeed, he was soon basking in the bright lights of the UFOs that were standard issue at a Funkadelic stage show.

3 JACO PASTORIUS

The bassists' bassist, Pastorius is probably most known by the general public for his work as part of the jazz-fusion group Weather Report. He played sessions with the best of the best before his life was cut tragically short at the age of 35.

2 JACK BRUCE

If you're in a band with Eric Clapton and Ginger Baker, you have to be one of the best. Despite well-publicised falling outs with Baker in the Graham Bond Organisation, Bruce's innovative lead style and innate musicality was the perfect match for Cream.

1 JOHN ENTWISTLE

Known as 'The Ox' and 'Thunderfingers', The Who's bassist, John Entwhistle, managed to produce a truly enormous sound and provide a much-needed tether for Keith Moon. He was incredibly dexterous too though, highlighted best perhaps by his famous solo from *My Generation*.

	ARTIST	BAND	LISTEN TO...
10	Robbie Shakespeare	Sly and Robbie	*Sly & Robbie Present Taxi (album)*
9	Flea	Red Hot Chilli Peppers	*Blood Sugar Sex Magik (album)*
8	Paul McCartney	The Beatles/Wings	*Revolver (album)*
7	John Paul Jones	Led Zeppelin	*Led Zeppelin II (album*
6	Donald 'Duck' Dunn	The MGs	*Melting Pot (album)*
5	Bernard Edwards	Chic	*C'est Chic (album)*
4	Bootsy Collins	Parliament/Funk-adelic/Bootsy's Rubber Band	*One Nation Under a Groove (album)*
3	Jaco Pastorius	Weather Report	*Heavy Weather (album)*
2	Jack Bruce	The Graham Bond Organisation/Cream	*Disraeli Gears (album)*
1	John Entwistle	The Who	*Meaty, Beaty, Big and Bouncy (compilation)*

TOP 10

Welsh hip-hop's Goldie Lookin' Chain's claim that, 'Guns don't kill people, rappers do' is clearly unfair. Firstly, the guns certainly have a part to play and, secondly, rappers are, on the whole, incredibly intelligent wordsmiths who have been demonized enough. This top ten celebrates the lyrical dexterity and rhythmic mastery of the very best.

RAPPERS

10 CHUCK D
Public Enemy came straight out of the gate with 1987's 'Yo! Bum Rush the Show'. An unapologetically political and confrontational record, it led the way for everything that followed. Direct and to the point, Chuck D is an angry, intelligent and important voice.

9 LL COOL J
One of the originals, LL Cool J (ladies love cool James) is a pioneer par excellence. A forthright, powerful delivery on tracks like 'Rock the Bells' and 'Mama Said Knock You Out' has seen his early work stand the test of time while much hasn't.

8 KRS ONE
Another deeply politicised lyricist, Boogie Down Production's KRS One's fierce intellect is clear to anyone lucky enough to have heard the album *By All Means Necessary*. His conflation of 'overseer' and 'officer' on 1993's 'The Sound of Da Police' is intelligent fury at its best.

7 SNOOP DOGG
Dogged by controversy stemming from a wayward past and criminal charges at the time of his first album, *Doggystyle*, Snoop, with his laid-back, melodic drawl and incredible ability to weave narrative, managed to carve out a place at the top of the game.

6 GHOSTFACE KILLAH
Arguably the best thing to come out of the revolutionary hip-hop crew Wu-Tang Clan, Ghostface Killah has also been incredibly prolific since 1996's *Ironman*. That his husky, guttural delivery has graced so many releases without sacrificing quality is an incredible feat.

5 MF DOOM
The masked man's lyrical flow is truly astounding. With a sense of the absurd and a facility for language that knows no bounds, Doom can – and does – make the mundane sound truly thrilling with a charming, childlike sense of abandon.

4 PHAROAHE MONCH
A one-time member of Organized Konfusion, Pharoah Monch showed a much more aggressive and hard-hitting style with 1999's solo debut 'Simon Says'. Crucially though, he never sacrificed his trademark timing, clever cadence and intricate rhymes that mark him out as one of the best.

3 RAKIM
Regarded as one of the most skillful MCs of all time, Rakim's place in the top 10 is assured. Rapping largely about what he knew best – himself – Rakim spoke with a considered and measured approach that was rare in 1986.

2 NAS

Debuts don't come stronger than Nas's 1994 album *Illmatic*, which arrived with the confident, lyrical swagger you might expect from an established star. Using some of the best producers available, Nas has continued to stay on top with his assured and literate approach.

1 THE NOTORIOUS B.I.G

Sadly, Biggie Smalls is remembered by most for his very public spat with Tupac Shakur and his early death, reflecting the violence he talked about in his music. He was, however, a masterful wordsmith and a clear contender for best rapper of all time.

	ARTIST	LISTEN TO...
10	Chuck D	*It Takes a Nation of Millions (album)*
9	LL Cool J	*Rock the Bells (album)*
8	KRS One	*By All Means Necessary (album)*
7	Snoop Dogg	*Doggystyle (album)*
6	Ghostface Killah	*Fishscale (album)*
5	MF Doom	*The Mouse and the Mask (album)*
4	Pharaohe Monch	*Internal Affairs (album)*
3	Rakim	*Paid in Full (album)*
2	Nas	*Illmatic (album)*
1	The Notorious B.I.G	*Ready to Die (album)*

TOP
10

Take one part melancholic melodies and two parts beat-heavy back line. Add a dash of laconic bass work and sprinkle liberally with feeling. Explaining what makes a country funk classic is nigh-on impossible, but you know it when you hear it – suddenly your head's moving and there's a smile on your face. These songs manage that and plenty more besides.

COUNTRY FUNK

10 DOLLY PARTON – 'JOLENE'
OK so it might not be technically funky, but there's a groove to this song that is undeniable and rare for such a popular hit. It's a phenomenal piece of writing and, if you haven't heard already, sounds great at 33 as well as 45rpm.

9 JERRY REED – 'OH WHAT A WOMAN'
While the lyrics to this patronizing ode belong to a time long gone, the combination of stuttering, scratchy guitar, lazy, rolling drums and lolloping bass will never grow old. So good Glen Campbell recorded a more up-tempo version on his Galveston LP.

8 THE BYRDS – 'FIDO'
This Ballad of Easy Rider album track is a perfectly pleasant tale of a stray dog until 1 minute 15 seconds in, when drummer Gene Parsons interrupts proceedings with exactly the sort of muscular funk you might expect of the Incredible Bongo Band. Nice!

7 BOBBIE GENTRY – 'FANCY'
With a rare talent for storytelling through song, Bobbie Gentry is a country legend. While Ode to Billie Joe may be more well-known, it lacks the percussive persuasiveness and killer horn stabs this tale of survival against the odds boasts.

6 JAKI WHITREN – 'NEW HORIZON'
Recorded when she was just 19 years old, this cut of Whitren's Raw and Tender LP has a sense of authority that belies her years. The guitar, banjo and voice are all Jaki's, but a mention also has to go to drummer Gerry Conway.

5 DON COOPER – 'BLESS THE CHILDREN'
Criminally underrated, Don Cooper's output was so consistent he should be a household name. The interplay between the shuffling drums, bouncing bass and his perfectly delivered vocals is typical, making this just one of many tracks that could hold a top 10 place.

4 TONY JOE WHITE – 'SOUL FRANCISCO'
They don't come funkier - or countrier - than Tony Joe. His voice sounds like a drunk Elvis on the wrong end of 40 Marlboro, while his guitar playing manages to sound bright, sharp and relaxed all at the same time. A neat trick.

3 LINK WRAY – 'FIRE AND BRIMSTONE'
As the title suggests, this is a big song. Big in scope, big in sound, big in drums. It's off the legendary guitarists 1971 album and, although not well-received at the time, has since been

covered by the Neville Brothers and Nick Cave.

2 DENNIS THE FOX - 'PILEDRIVER'
From the 1975 LP Mother Trucker, this
track begins almost like a out-and-out funk tune
with the beat-heavy, locked down drums and
mellow Hammond sound. Then comes the voice
sounding simultaneously out-of-its-time and
utterly perfect.

1 JIM FORD – 'I'M GOING TO MAKE HER LOVE ME'
A simple, powerful but effective backbeat sets
the tone before the wonderful melody of the
refrain comes in with such startling confidence
you end up believing there's nothing Jim Ford
couldn't make love him simply by singing at it.

	ARTIST	SONG	ALBUM
10	Dolly Parton	'Jolene'	*Jolene*
9	Jerry Reed	'Oh What a Woman!'	*Oh What a Woman!*
8	The Byrds	'Fido'	*The Ballad of Easy Rider*
7	Bobbie Gentry	'Fancy'	*Fancy*
6	Jaki Whitren	'New Horizon'	*Raw but Tender*
5	Don Cooper	'Bless the Children'	*Bless the Children*
4	Tony Joe White	'Soul Francisco'	*Black and White*
3	Link Wray	'Fire and Brimstone'	*Link Wray*
2	Dennis the Fox	'Piledriver'	*Mother Trucker*
1	Jim Ford	'I'm Going to Make Her Love Me'	*Harlan County*

As the Sixties rolled on and boundaries blurred between genres, new ones emerged. Of these, folk-rock was one of the broadest, including as it did rock acts who took their influences from the folk scene as well as folk musicians who plugged in, turned on and tuned up. Both are featured in this top 10.

FOLK ROCK

10 TREES
A band for whom commercial success proved elusive at the time, Trees' two 1970 albums, *The Garden of Jane Delawney* and *On the Shore* have retrospectively become classics of the genre with a heavier feel than most and a distinctive, psychedelic edge.

9 BUFFALO SPRINGFIELD
Along with The Byrds, Buffalo Springfield led the way for both folk rock and country rock in the States. Not as steeped in traditional music as their British counterparts, the light acoustic lilt of songs like 'For What it's Worth' had huge impact.

8 ESPERS
Greg Weeks' band are the only contemporary inclusion on this list but more than hold their own in such illustrious company. Their intense 2004 self-titled debut set the bar high with melancholic melody and psychedelic flourishes, but they've more than maintained the standard.

7 MELLOW CANDLE
The band's only album, *Swaddling Songs*, is a beautiful collection, made all the more extraordinary when you consider they were just 19 and 20 at the time of its 1972 release. Ignored then, it's become regarded as a classic, and rightly so.

6 CLANNAD
Forget the dreamy wash of Harry's Game for a moment, as it's Clannad's first two albums that have got them here. More folk than rock, there are nonetheless some truly great grooves, most notably on *Nil Sé Ina Iá* and *Dheanainn Súgradh*.

5 STEELEYE SPAN
When Fairport's Ashley Hutchings wanted a more traditional sound, he left to form Steeleye Span. Although best known for *All Around My*

Hat, it's their first two albums, *Hark! The Village Wait* and *Please to See the King* that stand up best today.

4 THE BYRDS

Combining folk music with the Sixties pop sound of the time might not seem like a big deal now, but when The Byrds took an Old Testament passage that had been set to music by Pete Seeger and came up with 'Turn, Turn, Turn', it was visionary.

3 PENTANGLE

Something of a folk supergroup, Pentangle consisted of guitarists Bert Jansch and John Renbourn, drummer Terry Cox, bassist Danny Thompson and the then unknown singer Jacquie McShee. The influence of their unique combination of folk, jazz and rock has never waned.

2 FAIRPORT CONVENTION

After a debut LP with a fairly transatlantic sound, Fairport looked closer to home for inspiration. This reached a pinnacle with their *Liege and Lief* album, where they combined traditional English folk and electric instruments, most notably on Tam Lin and Matty Groves.

1 BOB DYLAN

When Bob Dylan picked up an electric guitar at the Newport Festival, it was seen as an act of betrayal. It wasn't, of course, he simply wanted to push the boundaries of what he could do. While he led, others were born to follow.

	ARTIST	LISTEN TO...
10	Trees	'On the Shore'
9	Buffalo Springfield	'Buffalo Springfield Again'
8	Espers	'Espers'
7	Mellow Candle	'Swaddling Songs'
6	Clannad	'Clannad 2'
5	Steeleye Span	'Hark! The Village Wait'
4	The Byrds	'Mr Tambourine Man'
3	Pentangle	'Basket of Light'
2	Fairport Convention	'Liege and Leaf'
1	Bob Dylan	'Bringing it All Back Home'

TOP 10

To many, fusion represents the very worst excesses of rock and jazz conveniently put together in one place so it's easier to ignore. They're missing out however on some inspiring and incredibly rewarding music for, once you get past the tricky time signatures and extended solos, there's beauty in them there albums.

FUSION FLINGS

8 FRANK ZAPPA – *HOT RATS*

Proving that fusion can be fun is the irreverent wit of Frank Zappa. This album, his first after the Mothers of Invention fell apart, is largely instrumental but tracks like *Peaches in Regalia* and *Willie the Pimp* manage to be both complex and immediate.

7 SOFT MACHINE – *THIRD*

A band that had several marked shifts in their style during their career, Third is, arguably, the most stark of these. On the original vinyl release, each side is a song (a fairly weighty statement of intent), but holds the interest with superb interplay and dynamics.

10 GARY BURTON – *GOOD VIBES*

After his work with the Gary Burton Quartet, who predated the fusion scene with their mix of disparate influences, came this beauty. The distorted, rock sound of the vibraphone and the loose, almost unhinged feel on tracks like Vibrafinger mark this out as essential.

9 ENERGIT – *S/T LP*

Not what you would call a well-known album, sure, but this self-titled album by the Czech band is an under-the-radar classic. Made up of just five tracks, including the epic 'Ráno (Part 1)', this is a relaxed, confident and very clever record indeed.

6 NUCLEUS – *ELASTIC ROCK*

Having left the Rendell-Carr Quartet, Ian Carr went on to form Nucleus with,

among others, versatile session guitarist Chris Spedding. This was their first album and is a defining one for jazz-rock, with 1916 'The Battle of Boogaloo' a particular favourite.

5 WEATHER REPORT – *BLACK MARKET*
While *Heavy Weather* may have been a commercial high point for the band this, the first album to feature bass player Jaco Pastorius

is, in truth, far more interesting, drawing, as it does, on African influences for its often drum heavy instrumentals.

4 BILLY COBHAM – *SPECTRUM*
An absolute classic of the genre, this album from drummer Billy Cobham came as the band he played in - Mahavishnu Orchestra - was starting to fade. It boasts some great guest

players, including Jan Hammer and is, in parts, a deeply funky affair.

3 HERBIE HANCOCK – *MWANDISHI*

After his experience playing with Miles Davis on 'In a Silent Way', Herbie Hancock took influences from far and wide. A wonderful record of odd grooves and exciting tension, it is uncompromising, beguiling and completely successful.

2 THE MAHAVISHNU ORCHESTRA WITH JOHN MCLAUGHLIN – *THE INNER MOUNTING FLAME*

The mercurial playing of John McLaughlin is intense and dynamic, as you might expect from the protégé who had recently worked with Miles Davis, but he's ably backed up by possibly the best band of its type.

1 MILES DAVIS – *IN A SILENT WAY*

Almost like an ambient album in parts, this is a recording of understated beauty and subtle musicality. It was a controversial release at the time, with both the rock and jazz audiences unsure about the direction. It has, quite rightly, become a classic.

	ARTIST	LISTEN TO...
10	Gary Burton	'Good Vibes'
9	Energit	'Energit'
8	Frank Zappa	'Hot Rats'
7	Soft Machine	'Third'
6	Nucleus	'Elastic Rock'
5	Weather Report	'Black Market'
4	Billy Cobham	'Spectrum'
3	Herbie Hancock	'Mwandishi'
2	The Mahavishnu Orchestra with John McLaughlin	'The Inner Mounting Flame'
1	Miles Davis	'In a Silent Way'

TOP
10

What makes a classic girl group? There's the songs, of course – you've got to have the hits, perfect pop but not too saccharine. And there's the image too... but there's something else, it's getting the mix right. Making sure that there's the perfect blend of voices and personality to keep the customer satisfied and the bands' egos in check.

GIRL GROUPS

10 GIRLS ALOUD
The winners of the UK TV show *Popstars: The Rivals* in 2002 confounded their critics by releasing a string of clever, sophisticated pop hits and ruling the British charts for a decade – which is like a century in pop years.

9 THE MARVELLETES
Not the best-known girl group, but hugely significant nonetheless – their 1961 No.1, a rendition of *Please Mr Postman* for the Tamla label, was the first Motown chart topper. Sadly, they ended up in a head-to-head career battle with The Supremes. They lost.

8 THE SHIRELLES
Schoolfriends discovered at a high-school talent show in 1957, their doo wop/pop cross gave them several hits including the timeless classic *Will You Love Me Tomorrow*, and pretty much invented the sound that

dominated girl groups for more than a decade.

7 THE SHANGRI-LAS
In an age of demure smiles and prom dresses, the Shangri-Las were like a slap in the face. Their look, and reputation as girls from the wrong side of the street, was a world away from anyone else.

Their career may have faded, their impact has not.

6 THE RONETTES
It was a phone call from Estelle Bennett to Phil Spector that launched one of the greatest girl groups of the Sixties. They had released records, but to no fanfare. The unique blend of their voices, his

WALKING IN THE RAIN
HOW DOES IT FEEL
THE RONETTES

RONETTES RECORDS – A Division of Phil Spector Productions

production and certified pop classics proved a surefire hit.

5 TLC
Taking up the challenge set by En Vogue, Lisa 'Left Eye' Lopez and co. released their 1993 album *CrazySexyCool*, which gave them the worldwide hit 'Waterfalls'. However, it was

1999 when they hit heights that few could hope to reach with the towering *No Scrubs*.

4 EN VOGUE
En Vogue combined talent, power and style without compromise and bagged hit singles and awards as if for fun. 'My Lovin' (You're Never Gonna Get It)' and 'Free Your Mind' broke new ground

and caused everyone – male and female alike – to raise their game.

3 SPICE GIRLS
Making no secret of the thinking behind their marketing, Sporty, Scary, Baby, Ginger and Posh became the biggest selling girl group of all time. That they did so on the back of some genuinely

brilliant pop songs is to their eternal credit.

2 DESTINY'S CHILD

The Beyoncé-fronted group conquered the planet during the late Nineties and Noughties – first with global hits such as 'Say My Name', 'Survivor' and 'Independent Women' and then with that Bootylicious dance. Sixty million albums sold. Reputation guaranteed.

1 THE SUPREMES

During the mid-Sixties there were few who could touch the Supremes' popularity as hit after hit kept Diana Ross, Mary Wilson and Florence Ballard at the top. However, when Berry Gordy appointed Ross leader, the balance was upset and the rot set in...

	ARTIST	COUNTRY	YEARS ACTIVE
10	Girls Aloud	UK	2002-13
9	The Marvelletes	USA	1960-70
8	The Shirelles	USA	1957-82
7	The Shangri-Las	USA	1963-68
6	The Ronettes	USA	1959-66
5	TLC	USA	1990-present
4	En Vogue	USA	1989-present
3	Spice Girls	UK	1994-2000/2007-8/2012
2	Destiny's Child	USA	1990-2006
1	The Supremes	USA	1959-1997

TOP 10

The secret to a successful boy band is as difficult to pin down as the perfect football team formation. Obviously, you play your star striker up front, but what then? A flat-back-four of pretty backing singers? Or do you go for a diamond formation with a supersub occasionally stepping up to shine? The following bands all got it spot on.

BOY BANDS

10 WESTLIFE
Inspiring utter devotion in their fans, it's clear that Westlife, never the most fashionable of bands, got something very right indeed. Their boy-next-door charm coupled with ballads composed with laser-like efficiency made for a winning combination.

9 BOYZONE
After a hilariously ramshackle debut on Ireland's *Late Late Show*, Boyzone went on to become one of the most successful boy bands in the UK. Unlike many groups, they seemed to genuinely like each other, which made the untimely death of Stephen Gately all the sadder.

8 ONE DIRECTION
The young pretenders in an all-time top 10? Well yes – they've earned it and then some. They're about as successful as it's possible for singers to be having worked tirelessly across America and the UK, and their tourbus shows no sign of slowing down.

7 NEW EDITION
The forerunners to the modern US boyband, New Edition's 1983 hit *Candy Girl* was as infectious as pop can be. It's the legacy that's important here though; the band launched Bobby Brown, Bel Biv Devoe and the New Jack Swing sound.

6 EAST 17
If Take That were the band you could take home to meet mum, East 17... weren't. The bad boy image didn't hamper their appeal – or their sales – but may have distracted from the fact that Tony Mortimer is a gifted and smart songwriter.

5 THE MONKEES
The original boy band, put together for a TV show, they had it all – hits, screaming fans, fame and fortune. Eventually, they wanted control and, despite record company fears the hits would dry up, it worked. Monkees - 1, The Man - 0.

4 TAKE THAT
With great songs and cheeky grins, Take That took the pop world by surprise. The devastation when they announced their split after six years showed how important they had become, as did the response to their comeback nearly 10 years later.

3 NEW KIDS ON THE BLOCK

Formed as a response to the success of New Edition, it wasn't until their second album, *Hangin' Tough*, that things started to happen for the band. What ensued was full-blown mania, with fans able to buy everything from dolls to NKOTB lunchboxes.

2 BACKSTREET BOYS

Theirs was not an overnight success and the boys put in the hours getting there. However, when they did, it was in style. 'I Want It That Way', 'Quit Playing Games' and 'Backstreet's Back' helped them to become the most successful boy band of all time.

1 JACKSON 5

Their impact was simply extraordinary. It seems strange to imagine it in an age of internet connectedness, but the Jacksons were everywhere when all they had was TV, radio and the papers. And those songs... Hell, best boyband? They may well be best band.

	ARTIST	COUNTRY	YEARS ACTIVE
10	Westlife	UK	1998-2012
9	Boyzone	UK	1993-2000 2008-present
8	One Direction	UK	2010-present
7	New Edition	USA	1978-1989 1996-1997 2002-present
6	East 17	UK	1991-1997 1998-1999 2006-present
5	The Monkees	USA	1966–1971, 1986–1989, 1993–1997, 2001–2002, 2010–present
4	Take That	UK	1990–1996 2005–present
3	New Kids on the Block	USA	1984–1994 2008–present
2	Backstreet Boys	USA	1993–present
1	The Jackson 5	USA	1964–1989, 2001, 2012–present

TOP 10

Music forces us all to be subjective. There are times when we grow to love a song – our judgments inevitably clouded by association and coloured by memories. There are others, however, where a tune sounds so immediately perfect, so right, that it's like it's been there forever just waiting to be unearthed. Like these for instance...

POP PERFECTION

10 EVERLEY BROTHERS – 'BYE BYE LOVE'

Written by Felice and Boudleaux Bryant, this song clearly struck a chord with the record-buying public of 1957. Don and Phil Everly's definitive version of the song, with its utter earworm of a chorus, propelled them to fame and fortune.

9 HUMAN LEAGUE – 'DON'T YOU WANT ME'

Probably the most hummed bassline in the whole of pop music, 1981's huge statement of intent by what was left of Human League, following the original line up splitting in two, showed a band reaching for pop perfection and grabbing it with ease.

8 DAVID BOWIE – 'LET'S DANCE'

This 1983 release came as something of a shock to many David Bowie's fans, particularly after the comparatively downbeat Scary Monsters. To everyone else however, it was an example of what can happen when someone gets the pop formula exactly right.

7 OUTKAST! – 'HEY YA!'

The rap duo may not have been most people's first bet for catchiest song of the Noughties, but Hey Ya was typical of their ambition and scope on their album *Speakerboxxx/The Love Below*. A timeless song and as catchy as chicken pox.

6 BRITNEY SPEARS – 'TOXIC'

It was always going to be a toss-up between this and 'Baby One More Time', though Britney's got more than a few instant pop classics up her sleeve. In short, Toxic wins for its mix of sophisticated melody, exotic strings and echo-drenched guitar.

5 THE RONETTES – 'BE MY BABY'

Phil Spector composed and produced this hit with customary flair and it's often

cited as the best example of his 'wall of sound' technique. That is coupled with a phenomenal vocal performance and those melodies, full of tension and resolution.

4 BEACH BOYS – 'GOOD VIBRATIONS'
Possibly the oddest pop song here, the sudden shifts in tempo and tone could prove a tricky listen. It's down to the genius of Brian Wilson and the pop sensibilities of Mike Love that it works. And the theremin, don't forget that.

3 THE MONKEES – 'I'M A BELIEVER'
A hit for The Monkees, it's actually a Neil Diamond song and one he occasionally performs live. It's easy to see why he'd want to keep ownership of it, but The Monkees' version - all

wide-eyed wonder and sunny optimism - wins out.

2 MICHAEL JACKSON – 'BILLIE JEAN'
Narrowing down Jackson's talent for immediate pop to one song *should* be difficult. 'Billie Jean' however, with its minor-key melody and rolling bass is almost impossible not to like. That 'Thriller' producer Quincy Jones thought it a weak link is gobsmacking.

1 ABBA – 'DANCING QUEEN'
Had you grown up in a forest, with no electricity, company or formal understanding of language, you'd still be singing along within 30 seconds of hearing 'Dancing Queen' for the first time. That's the genius of Benny, Björn, Agnetha and Anni-Frid for you.

	ARTIST	SONG
10	Everley Brothers	'Bye Bye Love'
9	The Human League	'Don't You Want Me?'
8	David Bowie	'Let's Dance'
7	Outkast!	'Hey Ya!'
6	Britney Spears	'Toxic'
5	The Ronettes	'Be My Baby'
4	The Beach Boys	'Good Vibrations'
3	The Monkees	'I'm a Believer'
2	Michael Jackson	'Billie Jean'
1	ABBA	'Dancing Queen'

TOP 10

'Can you see the real me?' sang Roger Daltrey. When it comes to these masters of disguise, the answer is a resounding 'no'. Popular music has always been about image, and performance through the ages has featured masks of all kinds. The most successful performers are acutely aware of this and have learnt how to use it to stunning effect.

MUSICAL PERSONAE

10 *SGT PEPPER'S LONELY HEARTS CLUB BAND*

When a whole band creates another persona, it had better be good. This was, and heralded one of the most important concept LPs of the Sixties. Although lasting for only one album, the image of Sgt Peppers-era Beatles is a truly iconic image.

9 MF DOOM

Still an underground figure to many, hip-hop's surreal genius is identifiable only by his metal mask (inspired by the Marvel character Dr Doom). It's one of Daniel Dumile's many alter egos, but the freedom it offers him make it one of the best there is.

8 AFRIKA BAMBAATAA

The elaborate name and image adopted by Kevin Donovan was a personal reinvention that defines him as a true original. He left the Black Spades street gang and adopted his Zulu moniker (Bambaataa means 'affectionate leader'), to unleash his pioneering electro on the world.

7 OZZY OSBOURNE

One of the biggest rock stars ever, Ozzy's on-stage persona has, at times, been difficult to separate from his off-stage behaviour. This blurring of lines is perhaps one of the reasons his persona was so successful, but also explains his one-time destructive tendencies.

6 INSANE CLOWN POSSE

Winning the 'jumping in with both feet' award is this US duo. The horrorcore hip hop act's sheer dedication to their own mythology means it's almost impossible to know where the theatre stops – they are also a professional wrestling tag team!

5 KISS

The evil cartoon creations taken up by US rock band inspired fans and media alike. As time mellowed characters and music alike, Marvel jumped in with a Kiss comic before NBC released a feature-length cartoon. It really doesn't get much bigger.

4 SLIM SHADY

When Eminem's crazed alter ego appeared, it was a stroke of (evil) genius. It gave the rapper the ability to lash out lyrically while also maintaining a degree of artistic distance from the words. Oh, and it made him an international superstar too.

3 ALICE COOPER

The fake blood, the snakes, the make-up... the world of Alice Cooper is pure theatre. It's a character so enduring that, while most choose to keep reinventing themselves, Vincent Furnier has been slapping on the make-up and reaching for the guillotine for nearly 50 years.

2 MADONNA — VARIOUS GUISES

Always different, yet always Madonna. Understanding, like David Bowie, the need to constantly reinvent her image, Madonna Ciccone does it better than almost anyone. Combining stark shifts in style with a deft knack of hiring cutting-edge producers, she has led the way for decades.

1 ZIGGY STARDUST

David Bowie is a man of many parts, but none quite as remarkable as the lightning flashed face of Ziggy Stardust. The androgynous, egotistical rock-star creation may have been short lived, but its musical and cultural impact is still felt today.

	ARTIST	PERSONAE	LISTEN TO...
10	The Beatles	Sgt Pepper's Lonely Hearts Club Band	Sgt Pepper's Lonely Hearts Club Band (album)
9	Daniel Dumille	MF Doom	Mm... Food (album)
8	Kevin Donovam	Afrika Bambaataa	'Planet Rock'
7	John Michael Osbourne	Ozzy Osbourne	Black Sabbath (album)
6	Joseph Bruce/ Joseph Utsler	Insane Clown Posse	The Amazing Jeckel Brothers (album)
5	Paul Stanley/Gene Simmons/Ace Frehley/Peter Criss (original line up)	Kiss	Alive! (album)
4	Eminem (Marshall Mathers)	Slim Shady	The Slim Shady (album)
3	Vince Furnier	Alice Cooper	School's Out (album)
2	Madonna	Various guises	The Immaculate Collection (compilation)
1	David Bowie	Ziggy Stardust	The Rise of Ziggy Stardust and the Spiders of Mars (album)

TOP 10

'We are family!' Sister Sledge's triumphant declaration stands as a show of strength, a defiant declaration to the world that together they are stronger than they would be alone. Is this true? The following examples suggest that, for some at least, keeping it in the family could be a very good thing indeed...

MUSICAL FAMILIES

10 THE OSMONDS Considered a joke in some quarters, family group and TV favourites The Osmonds smuggled some real quality among the pop hits that gave them worldwide adulation. There's 'Crazy Horses', obviously, but listen to 'Traffic in My Mind' as well and prepare for a shock.

9 OASIS It's unclear how the relationship between the famously warring Gallagher brothers affected Oasis' music other than at gigs, where no-shows and mid-gig walkouts illustrated how sibling rivalry can boil over even when you're both in one of the biggest bands on the planet.

8 JESUS & MARY CHAIN One of the most revolutionary bands in British rock history, brothers Jim and William Reid created a tense, angry and chaotic sound unlike anything that had gone before that seemed to stem directly

from their volatile - and often violent - relationship.

7 THE CARPENTERS Brother and sister Richard and Karen were one of the best pop duos of all time. Before Karen's death at the age of just 32, they had amassed hits including a John Lennon-endorsed cover of 'Ticket to Ride' and proved themselves phenomenal musicians.

6 JACKSON 5 The chemistry between this band of brothers made them one of pop's all-time greats. Growing up in public is tricky though and, behind the smiles and showy stagecraft, inevitable resentment began to simmer particularly as Michael's solo star started to rise.

5 KINKS More musical brothers, another tricky relationship that produced fantastic music. Perhaps it was creative tension that sparked some of their most enduring hits but, crucially, the warring between Ray Davies and younger brother Dave never managed to drown out the songs.

4 THE BEACH BOYS
'I may not always love you,' sang Carl Wilson in his brother Brian's song 'God Only Knows' and there isn't a better examination of family ties – or band dynamics – in pop. Three brothers, one cousin and a friend who took the world by storm.

3 BEE GEES
The brothers Gibb formed a group where perfect harmony, particularly when set against a driving disco backbeat, was to gain them worldwide popularity. Although 'Saturday Night

Fever' was a commercial high point, they already had a fine body of work behind them.

2 SISTER SLEDGE
The archetypal sibling act, not least due to the all-encompassing popularity of their 1979 hit 'We Are Family', Sister Sledge's Chic-produced, pop-disco breakthrough, ensured huge and lasting success. And, apart from the departure of Kathy, they've stayed together through it all.

1 THE ISLEY BROTHERS
No dramas, no public spats, no shortage of hits. Five brothers have passed through the ranks of this band, whose career is so diverse it defies categorization. The one constant has been quality, from their gospel beginnings to the smooth funk of 'Summer Breeze'.

	ARTIST	YEARS ACTIVE
10	The Osmonds	1958-present
9	Oasis	1991-2009
8	The Jesus & Mary Chain	1983–1999, 2007–present
7	The Carpenters	1969–1983
6	The Jackson 5	1964–1989, 2001, 2012–present
5	The Kinks	1963–1996
4	The Beach Boys	1961–present
3	Bee Gees	1958-2003, 2009-2012
2	Sister Sledge	1971–present
1	The Isley Brothers	1954–present

TOP
10

It could be the genes, learnt behaviour or just the luck of the draw, but there seems to be a lot of rock stars whose children end up following them into the business – whether they have the requisite talent or not. Having said that, often the good example set for them pays off...

ROCK STAR CHILDREN

10 JULIAN/SEAN LENNON
John's boys have split the judges, so they've been included as a two-for-one. Julian, from John's first marriage to Cynthia, and Sean, who's mum is Yoko Ono, have never managed to achieve the fame of their father, but then, who could?

9 MILEY CYRUS
The daughter of country star Billy Ray Cyrus made the transition from child TV star to pop star seamlessly enough with a string of hits. More recently, she's hit the big time, but who knows what Billy must think of that 'Wrecking Ball' video?

8 CHARLOTTE GAINSBOURG
After a controversial start to Charlotte's career, aged 12, when she sang with her father, Serge, on the risqué 'Lemon Incest', there was a

20-year gap before 5.55 – an assured album on which she collaborated with French band Air and Jarvis Cocker.

7 MARTHA WAINWRIGHT/RUFUS WAINWRIGHT
Rather than have the children of folk singer Loudon Wainwright III and Kate McGarrigle each occupy a space on the list, we've put them together. Both acclaimed singer-songwriters, both from musical royalty, both utterly deserving of a top 10 spot.

6 NORAH JONES
One of Ravi Shankar's two musician daughters (his other, Anoushka, is an award-winning sitar player), Norah's soft, jazz-inflected style has won her nine Grammys during a recording career that included the enormous 2002 hit album *Come Away with Me*.

5 NENEH CHERRY
Taking the surname of her stepfather, jazz musician Don Cherry, Neneh first found fame in 1988 with singles including *Buffalo Stance* and *Manchild*, and continues to produce outstanding work including 2012's *The Cherry Thing* and 2014's *The Blank Project*.

4 ZIGGY MARLEY
Bob's eldest son, Ziggy, has carried on the family tradition with huge success. His brother, Stephen, has also managed to grab a Grammy or nine along the way too, but Ziggy edges it for having written the music to the children's show, *Arthur*.

3 FEMI KUTI
While some claim that it is Seun Kuti, who performs with his father's old band, the Egypt 80, who is the rightful heir to the afrobeat crown, it is eldest son Femi who has

gained the international plaudits. In truth, both are worthy successors.

2 **JEFF BUCKLEY**
The singer-songwriter followed in dad Tim's footsteps with a career in the music business – a career that produced the breathtaking album *Grace*. Sadly, his life was to mirror his father's in other ways too, and he died in 1997 aged just 30.

1 **NANCY SINATRA**
Keeping up the family tradition, Nancy was both singer and actress. Her best known moment is undoubtedly the 1966 hit, 'These Boots Are Made for Walkin'', but it's the albums she recorded with Lee Hazlewood that impress the most.

	ARTIST	PARENT(S)
10	Julian/Sean Lennon	John Lennon
9	Miley Cyrus	Billy Ray Cyrus
8	Charlotte Gainsbourg	Serge Gainsbourg and Jane Birkin
7	Martha Wainwright/Rufus Wainwright	Loudon Wainwright III and Kate McGarrigle
6	Norah Jones	Ravi Shankar
5	Neneh Cherry	Don Cherry (stepfather)
4	Ziggy Marley	Bob Marley
3	Femi Kuti	Fela Kuti
2	Jeff Buckley	Tim Buckley
1	Nancy Sinatra	Frank Sinatra

TOP 10

One of the most potentially controversial categories as everyone has their favourite gig. The one where they met their partner, finally getting to see their most-loved band… and that's exactly the point when compiling a list like this – context becomes everything and the word 'best' is rendered redundant.

GREAT GIGS

10 SEX PISTOLS – RIVER THAMES 1977

Not really a gig as such but, in the spirit of things, let's be controversial, shall we? On the Queen's Silver Jubilee, 7th June 1977, the Sex Pistols set sail on the Thames to play their anti-monarchy anthem 'God Save the Queen'.

9 THE VELVET UNDERGROUND & NICO, THE EXPLODING PLASTIC INEVITABLE, 1966-7

A series of 'happenings' organized by pop artist Andy Warhol, these included screenings of films and multimedia performances by artists including the Velvet Underground and Nico. The raw, vital energy of these shows is still talked about today.

8 STONE ROSES – SPIKE ISLAND 1990

Another gig beset by problems both with sound and organization (not least the decision to hold it on a reclaimed toxic waste site), the Roses' 1990 folly has, nonetheless, achieved near mythical status for its cultural significance alone - and quite right.

7 PULP – GLASTONBURY 1995

When the Stone Roses pulled out of 1995's Glastonbury festival, Pulp, whose hit single 'Common People' had been released the month before, stepped up. Their amazing performance won over a potentially difficult crowd and marked their arrival in the big league.

6 BEATLES – APPLE STUDIOS ROOFTOP GIG 1969

Although they had stopped gigging in 1966, this seemingly impromptu gig in central London was the Fab Four's last public performance. With 'fifth Beatle' Billy Preston on keyboards, they gave shoppers a bargain with a free concert before police called a halt.

5 LAST GIG OF THE ZIGGY STARDUST TOUR 1973

It was at the Hammersmith Odeon Theatre, London on the 3rd July 1973 that David Bowie announced the retirement of Ziggy Stardust. It came as a huge shock to fans, the majority of the press and, unfortunately, most of his band, too.

4 NIRVANA – READING 1992

In three years, Nirvana had gone from playing a small room at London's School of Oriental and African Studies to headlining one of the biggest festivals in Britain. The gig was blistering, one of their best and, sadly, their last in Britain.

3 JIMI HENDRIX – WOODSTOCK 1969

With delays and hitches, by the time Hendrix stepped on stage to close the Woodstock festival it was 9.00am on Monday morning, half of the audience had left and there were people collecting litter. Even so, it was a jaw-dropping performance.

2 BOB DYLAN – NEWPORT FOLK FESTIVAL 1965

The moment that broke a thousand folk fans' hearts has to go down as a landmark moment. In truth, the gig itself was short and the sound not great, but Dylan's insistence on playing with an amplified band changed everything.

1 LIVE AID 1985

Now this might seem a bit of a cheat - it's about a thousand gigs in one, but the sheer scale of the live culmination of Bob Geldof's fundraising project was staggering. Not just a gig, more a worldwide cultural phenomenon.

	ARTIST	VENUE
10	Sex Pistols	River Thames, London
9	The Velvet Underground & Nico	(Various) The Exploding Plastic Inevitable
8	The Stone Roses	Spike Island
7	Pulp	Glastonbury
6	The Beatles	Apple studios rooftop, London
5	David Bowie	Hammersmith Odeon, London
4	Nirvana	Reading Festival
3	Jimi Hendrix	Woodstock
2	Bob Dylan	Newport Folk Festival
1	Live Aid	Various

TOP
10

Time to put pen to paper and create your own top 10 list of gigs you've been to/wished you'd been to...

10

9

8

7

6

5

4

3

2

1

TOP
10

Tickets to see your favourite band lose something of value if they're playing in a venue so big you can barely see them. Similarly, it's nice to know that the small details are taken care of, like basic sanitation and fire exits. Thankfully, the world is full of phenomenal venues – and not all of them obvious.

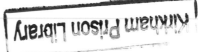

GIG VENUES

10 EFFENAAR, EINDHOVEN

Opened in 1971, this venue is steeped in political history and was intended as a forum for young people to express their discontent with society. The original venue was rebuilt in 2005 and now stands as a testament to architecture as well as music.

9 PARADISO, AMSTERDAM

Amsterdam is well served by superb mid-size venues, also boasting the excellent Melkweg. Pipping it at the post though is the gorgeous, 19th-Century former church. Keith Richards said the 1995 gigs the Rolling Stones played there were the best of their career.

8 LA BATACLAN, PARIS

Still hosting gigs today, this distinctive and fascinating Parisian venue is steeped in history. Opened in the mid-19th Century, it has seen acts as varied as Edith Piaf, the Clash and The Manic Street Preachers cross the disctinctive, Chinese-influenced threshold.

7 EMPRESS BALLROOM, BLACKPOOL

A Grade-II listed Victorian building, complete with wooden roof and chandeliers, the Empress Ballroom has more than a touch of vintage glamour about it and has gained fans worldwide – not least the White Stripes, who recorded a live DVD here.

6 TROUBADOUR, LA

While the Whisky a Go Go was rocking out with the Doors on Sunset, West Hollywood's Troubadour gave itself a slightly wider remit – from Buffalo Springfield, The Byrds, Love and Joni Mitchell through to comedians including Steve Martin and George Carlin.

5 THE ROUNDHOUSE, LONDON

A former railway engine shed in north London, it has been converted into an impressive concert venue. And its not just the architectural history that's impressive, the venue has hosted The Doors, Led Zeppelin, Jimi Hendrix, and is still going strong today.

4 THE LONDON ASTORIA

This much-missed venue was modest in size, but big on sound. Large enough to move, but retaining an intimate feel, it was the perfect choice to see successful bands and hugely important to the LBGT scene for its G-A-Y club nights.

3 THE FILLMORE

The people of San Francisco who wore flowers in their hair were almost certainly doing so at the Fillmore, the premier place to see the psychedelic acts of the time. Hendrix, Jefferson Airplane, Pink Floyd, The Velvet Underground... the list appears endless.

2 RED ROCKS

This amphitheatre, near Denver, Colorado, is quite something to behold – carved out of the surrounding rock. The only problem you're likely to encounter is that the breathtaking natural beauty of your surroundings may well outshine any act performing there.

1 CBGB'S

Not scoring particularly high on basic sanitation if we're honest, this Manhattan venue is nonetheless legendary. The place to see the *enfants terrible* of the New York scene grow up in public, Talking Heads, the Ramones and Blondie are among its alumni.

	VENUE	CITY	COUNTY
10	Effenaar	Eindhoven	The Netherlands
9	Paradiso	Amsterdam	The Netherlands
8	La Bataclan	Paris	France
7	Empress Ballroom	Blackpool	England
6	Troubadour	Los Angeles	USA
5	The Roundhouse	London	England
4	The Astoria	London	England
3	The Fillmore	San Francisco	USA
2	Red Rocks	Denver	USA
1	CBGB's	New York	USA

TOP
10

The best live albums capture not just the songs, but the whole atmosphere of a gig – the feeling in the room. When done well, they can transport the avid listener to a specific moment in time and bestow upon them all the thrills of a front row seat, and with better toilet facilities to boot.

LIVE RECORDINGS

10 CRAMPS – SMELL OF FEMALE 1983

The Peppermint Lounge – purportedly the birthplace of go go dancing – was the perfect venue for the seductive sleaze of pyschobilly legends The Cramps to record this thrilling live album that captures perfectly their primitive and frenzied sound.

9 BOB DYLAN – ROYAL ALBERT HALL 1966

This legendary album was actually recorded at the Manchester Free Trade Hall in 1966. The first half saw Dylan play an acoustic set before 'going electric' with his band in the second. Cue heckles and one famous shout of 'Judas!'

8 PINK FLOYD – LIVE AT POMPEII 1972

Another live film, this is lacking only one thing – an audience. Performing in front of no one apart from a film crew at the ancient Roman amphitheatre in Pompeii, Pink Floyd recorded one of the most engrossing live performances of all time.

7 NEIL YOUNG – LIVE RUST 1978

To capture the sheer impact of a Neil Young live gig seems almost an impossible task, yet listening to this 1978 release, it feels like pure emotion has been transferred to magnetic tape, particularly on his rendition of 'Needle' and 'The Damage Done'.

6 TALKING HEADS – STOP MAKING SENSE 1984

Actually a soundtrack to a self-financed live film, this 'gig' was in fact shot over three nights in Hollywood. A great sense of theatre and phenomenal songs jostle for prime position, a battle eventually won by David Byrne's big suit.

5 JAMES BROWN – LIVE AT THE APOLLO 1962

MC5's Wayne Kramer has said that this LP, recorded at the world-famous Apollo theatre, was the inspiration for 'Kick out the Jams'. While the connection isn't perhaps obvious, the urgency, fire and raw energy of James Brown's recording certainly is.

4 JOHNNY CASH – AT FOLSOM PRISON 1968

A landmark album for Cash, who was no stranger to performing in prisons and would do so again, most notably in San Quentin. It was his first show at Folsom however (only two cuts from the second made the album) that shone.

3 ARETHA - LIVE AT FILLMORE WEST 1971

The main problem when talking about Aretha Franklin's second live album is finding

new superlatives. Remastered
and repackaged with alternate
takes and extra material,
you're better off sticking
to the original and its 10
faultless renditions by this
incomparable singer.

2 MC5 – KICK OUT THE JAMS 1968

Releasing a live album as
your debut either shows
confidence in your ability and
determination to catch a raw,
incendiary sound, or that
you can't afford studio fees.
Recorded in 1968 at Detroit's
Grand Ballroom, this is an
essential recording.

1 THE WHO - LIVE AT LEEDS 1970

Having ordered the
destruction of all live tapes
from their 1969 tour, it's just
as well that this recording
survived and went on to
earn them universal praise.
The songs here, including a
14-minute 'My Generation',
capture the band at their peak.

	BAND	ALBUM
10	The Cramps	*Smell of Female*
9	Bob Dylan	*The "Royal Albert Hall" Concert*
8	Pink Floyd	*Live at Pompeii*
7	Neil Young	*Live Rust*
6	Talking Heads	*Stop Making Sense*
5	James Brown	*Live at the Apollo*
4	Johnny Cash	*Live at Folsom Prison*
3	Aretha Franklin	*Live at Fillmore West*
2	MC5	*Kick out the Jams*
1	The Who	*Live at Leeds*

CHAPTER 2
IN THE CLUB

TOP 10

The days of smoking in bars and clubs may be gone, but the image of watching musicians through a smoky haze endures. Despite knowing how bad it is for us, the cigarette holds an unmistakable allure, and the musician is just as susceptible. Probably more so, given they don't have to stand outside an office in the rain to light up...

SONGS ABOUT SMOKING

10 ELLA FITZGERALD – 'WHEN I GET LOW I GET HIGH'
A word of warning - Ella may not be talking about 'normal' tobacco in this 1936 riff on jazz cigarettes. Backed by Chuck Webb & his Orchestra, it's certainly a world away from the Ella we're used to, but it's fun nonetheless.

9 ARCTIC MONKEYS – 'CIGARETTE SMOKE'
Alex Turner's trademark tale of gritty urban realism was eventually reworked into 'Cigarette Smoker Fiona', but it's this early version that we've plumped for here, partly for the narrative and partly because it repeats the word 'cigarette' far more often.

8 SPIRITUALISED – 'DON'T JUST DO SOMETHING'
From 2001's 'Let it Come Down', this bittersweet ballad showcases some of Jason Pierce's best lyrics as the sprawling, ambitious arrangement builds to a blistering climax before fading to nothing as Jason opines, 'And life ain't good without cigarettes.'

7 MY BLOODY VALENTINE – 'CIGARETTE IN YOUR BED'
Like most My Bloody Valentine songs, the exact meaning is lost under swathes of distortion and rich, lush texture, but to say that there's some unsettling imagery going on here is putting it very mildly. It remains, however, a stunning piece of music.

6 FRATERNITY OF MAN – 'DON'T BOGART ME'
Featured on the *Easy Rider* soundtrack, the title of this silly, intentionally funny ditty says it all really - 'bogart' means to hog something - in this case a joint. It proved a popular song to cover, with versions by The Grateful Dead, Little Feat and Country Joe & The Fish.

5 SUPER FURRY ANIMALS – 'SMOKIN''
Another song about the joys of 'rolling your own', this time from Super Furry Animals. The lines, "Gonna manage my time, Just like Johann Cruyff, If we do it together, We've got meaning of life," indicate that considerable research had been undertaken.

4 OTIS REDDING – 'CIGARETTES AND COFFEE'
It's quarter to three, and Otis is still awake. Hardly surprising since he's smoking cigarettes and drinking coffee. He's watching his health though, and abstaining from cream and sugar on the basis that his girlfriend's sweet enough. What a song!

3 SIMON & GARFUNKEL – 'AMERICA'

This tale of young lovers on a voyage of discovery contains the beautifully weighted words, '"Toss me a cigarette, I think there's one in my raincoat", "We smoked the last one an hour ago"', which neatly sums up the whole song in three lines.

2 OASIS - 'CIGARETTES AND ALCOHOL'

Has there ever been a more celebratory ode to all that is bad for us? 'All I need are cigarettes and alcohol', sings Liam with his trademark sneer and such carefree abandon that you're half-tempted to join him.

1 PATSY CLINE – 'THREE CIGARETTES IN AN ASHTRAY'

Using fags as a nifty narrative device, Patsy tells the story of a woman resigned to losing her lover to another woman and watching the ash form on the last remaining cigarette as he leaves. It's truly affecting, heartbreaking stuff.

	ARTIST	SONG	YEAR
10	Ella Fitzgerald	'When I Get Low I Get High'	1936
9	Arctic Monkeys	'Cigarette Smoke'	2004
8	Spiritualised	'Don't Just Do Something'	2001
7	My Bloody Valentine	'Cigarette in Your Bed'	1988
6	Fraternity of Man	'Don't Bogart Me'	1969
5	Super Furry Animals	'Smokin''	1998
4	Otis Redding	'Cigarettes and Coffee'	1966
3	Simon & Garfunkel	'America'	1968
2	Oasis	'Cigarettes and Alcohol'	1994
1	Patsy Cline	'Three Cigarettes in an Ashtray'	1957

TOP 10

It's one of the biggest motifs in popular music and has been both muse and unkind mistress to many. Whether it's a celebration or drowning your sorrows, there's bound to be a song to fit the occasion, such is the musician's preoccupation with drinking. So raise your glasses and be upstanding please... to *booze*!

DRINKING SONGS

10 JOHN LEE HOOKER – 'ONE BOURBON, ONE SCOTCH, ONE BEER'
At odds with Dr Feelgood's suggestion that 'They got him on milk and alcohol', this song suggests that John Lee Hooker has a much wider palette than previously thought. An example of both a great drinking song and great jump blues.

9 KRIS KRISTOFFERSON – 'SUNDAY MORNING COMING DOWN'
Johnny Cash popularized the song, but it's Kris's hangover, so he makes the list. A thoroughly downbeat tale of woe, it also contains as eloquent a description of the morning after the night before as you're ever likely to hear.

8 BEASTIE BOYS – 'BRASS MONKEY'
Not a song about a brass monkey at all, or being cold – as suspected by some English folk. No, the brass monkey in question is actually a cocktail... although the recipe seems as tricky to pin down as the excitable Beasties.

7 SNOOP DOGG – 'GIN & JUICE'
After introducing himself on first single 'What's My Name?' Snoop's second hit left us in no doubt what to get him should we get served first. It's an insight into a lifestyle of wild parties and being curiously preoccupied with his money.

6 MF DOOM – 'ONE BEER'
Using a neat sample from French jazz-funk outfit Cortex, Doom begins this track with a ramshackle (presumably drunk) rendition of Cole Porter's 'I Get a Kick Out of You', before launching into his rambling rap. It's dumb, funny and a bit like being drunk.

5 THE HOUSEMARTINS – 'HAPPY HOUR'
The band from Hull's first big hit, the music and delivery may have been relentlessly upbeat and delightfully goofy, but the lyrics served up something altogether more, well... sobering, with a caustic appraisal of corporate culture and boorish male attitudes.

4 UNDERWORLD – 'BORN SLIPPY .NUXX'
After featuring on the soundtrack to *Trainspotting*, the song's refrain, 'Shouting lager lager lager lager,' was belted out in thousands of pubs at weekends, mainly by people who perhaps didn't quite get singer Karl Hyde's intention to vocalize an alcoholic's internal dialogue.

3 THIN LIZZY – 'WHISKEY IN THE JAR'
In answering once and for all the question, 'Where's the whisky?', Thin Lizzy delivered

one of the best alcohol-related tracks ever recorded. A traditional Irish song, it's perfectly designed for singing along to, preferably after a few drinks.

2 DR FEELGOOD – 'MILK & ALCOHOL'
Dr Feelgood were, appropriately enough, known as the UK's premier pub-rock act. This song, written for them by songwriter Nick Lowe, tells the tale of the author's comeuppance after one too many Kahlúas at a John Lee Hooker gig.

1 THE CHAMPS – 'TEQUILA'
Latin-influenced American band The Champs recorded a drinking classic with this two-minute, largely instrumental track. Originally recorded and released almost as an afterthought, it's as instantly affecting as a shot of the hard stuff and less likely to leave you hungover.

	ARTIST	SONG	YEAR
10	John Lee Hooker	'One Bourbon, One Scotch, One Beer'	1966
9	Kris Kristofferson	'Sunday Morning Coming Down'	1970
8	Beastie Boys	'Brass Monkey'	1986
7	Snoop Dogg	'Gin & Juice'	1993
6	MF Doom	'One Beer'	2004
5	The Housemartins	'Happy Hour'	1968
4	Underworld	'Born Slippy .NUXX'	1996
3	Thin Lizzy	'Whiskey in the Jar'	1972
2	Dr Feelgood	'Milk & Alcohol'	1979
1	The Champs	'Tequila'	1958

TOP 10

A world with no blues is one with no popular music. Thought to have arisen from a combination of West African storytelling, the work songs of African slaves and early forms of folk music, over the years it developed into what we would identify as the blues with standards forming the basis for pretty much everything that has come since.

BLUES ROOTS

10 KANSAS JOE AND MEMPHIS MINNIE – 'WHEN THE LEVEE BREAKS'
The title will be familiar due to Led Zeppelin's rock reworking of the song for their Led Zeppelin IV album. It's easy to see why they chose it, as this 1929 song by the blues duo, written in the light of the great Mississippi flood of 1927, is truly great.

9 LEAD BELLY - 'HOUSE OF THE RISING SUN'
While everyone is familiar with The Animals' version of this traditional American folk song, it had been covered countless times before. Lead Belly's deft and definitive 12-string version, dating from the 1940s, is almost completely different in all but lyrics.

8 SONNY BOY WILLIAMSON – 'NINE BELOW ZERO'
The second musician to go by this name, the harmonica player and singer was another musician to have considerable sway over the blues revival scene. His charismatic delivery and irresistible tone are all over this recording of his self-penned classic.

7 BIG BILL BROONZY – 'BABY PLEASE DON'T GO'
Broonzy's influence as a guitar player is second to none. Muddy Waters, Memphis Slim and even folk legend John Renbourn claim to have taken inspiration from his distinctive style. His version of the classic blues song is a laid-back masterpiece.

6 BLIND WILLIE MCTELL – 'LORD SEND ME AN ANGEL'
Ragtime and blues singer and guitarist Blind Willie McTell was another figure whose legacy has proved to be lasting. His output was prolific, though lacking in hits, but this 1933 song, covered in 2000 by the White Stripes, is truly timeless.

5 SISTER ROSETTA THARPE – 'DIDN'T IT RAIN CHILDREN'
The guitarist, singer and songwriter was one of the true pioneers of what was to become rock 'n' roll. She enjoyed a resurgence of interest with the UK blues revival and the version of this song recorded in Manchester, 1964, is astounding.

4 JOHN LEE HOOKER – 'BOOM BOOM'
The point where blues edges into pop, this irresistible 1962 hit track by John Lee Hooker was a massive hit at the time of its release and proved to be hugely influential, particularly on the 1960s blues revival scene in the UK.

3 ROBERT JOHNSON – 'ME AND THE DEVIL BLUES'
The life of the blues guitarist is shrouded in mystery. Initially regarded as a poor guitarist, the sudden and showy ability

he displayed was thought by many to be the result of a deal with the Devil rather than, say, practise.

2 BB KING – 'THE THRILL IS GONE'

BB King plays guitar like he's not even trying, so effortless is his style. The feel, however, is unmistakable. This 1969 release of a 1931 song marked something of a departure in style for him at the time, but remains a classic.

1 HOWLIN WOLF – 'SMOKESTACK LIGHTNIN''

Although released in 1956, Howlin' Wolf had been performing this song for at least two decades. It's an odd song, propelled by just one chord and with no discernable verse or chorus, but it somehow manages to be goosebump-inducingly effective.

	ARTIST	SONG	YEAR
10	Kansas Joe and Memphis Minnie	'When the Levee Breaks'	1929
9	Lead Belly	'House of the Rising Sun'	1948
8	Sonny Boy Williamson	'Nine Below Zero'	1951
7	Big Bill Broonzy	'Baby Please Don't Go'	1952
6	Blind Willie McTell	'Lord Send Me an Angel'	1933 (recorded) 1979 (released)
5	Sister Rosetta Tharpe	'Didn't It Rain Children'	1948
4	John Lee Hooker	'Boom Boom'	1962
3	Robert Johnson	'Me and the Devil Blues'	1937
2	BB King	'The Thrill Is Gone'	1969
1	Howlin Wolf	'Smokestack Lightnin''	1965

TOP 10

With a new generation besotted by the blues, it was inevitable that they would bring to it a new approach. Add to this established artists keen to push the form as far as it would go and others who wanted to progress the more dancefloor sound of R&B, the stage was set for some truly original sounds...

BLUES AND BEYOND

10 BLUES INCORPORATED – 'A LITTLE BIT GROOVY'
Primarily a live act, and one intended to have a fluid line-up, the list of members to have passed through Alexis Korner's outfit reads like a who's who of British Blues. This track, off their 1965 album, shows a much jazzier feel than you might expect.

9 BLOOMFIELD, KOOPER, 'STILLS – SEASON OF THE WITCH'
The brainchild of Al Kooper, the LP this track is from features two of the best guitarists of the day, though not at the same time. This track comes from the Stephen Stills side and extends a blues take of a Donovan song over 10 minutes.

8 BUTTERFIELD BLUES BAND – 'GOT MY MOJO WORKING'
A talented blues harmonica player, Paul Butterfield formed the Butterfield Blues Band with the twin guitar attack of Mike Bloomfield and Elvin Bishop. This track from their first LP brings an urgent, driving rock feel to the blues along with supreme musicianship.

7 CCS – 'SALOME'
In 1970, British blues musician Alexis Korner formed CCS (The Collective Consciousness Society). Their hits include a cover of 'Whole Lotta Love', but it's this b-side to their 1971 single 'Walkin'' that best conveys their combination of blues feel and rock rhythms.

6 JOHN MAYALL AND THE BLUESBREAKERS – 'ALL YOUR LOVE'
From the 1966 album *Bluesbreakers* with Eric Clapton, this track combines a more traditional take on the blues with the energy and distortion of rock and a treatment on the vocals that sounds almost psychedelic before launching into heads-down, 12-bar bliss.

5 THE ANIMALS – 'INSIDE-LOOKING OUT'
This 1966 single by the British band is about as hard-hitting a take on the blues as you're ever likely to hear. A single note builds with the vocals gradually building in intensity until the whole thing explodes. To many, this is The Animals' best moment.

4 MUDDY WATERS – 'MANNISH BOY'
An absolute visionary, Muddy Waters first recorded this track in 1955. For the purposes of this list however, it's the heavy, sprawling 1968 version on the Electric Mud LP. Apparently, Waters wasn't at all happy with it, though it's hard to hear his apathy in the recording.

3 GRAHAM BOND ORGANISATION – 'HARMONICA'
A British rhythm and blues

group which included Ginger Baker and Jack Bruce, their hard hitting - in every sense - style brought them infamy. It's perhaps surprising then, that this wonderful cut is from the goofy 1965 sci-fi film *Gonks Go Beat*.

2 BOOKER T – 'MELTING POT'
Putting the rhythm in Rhythm and Blues, the title track of the 1971 album was among the last recordings to feature the classic line-up and shows all members of the band playing fast and loose. Almost impossible not to dance to.

1 BO DIDDLEY – 'ELEPHANT MAN'
Bo Diddley was a musician who rarely stood still. This track, from his 1970 LP *The Black Gladiator* takes the urgent energy of funk and a raw rock sound while retaining his unmistakable blues stylings to create something altogether more psychedelic.

	ARTIST	SONG	YEAR
10	Blues Incorporated	'A Little Bit Groovy'	1965
9	Bloomfield, Kooper, Stills	'Season of the Witch'	1968
8	Butterfield Blues Band	'Got My Mojo Working'	1965
7	CCS	'Salome'	1971
6	John Mayall and the Bluesbreakers	'All Your Love'	1966
5	The Animals	'Inside-Looking Out'	1966
4	Muddy Waters	'Mannish Boy'	1968
3	The Graham Bond Organisation	'Harmonica'	1965
2	Booker T & The MGs	'Melting Pot'	1971
1	Bo Diddley	'Elephant Man'	1970

TOP
10

While some musicians are content to carry on doing what they do best, others, when left to their own devices, have tried to forge a path that is all their own. Often choosing quite different routes, the singers and songwriters on this list all ended up at the same destination – waaay out there.

TRIPPY TROUBADORS

10 BILL QUICK – 'BEAUTIFUL PEOPLE'
A lost gem that was rediscovered way after its time, this track is by a travelling hippy who ended up in Madrid in the early seventies. A chance meeting led to him recording an album which boasts this gentle and beautifully optimistic folk gem.

9 JONATHAN WILSON – 'DEAR FRIEND'
Singer-songwriter Jonathan Wilson pays no heed to current fads, instead content to do what he does. In this case, it's veering from waltz-time fairground fancy to 4/4 space rock with an assurance that makes you wonder why all songs don't follow suit.

8 SUSAN CHRISTIE – 'PAINT A LADY'
Christie is an American singer-songwriter who was destined to languish in obscurity after this album was shelved by

Columbia in 1970. Thankfully, it received a reissue from the wonderful Finders Keepers label so we can all revel in her far-out folk.

7 D.R. HOOKER – 'FORGE YOUR OWN CHAINS'
Like scores of musicians before him and many more after, DR Hooker, a quasi-religious philosopher musician, privately pressed copies of his album. This isn't usually a guarantee of quality, but this out-there psychedelic oddity is an amazing exception.

6 RITCHIE HAVENS – 'BACK TO MY ROOTS'
Boasting a supremely rhythmic guitar style and unique soulful voice, Richie Havens found a worldwide audience after his appearance at Woodstock. Originally written by Lamont Dozier, Havens made this song every bit his own and took it somewhere totally different.

5 DONOVAN – 'GET THEY BEARINGS'
To some, he's the poor man's Dylan, but to anyone who's really listened, he's the one and only Donovan. There are

a huge number of tracks that could have made this list, but this edges it for its elegant musical and lyrical simplicity.

4 ANNETTE PEACOCK - 'PONY'

Unafraid to experiment with electronics and poetry, singer, multi-instrumentalist and avant-garde composer Peacock produced some extraordinary music. This track features a lolloping groove, distorted vocals and unsettling, squelching synth stabs to wonderful effect.

3 TIM BUCKLEY – 'SWEET SURRENDER'

A musician who often shifted styles, Tim covered folk, rock, soul and psychedelia in his short career. In this song, from his *Greetings from LA* album, he embraces a range in his voice and arrangement that creates a feeling all of his own.

2 DAVID CROSBY – 'ORLEANS'

Well-known for his time in Crosby, Stills, Nash & (occasionally) Young, Croz's solo album, *If Only I Could Remember My Name*, is a trippy troubadour triumph and 'Orleans', a short piece featuring just guitar and voice, is its dreamy masterpiece.

1 EDEN AHBEZ – 'FULL MOON'

Was Eden Ahbez the first hippy? Born in 1908, he wore his hair long and lived as close to nature as he could, even sleeping outdoors. He had followers, too, called Nature Boys after the song he wrote, made famous by Nat King Cole.

	ARTIST	SONG	YEAR
10	Bill Quick	'Beautiful People' (Maravillosa Gente)	1972
9	Jonathan Wilson	'Dear Friend'	2013
8	Susan Christie	'Paint a Lady'	1970 (recorded) 2006 (released)
7	D.R. Hooker	'Forge Your Own Chains'	1972
6	Ritchie Havens	'Back to My Roots'	1980
5	Donovan	'Get They Bearings'	1968
4	Annette Peacock	'Pony'	1972
3	Tim Buckley	'Sweet Surrender'	1972
2	David Crosby	'Orleans'	1971
1	Eden Ahbez	'Full Moon'	1960

TOP 10

There are times when only a crushed-velvet lounge suit and a martini will do, and those times are best soundtracked by the greats of easy listening. It's true that occasional slips in sartorial style haven't helped the giants of this genre to be taken altogether seriously, but the bow ties and bellbottoms disguise some wonderful arrangements and superb musicianship.

EASY LISTENING

10 RONNIE HAZLEHURST – 'THE TWO RONNIES THEME'

A much-maligned composer, history will surely remember Ronnie very fondly indeed. It takes a special kind of genius to come up with the consistently effective earworms that he did, and the 'Two Ronnies Theme' stands as tall as any of them.

9 KEITH MANSFIELD – 'FUNKY FANFARE'

Another easy listening classic that's proved rich pickings for hip hop producers (Dangermouse used it as the main refrain in 'Old School' with MF Doom and Talib Kweli), this song, put simply, is a stone-cold classic, with absolutely huge drums.

8 THE RAY MCVAY ORCHESTRA AND SINGERS – '2001: A SPACE ODYSSEY'

From The Ray McVay Road Show, this big-band belter breaks all speed limits as it takes flight into the stratosphere. With flourishes of flute and the drums and bass propelling things forward at an impressive pace, it's out of this world!

7 MARTIN DENNY – 'QUIET VILLAGE'

Exotica par excellence, composer Martin Denny's most famous moment is so evocative, you'll swear that you're sitting on the porch of a bamboo bungalow while the sun sets over an unfamiliar ocean and waiters bring you endless margaritas.

6 KLAUS WUNDERLICH – 'SUMMERTIME'

While the Seventies German Moog ace may look like an extra from *When Polyester Attacks,* he produced some startlingly good, futuristic music (see the opening and closing minutes of 'Krimooglulus'). It's the amazing Gershwin groove of 'Summertime' that works best however.

5 JAMES LAST – 'SE A CABO'

Last's prodigious output is full of hidden gems. This prime example from the *Voodoo Party* LP (exactly how many Voodoo parties have been soundtracked by it is unclear) is Latin-tinged groovy rock of the sort you might expect on a decent Santana LP.

4 BIRDS 'N' BRASS – 'FRITZY BABY'

Boasting flute, scratchy wah-wah guitar and funk-filled back line, this track is notable not just for the soaring singers, but also the fact that the guitarist is able to make his instrument sound exactly like a cat. As for the name... well, it was the Seventies.

3 GUNTER KALLMAN CHOIR - 'DAYDREAM'

Heavily sampled by both the Beta Band and I, Monster in the early Noughties, it's easy to see the allure of this beautiful German lounge version of the Wallace Collection song that manages to sound exactly like falling asleep in a wildflower meadow.

2 GEOFF LOVE – 'THREE DAYS OF THE CONDOR'

The easy listening maestro made a career out of reinterpreting existing film and TV scores in a lounge-friendly style. Of his impressive back catalogue, the horizontal funk of his take on Dave Grusin's original theme is the stand-out.

1 BUTTON DOWN BRASS FEATURING RAY DAVIES – 'SUPERSTITIOUS'

Not the Kinks frontman, but a musician who, with his funky trumpet, brought considerable groove into the lounge. This version of Stevie Wonder's classic doesn't go head-to-head with the original, but instead offers a very alternate – and very successful – take on it.

	ARTIST	SONG
10	Ronnie Hazlehurst	'The Two Ronnies Theme'
9	Keith Mansfield	'Funky Fanfare'
8	The Ray McVay Orchestra and Singers	'2001: A Space Odyssey'
7	Martin Denny	'Quiet Village'
6	Klaus Wunderlich	'Summertime'
5	James Last	'Se a Cabo'
4	Birds 'n' Brass	'Fritzy Baby'
3	Gunter Kallman Choir	'Daydream'
2	Geoff Love	'Three Days of the Condor'
1	Button Down Brass featuring Ray Davies	'Superstitious'

TOP
10

While their opposite numbers in the rock fraternity get all the plaudits for their showmanship and solos, the deft touch and amazing dexterity of the folk guitarist shouldn't go unrewarded. Often showcasing their skills in small clubs to few people, their talent, nonetheless, is huge. Here are 10 of the best.

FOLK FINGERPICKERS

10 NICK DRAKE
With a gentle, hushed style that belies its impact, Nick Drake's guitar playing was perfectly suited to his voice. Not a showy or flashy player, it also suited his personality, never pushing in, always in the background but always perfectly right.

9 JOHN MARTYN
A hugely talented performer, Martyn's distinctive, drawling vocal style along with his use of tape delay on guitar tracks made for an unmistakable sound in his Seventies heyday. He also recorded earlier albums with former wife Beverley, including the faultless *Stormbringer* LP.

8 JACKSON C FRANK
A troubled soul, Frank proved a huge influence on artists including Sandy Denny and Paul Simon (who produced his debut album). His songs were often covered, most

successfully by Bert Jansch ('Blues Run the Game') and Bonnie Dobson ('Milk and Honey').

7 JOHN RENBOURN
Taking influence from jazz, classical and baroque music as well as folk, John Renbourn has a distinctive style all of his own. It was one that found a perfect foil in Bert Jansch with whom he collaborated individually and as part of Pentangle.

6 SANDY BULL
First coming to prominence in the late Fifties, Sandy Bull's proficiency on several instruments including the oud and his extended, modal jams that incorporated jazz and foreign styles ensured no one sounded like Sandy Bull back then. That many do today shows his lasting impact.

5 JOHN FAHEY
Fahey's best recordings

weave wonderful, intricate melodies onto beautiful, droning backdrops. Though most obviously a blues and folk guitarist his style took on board everything from classical music to Gregorian chants. He was a true American original.

4 WIZZ JONES
Thought by many, including Bert Jansch, to be the most underrated guitarist ever, the evidence seems to agree. His second album, in particular, is a classic in the folk cannon, including his masterful versions of 'Beggar Man' and 'Keep Your Lamp Trimmed and Burning'.

3 BERT JANSCH
Jansch's rendition of the Davy Graham-penned instrumental 'Angie', done in one take at producer Bill Leader's home is a good indication of his singular style. Neil Young called him 'the Jimi

Hendrix of the acoustic guitar', a description that anyone would struggle to better.

2 RICHARD THOMPSON

Considered the best there is in folk rock, Thompson's dexterity and versatility are staggering. Even at the tender age of 18, while in the fledgling Fairport Convention, it was the sophistication of his playing that endeared them to producer Joe Boyd, who signed them up.

1 DAVY GRAHAM

Possibly the single most influential figure of the British folk revival, Graham's dexterity and encompassing of musical styles from other cultures set him apart. Just 19 when he wrote the instrumental touchstone Anji, his *Folk Blues & Beyond* album is absolutely essential.

	ARTIST	LISTEN TO...	YEAR
10	Nick Drake	*Five Leaves Left*	1969
9	John Martyn	*Solid Air*	1973
8	Jackson C Frank	*Jackson C Frank*	1965
7	John Renbourn	*Faro Annie*	1971
6	Sandy Bull	*Fantasias for Guitar and Banjo*	1963
5	John Fahey	*The Transfiguration of Blind Joe Death*	1965
4	Wizz Jones	*The Legendary Me*	1970
3	Bert Jansch	*Bert Jansch*	1965
2	Richard Thompson	*I Want to See the Bright Lights Tonight*	1974
1	Davy Graham	*Folk, Blues and Beyond*	1965

Very much the unsung heroes of rock and pop, the jobbing musician may not get the plaudits, the fame or the royalties, but they do get a solid daily rate and are able to pop to the shops without being papped. These largely anonymous musicians are responsible for some of the most recognizable moments in popular music...

SESSION MUSICIANS

10 ALAN PARKER
Having played for artists as big as Frank Sinatra and Ella Fitzgerald, guitarist Parker later churned out hits for tartan clad teen dreams Bay City Rollers. His work for library labels KPM and De Wolfe, Alexis Korner's CCS and David Bowie more than absolve him.

9 BIG JIM SULLIVAN
Called 'Big' to differentiate him from the other Jim on the session scene (Jimmy Page) Jim Sullivan's versatility soon saw him become one of the most sought after guitarists around and pioneered the use of the wah-wah and fuzz guitar pedals.

8 BERNARD PURDIE
Any drummer good enough for James Brown is good enough for this list. As well as laying down the good grooves for the Godfather of funk, Bernard Purdie has played for artists as diverse as Aretha Franklin, Steely Dan, Tim Rose and guitarist Sandy Bull.

7 CAROL KAYE
A bass player who came up with a line so distinctive it should have earned a writing credit, Carol was responsible for the best bit bar none of the Beach Boys' 'Good Vibrations'. Quincy Jones is also a huge fan.

6 HERBIE FLOWERS
With a tone so distinctive it's a sonic calling card, Herbie Flowers has played bass for the best. That bit in 'Walk on the Wild Side'? That was him. 'Space Oddity'? Him too. And he's all over the recordings of French maverick Serge Gainsbourg too.

5 BILLY PRESTON
Singled out in the keyboard players top 10, Billy gets a mention here for the sheer volume of artists who have sought out his talents. Little Richard, Clapton, Sly Stone and the Red Hot Chili Peppers are among those who would give glowing references.

4 MUSCLE SHOALS RHYTHM SECTION
Also known as The Swampers, this group of session players defined an entire sound. Keen

to benefit from their expertise, artists travelled from far and wide to work with them, including the Stones, Wilson Pickett and the peerless Tony Joe White.

3 BOOKER T AND THE MGS

Although it feels odd including a band as well known as this in the session musicians top 10, that's exactly what they were. It was their style that gave Stax its identity and as such there's a whole roster of artists who owe them a great debt.

2 THE FUNK BROTHERS

Motown's go-to backing band, the Funk Brothers are another group with a fluid and shifting line-up. The quality was consistent though, and the sound utterly unmistakable, which proved unfortunate when the band tried to moonlight for other labels!

1 THE WRECKING CREW

Given their name by drummer Hal Blaine, The Wrecking Crew's alumni includes Glen Campbell and Dr John. Though best known for their work creating Phil Spector's infamous 'wall of sound' they were the first choice of any producer worth their salt in Sixties America.

	ARTIST	APPEARS ON	BY	YEAR
10	Alan Parker	'Hurdy Gurdy Man'	*Donovan*	1968
9	Big Jim Sullivan	'Histoire de Melody Nelson'	*Serge Gainsbourg*	1971
8	Bernard Purdie	'Morning Dew'	*Tim Rose*	1967
7	Carol Kaye	'Wichita Lineman'	*Glen Campbell*	1968
6	Herbie Flowers	'Walk on the Wild Side'	*Lou Reed*	1972
5	Billy Preston	'Miss You'	*Rolling Stones*	1978
4	The Funk Brothers	'Papa Was a Rolling Stone'	*The Temptations*	1972
3	Booker T and the MGs	'Try a Little Tenderness'	*Otis Redding*	1967
2	Muscle Shoals Rhythm section	'Gotta Serve Somebody'	*Bob Dylan*	1979
1	The Wrecking Crew	*Pet Sounds (album)*	*The Beach Boys*	1966

TOP
10

Taking inspiration from the American originators, the British exponents found their own, distinctive voice over time, taking influence from far and wide. However, while history has ensured many of their peers over The Pond are household names, little is known of these British originals. This seems as good a time as any to attempt to redress that balance...

BRITISH JAZZ HEROES

10 COURTNEY PINE
The saxophonist came to fame during the Eighties and his work has been notable for taking influence from contemporary popular music, including drum and bass. He has done more than most to ensure that jazz is constantly developing in the new millennium.

9 BASIL KIRCHIN
First playing drums in his father's band, Kirchin then began writing music. His percussive-heavy compositions featured on film and TV and he built up a wealth of unreleased material that has, more recently, found an outlet through the consistently impressive Trunk records imprint.

8 MICHAEL GARRICK
The pianist is notable for being largely self-taught and for experimenting with combinations of jazz and poetry. A member of the Rendell-Carr quintet, he is another composer whose work (including the Moonscape album) has been rediscovered recently to great acclaim.

7 GRAHAM COLLIER
A pioneer in many ways – bass player Collier was at the forefront of a British jazz scene beginning to cut the cord from its US parentage and his ensemble, Graham Collier Music, gained a reputation for innovative, progressive jazz.

6 MIKE WESTBROOK
Considered one of the most influential big band leaders and heralded for his skill as an arranger as well as a pianist, his Mike Westbrook Concert Band produced musically progressive and politically charged music including 1969's pacifist album *Marching Song Vol. 2*.

5 IAN CARR
The prodigious, self-taught trumpet player was a true visionary, forming the Rendell-Carr Quintet in 1963 and then, subsequently, the groundbreaking jazz-rock band Nucleus, which led to international acclaim and recognition.

4 NORMA WINSTONE
Singer Winstone started out singing jazz standards, but soon became interested with the avant garde and a wordless, improvisational approach to her singing. Hers is a unique, beguiling voice that has graced recordings by the very best in British jazz.

3 TUBBY HAYES
A multi-instrumentalist, best known for his work on the alto sax, Hayes played with Kenny Baker's sextet at the tender age of 16. He is widely credited with raising the UK game in jazz and his 1961 residency in New York gained him fans including Miles Davis.

2 KENNY BAKER

One of the most highly regarded British jazz players in the world, Baker paved the way for much of what was to come. 'While we have Kenny Baker who needs Louis?' said the musician's union of their ban on visiting US musicians. Quite.

1 JOHN DANKWORTH

A phenomenal composer, incredibly gifted saxaphone player and driven by a desire to open both ears and minds, John Dankworth was a true British Jazz legend. Along with his wife, Cleo Laine, he was also a totemic figurehead for the scene.

	ARTIST	PRIMARY INSTRUMENT	BUT ALSO...
10	Courtney Pine	Saxophone	Flute, clarinet, bass clarinet, composer and bandleader
9	Basil Kirchin	Drums	Composer
8	Michael Garrick	Piano	Composer, bandleader
7	Graham Collier	Bass	Composer, bandleader
6	Mike Westbrook	Piano	Composer, bandleader
5	Ian Carr	Trumpet	Composer, bandleader
4	Norma Winstone	Singer	Lyricist
3	Tubby Hayes	Saxophone	Flute, vibraphone, composer and bandleader
2	Kenny Baker	Trumpet	Cornet, flugelhorn, composer and bandleader
1	John Dankworth	Saxaphone, clarinet	Clarinet, composer and bandleader

TOP
10

Time to put pen to paper and create your own top 10 list of end of night classics...

10

9

8

7

6

5

4

3

2

1

TOP
10

After heavy metal was largely co-opted by backcombed boys in spandex as the Eighties progressed, it was inevitable that the tide would turn. Towards the end of the decade these bands, largely from the US coastal port of Seattle and favouring a look that said 'My day job is as a lumberjack', paved the way for a monumental shift in guitar music.

GRUNGE GREATS

8 THE FLUID - 'COLD OUTSIDE'

The first non-Seattle band to sign with the hugely important Sub Pop label, The Fluid released their album *Clear Black Paper* in 1988. It was lighter, leaner and punkier than many of their new labelmates, but none the worse for that.

7 AFGHAN WHIGS – 'RETARDED'

Greg Dulli's Cincinatti band Afghan Whigs had a more thoughtful, soulful approach than many bands of the time. This 1990 track however, provides a good indication of what could have happened if J Masics had ever decided to join forces with Nirvana.

10 LEMONHEADS – 'LI'L SEED'

True, Evan Dando's distorted, melodic offerings were far removed from the fuzz and the filth of grunge. However this standout from the 1990 LP Lovey, has much more in common with its sentiment than anything on Pearl Jam's AOR debut 10.

9 SCREAMING TREES – 'BLACK SUN MORNING'

While some might go for the lighter, jauntier rock of 'I Nearly Lost You', Mark Lanegan's often overlooked outfit make it on to the list with this, from their 1989 LP *Buzz Factory*. It's earlier darker, noisier and...more grunge.

6 MELVINS – 'ANACONDA'

The Melvins have been called the godfathers of grunge and were certainly hugely important in its development. The slow, punishing sludge

groove of this track, from their third album, *Bullhead*, owes more than a nod to the heavy riffs of Black Sabbath.

5 SOUNDGARDEN – 'FLOWER'
More conventionally 'rock' that any of their Seattle stablemates, future rock gods Soundgarden's early sound, though polished,

still has that sense of urgency and abandon that the best of the grunge scene shared. And riffs as heavy as anything the Sixties could offer.

4 TAD – 'SEX GOD MISSY'

Sharing more in common musically with Nirvana than most, Tad were the obvious choice for the 1989 double headline tour that saw both bands hit the UK. This amazing track is as heavy as frontman Tad Doyle himself (about 350 pounds at a guess).

3 GREEN RIVER – 'COME ON DOWN'

The forefathers of the scene, comprising future members of Mudhoney and Pearl Jam, when this band reformed for live gigs in 2008 it could legitimately be called a supergroup. Off their 1985 EP, this cut is as good an indication as you can get of where things were heading.

2 NIRVANA – 'SCHOOL'

While Nevermind got all the plaudits, Nirvana's first LP, *Bleach*, was already a classic among the converted. This track perfectly combines the energy, dumb-not-dumb riffs and screaming warts-and-all intensity that made them such an enthralling live band.

1 MUDHONEY – 'TOUCH ME I'M SICK'

Living, breathing proof that 'If it ain't broke, don't fix it', Mudhoney haven't changed the blueprint in more than 20 years. When that blueprint is as perfectly pitched as this sneering grunge-punk blast though, you probably don't need to.

	ARTIST	SONG	ALBUM	YEAR
10	Lemonheads	'Li'l Seed'	*Lovey*	1990
9	Screaming Trees	'Black Sun Morning'	*Buzz Factory*	1989
8	The Fluid	'Cold Outside'	*Clear Black Paper*	1988
7	Afghan Whigs	'Retarded'	*Up in It*	1990
6	The Melvins	'Anaconda'	*Bullhead*	1991
5	Soundgarden	'Flower'	*Ultramega OK*	1988
4	Tad	'Sex God Missy'	*God's Balls*	1989
3	Green River	'Come on Down'	*Come on Down (EP)*	1985
2	Nirvana	'School'	*Bleach*	1989
1	Mudhoney	'Touch Me I'm Sick'	*Superfuzz Bigmuff*	1988

TOP 10

Trying to pin down what constitutes a Mod classic is like trying to swallow a hedgehog – difficult and a prickly issue. Go to a big Mod event and you'll find vintage R&B and Ska classics in one room and, next door, obscure 60s psych unearthed by dedicated diggers. With that in mind, this is a top 10 with some unashamedly broad strokes.

MOD MOVERS

10 *PAUL NICHOLAS – 'RUN SHAKER LIFE'*
You know the actor? Hair? Just Good Friends? Yep him. No, seriously. And it's really good too! Something of an unexpected delight, the B-side of his 'Freedom City' single is a built for dancing and copies can command a fair sum, too.

9 DON FARDON – 'I'M ALIVE'
A hit in Holland when recently reissued, it just goes to show the timeless quality of Don Fardon's cover of the Tommy James & The Shondells tune. A huge hitter on the more progressive Mod dancefloors, it has an absolutely irresistible groove.

8 THE SKATALITES – 'DR RING DING'
Often listed as a solo release by Skatalites member and Ska legend Jackie Mittoo, this joyous, horn-led track was released on the Studio One label. It's easy to see why this was a tune many took to their hearts.

7 THE KINKS – 'TIL THE END OF THE DAY'
Well, we did say unashamedly broad... despite being ostensibly a pop band, this 1965 track has razor sharp beats that marry the fuzz guitar perfectly to irresistibly on-point harmonies, and manages better than most pop hits to capture that sound.

6 LITTLE SONNY – 'WADE IN THE WATER'
Given the number of versions of this spiritual song there are, the claim that this is the best is a strong one. Still, no matter – it's a claim we're going to make as the raw, harmonica-led stomp has an energy that few can possibly match.

5 THE CREATION – 'MAKING TIME'
There are a few Creation songs that could have made this chart, this 1967 release edged it for two reasons: one – you can actually dance to it, two – as far as debut singles go, this is a brave and bold opening statement.

4 RUFUS THOMAS – 'CAN YOUR MONKEY DO THE DOG'
Another R&B monster to make the list, this 1964 single asks

two questions, the first is obvious, the second is, 'After singles 'The Dog', 'Walking the Dog', 'Somebody Stole My Dog' and this... why on Earth is Rufus Thomas so obsessed with dogs?'

3 SHARON TANDY & FLEUR DE LYS — 'HOLD ON'

The South African singer teamed up with the best blue-eyed soul band in town to record this single – an absolutely stomping tune guaranteed to fill a dancefloor and also boasting the best one-note guitar solo in pop history. Probably.

2 JACKIE EDWARDS – 'KEEP ON RUNNING'

The original and still the best! Initially recorded for Edwards' own album, *Come on Home*, The Spencer Davis Group took it to number one the next year with a radical overhaul. The original is wonderful, lilting Jamaican R&B perfect for dancing.

1 THE SMALL FACES – 'WATCHA GONNA DO ABOUT IT'

In just four years, The Small Faces managed to go from the urgent rhythm and blues of this wonderful debut to the ambitious psychedelic steam train of their *Odgen's Nut Gone Flake* concept LP without once missing a beat.

	ARTIST	SONG	YEAR
10	Paul Nicholas	'Run Shaker Life'	1970
9	Don Fardon	'I'm Alive'	1969
8	The Skatalites	'Dr Ring Ding'	1964 (reissued 1970)
7	The Kinks	'Til the End of the Day'	1965
6	Little Sonny	'Wade in the Water'	1970
5	The Creation	'Making Time'	1967
4	Rufus Thomas	'Can Your Monkey Do the Dog'	1964
3	Sharon Tandy & Les Fleur de Lys	'Hold On'	1967
2	Jackie Edwards	'Keep on Running'	1965
1	The Small Faces	'Watcha Gonna Do About It'	1966

TOP 10

It seemed for a while that Goths had died a death. Although that's not unusual for Goths – probably the make-up. Thankfully, rumours of their demise had been exaggerated, as had the notion that they sat in darkened rooms drinking snakebite and black and reading Victorian horror. Goths can (g)rave it up with the best of them – as this top 10 shows.

GOTH GROOVES

10 DANIELLE DAX – 'OSTRICH'

There is some debate as to whether Danielle Dax counts as Goth. She does. Right, now we've got that cleared up, we can concentrate on the shuffling groove-led drums, jangling guitar and punctuated bass of this brilliant 1984 precursor to indie dance.

9 THE CURE – 'FASCINATION STREET (EXTENDED MIX)'

Notable for its walloping four-minute long instrumental passage before Robert Smith so much as opens his lipstick-smeared mouth, this is another track to end the night while people sway, arms extended, in the chiming, epic grandeur of it all.

8 THE MISSION 'TOWER OF STRENGTH' (BOMBAY MIX)

Formed by former members of Sisters of Mercy in 1986, the band released this single two years later. This remix (produced by Led Zeppelin's John Paul Jones) has a rhythmic chug that has made it an end-of-night classic in some quarters.

7 KILLING JOKE – 'BLOODSPORT'

Technically post-punk rather than Goth, but that's crossover for you – it fits, so it's in! Along with Ministry, this is the nearest thing to an all-out dancefloor track on this list, and would be a guaranteed floorfiller in any number of clubs.

6 MARILYN MANSON – 'TAINTED LOVE'

It's easy to forget that this is a cover of a Soft Cell cover version so well does Manson manage to make it his own. In fact, with synths set to 'sandblast' and drums to 'punish' this is as far removed from Gloria Jones' original as possible.

5 THE CULT – SHE SELLS SANCTUARY

Before Ian Astbury and co.

discovered America, heavy rock and leathers so tight they had to be surgically removed, they used to be masters at anthemic and melodic Goth-rock of which this, with Billy Duffy's signature strumming, is the pinnacle.

4 NINE INCH NAILS – 'HEAD LIKE A HOLE'

The go-to track on Nine Inch Nails' album, *Pretty Hate Machine*, this takes its lead from Ministry's later sound. It works though, and there's no denying the powerful mix of electronic elements, rock posture and extreme anger. Trent Reznor is very, very cross.

3 BAUHAUS – 'BELA LUGOSI'S DEAD'

Echoed rimshots and stuttering electronic effects work in perfect harmony with the building treble of the guitars to create a genuinely haunting atmosphere in what is largely considered to be the first ever Goth rock single, released in 1979.

2 SISTERS OF MERCY – 'LUCRETIA MY REFLECTION'

With its hard, driving beat and raw, incessant bass, this single was an instant hit on its 1988 release. It combined a distinct, rocky edge to the dark introspection that emanated from Eldritch, ensuring many snakebite and blacks were spilled dancing to this.

1 MINISTRY – COLD LIFE

Before Al Jourgensen's outfit went all industrial and shouty, Ministry were a synthpop outfit - albeit one with dark and brooding lyrics. This first single was unashamed pop aimed at the dancefloor complete with slap bass and soaring synths. It's brilliant, too!

	ARTIST	SONG	YEAR
10	Danielle Dax	'Ostrich'	1984
9	The Cure	'Fascination Street (Extended mix)'	1989
8	The Mission	'Tower of Strength' (Bombay Mix)	1988
7	Killing Joke	'Bloodsport'	1980
6	Marilyn Manson	'Tainted Love'	2001
5	The Cult	'She Sells Sanctuary'	1985
4	Nine Inch Nails	'Head Like a Hole'	1989
3	Bauhaus	'Bela Lugosi's Dead'	1979
2	Sisters of Mercy	'Lucretia My Reflection'	1987
1	Ministry	'Cold Life'	1982

TOP 10

Following the filth and fury of punk, a generation of kids scrubbed up, stuck on a bit of make-up and decided that there was nothing wrong with a bit of glamour. All over the UK, clubs vibrated to a new kind of sound as bands took their lead from Bowie and Roxy music as well as the avant garde art world.

NEW ROMANTIC CLUB HITS

10 JAPAN – 'GHOSTS'
The ethereal, unnerving introduction of this single off final album, *Tin Drum*, shows the willingness of the band to embrace an experimental approach. Underneath it all though, it's a great pop melody, marking it out as a classic of the time.

9 SOFT CELL – 'MEMORABILIA'
While the band never thought themselves a New Romantic act, many other people did. This track, while not their most immediate, is almost purpose-built for clubs, sounding in many ways like a proto-house track. However you wish to label it, it's genius.

8 HUMAN LEAGUE – 'LOVE ACTION'
Following the departure of founding members Martyn Ware and Ian Marsh, The Human League changed direction and became

associated with the new romantic scene. The polished pop perfection of this single from the album *Dare*, is a prime example.

7 ROXY MUSIC – 'LOVE IS THE DRUG'
A song that inspired, rather than came directly from, the scene, Roxy Music's flamboyant fashion and art-house pop transformed the band into idols in the eyes of these wannabe stars and influenced not just the music but the look too.

6 ULTRAVOX – 'SLOW MOTION'
Produced by Krautrock legend Conny Plank (who also produced the Eurythmics first LP, *In the Garden*), this is a world away from their later hits. With a guitar tone straight out of Neu! this is a very different side to the new romantic sound.

5 DAVID BOWIE – 'HEROES'
While not a New Romantic himself, Bowie was one of the artists who inspired the scene, and this track was something of an anthem at the Blitz Club. In fact, Bowie turned up to the club and hand-picked Steve Strange to be in the 'Ashes to Ashes' video!

4 SIMPLE MINDS – 'I TRAVEL' (EXTENDED MIX)
Often called a New Romantic band, whether Simple Minds truly fit the category is a moot subject. Early on however, they had the look and the electronic Germanic sound that fits the bill. They also had a consistently brilliant output that no one could match.

3 DURAN DURAN – 'PLANET EARTH'
The most glamorous thing to come out of Birmingham for some time, Duran Duran

assaulted the charts and the pop consciousness like few others. No wonder when this debut single managed to get absolutely everything spot on right from the start.

2 SPANDAU BALLET - 'CHANT NO. 1'
This band of Blitz club kids introduced the funk to the new romantic scene with this single off their second album. It was also to set the tone for much of the chart pop that was to follow, and proved a clear inspiration for Wham! among others.

1 VISAGE – 'FADE TO GREY'
Founder members Steve Strange and Rusty Egan were the people behind London's infamous Blitz club, where the New Romantic scene was born, so it's no surprise that they should be behind one of the biggest – and best – records of the genre.

	ARTIST	SONG	YEAR
10	Japan	'Ghosts'	1981
9	Soft Cell	'Memorabilia'	1982
8	Human League	'Love Action'	1981
7	Roxy Music	'Love is the Drug'	1975
6	Ultravox	'Slow Motion'	1978
5	David Bowie	'Heroes'	1977
4	Simple Minds	'I Travel' (Extended mix)	1980
3	Duran Duran	'Planet Earth'	1981
2	Spandau Ballet	'Chant No.1'	1982
1	Visage	'Fade to Grey'	1980

TOP
10

As the Eighties became the Nineties, many young UK bands stopped looking to the past or the future for their inspiration and focused on their shoes instead. In truth, this on-stage heads-down habit (which led to the term 'shoegaze') was probably down to shyness, but it became a handy adjective for a whole new sound – ethereal, dreamy and epic.

SHOEGAZE SWAYERS

10 THE EARLY YEARS – 'FALLEN STAR'
A band from the pioneering shoegaze label Sonic Cathedral stable, East London's The Early Years also manage to combine a krautrock influence with dreamy, textured guitars, but the sheer weight of their layered sound gives them a gravitas all of their own.

9 CHAPTERHOUSE – 'FALLING DOWN'
Beginning with a wah-wah guitar over a baggy beat, you could be forgiven for thinking that this was just another band capitalizing on the Madchester bandwagon. However, it soon morphs into something altogether more interesting and greater than the sum of its parts.

8 BELONG – 'PERFECT LIFE'
Released in 2011, this album took the My Bloody Valentine-influenced music concrete that US duo Turk Dietrich and Michael Jones had previously released and added a dash of The Cure to create a sound that, while indebted to the past, was rooted in the present.

7 LORELLE MEETS THE OBSOLETE – 'WHAT'S HOLDING YOU?'
Another release from the Sonic Cathedral stable, this track, from the band's third album, Chambers, blends the sonic template of shoegaze with the heads-down, no-nonsense motorik beat of krautrock to produce a thrilling and vital record.

6 PALE SAINTS – 'SIGHT OF YOU'
With a fine pop sensibility and a good ear for melody, Leeds band the Pale Saints came to the attention of the indie world with their 1989 EP Barging into the Presence of God, of which this is the stand-out track.

5 ULRICH SCHNAUSS – 'WHEREVER YOU ARE'
If German synth pioneers Tangerine Dream had been teenagers at the height of shoegaze, it's entirely possible that they would have ended up sounding like Ulrich Schnauss. This 2001 track highlights the very best of the producer's unique tone and touch.

4 LUSH – 'THOUGHTFORMS'
Re-recorded with the trademark chorus overdrive of Cocteau Twins' Robin Guthrie, it's the untreated version from the bands debut mini LP, Scar, that holds the real treats. Devoid of production trickery, still chimes and enchants in equal measure.

3 RIDE – 'VAPOUR TRAIL'
Without doubt one of the most important bands of the shoegaze scene, Ride's first four EP's were absolutely essential listening. This track

from their album, *Nowhere*, takes a softer approach, combining cellos but is no less impactful for doing so.

2 SLOWDIVE – 'CATCH THE BREEZE'

Recently reformed, Slowdive make a big and beautiful sound that is unashamedly progressive. On this, their biggest hit, there's fragility and tension but, ultimately, listening to them is like being allowed to lie down in the comfiest bed ever.

1 MY BLOODY VALENTINE – 'SOON'

While tempting to include something from their first album proper, *Isn't Anything*, it is this track from Loveless that proved to be the most influential, not least due to the astonishing remix from Andrew Weatherall that introduced distortion to the dancefloor.

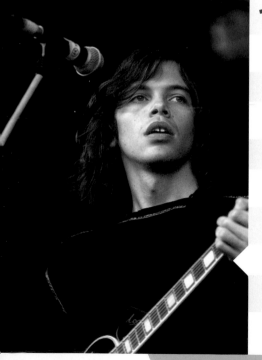

	ARTIST	SONG	YEAR
10	The Early Years	'Fallen Star'	1984
9	Chapterhouse	'Falling Down'	1991
8	Belong	'Perfect Life'	2011
7	Lorelle Meets the Obsolete	'What's Holding You?'	2013
6	Pale Saints	'Sight of You'	1990
5	Ulrich Schnauss	'Wherever You Are'	2002 (CD 2006 (vinyl)
4	Lush	'Thought-forms'	1989
3	Ride	'Vapour Trail'	1990
2	Slowdive	'Catch the Breeze'	1991
1	My Bloody Valentine	'Soon'	1990

TOP 10

Whether on terrace bars as the day's embers slowly fade, in rooms in which to escape the frantic pace of a club or simply soundtracking falling energy levels in a sitting room at dawn, there's always a place for chill-out tunes. This list comprises a mixture of single tracks and albums because sometimes it's just too much trouble to get off the sofa.

CHILL-OUT TUNES

9 BUGGE WESSELTOFT – 'EXISTENCE'

A sampled jazz drum loop, a simple piano line, some synth pads and an upright bass are the main ingredients in this fabulous piece of music that manages to sound simple and complex, laid-back yet urgent and simultaneously soothing and exciting.

8 LAMBCHOP – 'UP WITH PEOPLE' (ZERO 7 REMIX)

An alt-country band might not be the first thing that springs to mind when you say the words 'chill-out', but production duo Zero 7 built layer upon beautiful layer around Kurt Wagner's voice to create something even better than the original.

10 THE ART OF NOISE – *THE AMBIENT COLLECTION*

Taking the band's songs and stitching them together with sounds and spoken word was a stroke of genius and instantly made this something altogether different from a run-of-the-mill compilation album. In fact, it made it something much... better.

7 THE CINEMATIC ORCHESTRA – 'CHANNEL 1 SUITE'

With an impressive body

of work behind them since they first appeared in 1999, it's difficult to know what to pick from Jason Swinscoe's project-turned-fully fledged band. However, this track, off their first album, *Motion*, wins for being the most like a big hug.

6 AIR – 'SOLIDISSIMO' (EDC REMIX)

Appearing on the *Super Discount* compilation, this remix manages the impressive feat of managing to take a track by French duo Air and 'calm it down a bit'. A thing of spine-tingling beauty, if it were any more laid back, it'd be practically horizontal.

5 SPACE – *S/T*

An album by KLF man Jimmy Cauty, this aural journey through the solar system was intended to be the first Orb album. Starting off at Mercury, the listener is taken on a fascinating ride past planets and through space though, interestingly, swerving Earth.

4 GLOBAL COMMUNICATION – *76:14*

While three minute guitar blasts were in fashion, Mark Pritchard and Tom Middleton released one hour, 16 minutes and 14 seconds of blissful, shimmering joy. When, in

2000, the track 12:18 was performed at London's Union Chapel with a 40-strong choir, grown adults wept at its beauty.

3 THE KLF – *CHILL OUT*

Part band, part performance

artists, when Bill Drummond and Jimmy Cauty did something, they really did it – from terrorising the Brit Awards with a dead sheep to burning a million quid for a film. So, when they chill out, they really chill out. Bliss!

2 THE ORB — 'LITTLE FLUFFY CLOUDS'

A classic of the genre, this Orb song isn't actually that chilled out. Jogging along at a respectable 105 bpm, that it still manages to feel so relaxing is down to some wonderful production and the drawling tones of Rickie Lee Jones.

1 APHEX TWIN — *SELECTED AMBIENT WORKS 85-92 (LP)*

The Aphex Twin is a singular talent - not least as, despite the name - there's just one of him. If the dates on the release are accurate, it suggests that some of Richard D James's haunting ambient masterpieces were created at the tender age of 14.

	ARTIST	SONG	YEAR
10	The Art of Noise	*The Ambient Collection (compilation)*	1990
9	Bugge Wesseltoft	*Existence*	1999
8	Lambchop	*Up With People (Zero 7 remix)*	2000
7	The Cinematic Orchestra	*Channel 1 Suite*	1999
6	Air	*Solidissimo (EDC Remix)*	1997
5	Space	*S/T (album)*	1990
4	Global Communication	*76:14 (album)*	1994
3	The KLF	*Chill Out (album)*	1990
2	The Orb	*Little Fluffy Clouds*	1990
1	Aphex Twin	*Selected Ambient Works 85-92 (album)*	1992

TOP
10

In reaction to the plaid shirts of grunge, British bands pulled on a Fred Perry, rediscovered the Kinks songbook and set about creating something as far removed from the sludgy drawl of America as you could get. Looking back – not in anger, of course – which have proved the most enduring tunes of the time?

BRITPOP

10 SUPERGRASS – 'CAUGHT BY THE FUZZ'
With the cheeky wink of 'Alright' proving to be something of a Marmite tune for many, the short, fuzzy blast of singer Gaz Coombe's brush with the law is a safer – and altogether better – bet. Celebratory, fun and as energetic as a toddler on tartrazine.

9 BOO RADLEYS – 'BARNEY AND ME'
The alarm-clock rock of 'Wake Up Boo!' notwithstanding, Boo Radleys don't get anywhere near the acclaim they should. The ambition of their *Giant Steps* album is staggering (psychedelic Britpop anyone?) and this upbeat slice of perfect pop an understated gem.

8 BLUETONES – 'SLIGHT RETURN'
Taking their cue from the Sixties jangle popularized a few years earlier on the Stone Roses' debut, the Bluetones were no copyists. Theirs was a much more classic sound than many of their peers, yet this tune seemed to catch the zeitgeist perfectly.

7 ELASTICA – 'WAKING UP'
While Oasis won plaudits for their 'talent borrows genius steals' approach to songwriting, people weren't so kind to Elastica and it's difficult to see why. This tune, though borrowing heavily from The Stranglers' 'No More Heroes', does so with class and sharp intelligence.

6 THE VERVE – 'BITTERSWEET SYMPHONY'
With a Stones sample borrowed from Andrew Loog Oldham and a video homage to Massive Attack's 'Unfinished Symphony', Richard Ashcroft's band nontheless created something startlingly original and utterly beguiling with this track from their *Urban Hymns* album.

5 SUEDE – 'ANIMAL NITRATE'
Brett Anderson with Bernard Butler and the band in tow brought something new to the pop party with androgynous imagery, rent-a-quote interviews and the wonderfully theatric overblown bluster of their debut album, from which this was the best track.

4 RADIOHEAD – 'JUST'
The Oxford band had already turned heads with the worldwide hit of 'Creep', but it's this track from the 1995 album *The Bends* that makes the list. An absolutely huge influence on bands that were to come, most obviously perhaps, Muse.

3 BLUR – 'POPSCENE'
Forget 'Parklife' (unlikely, it's quite catchy isn't

it?) this single-only release from 1992 was where it all started. Blur's short, angry, horn-backed, stab marked a huge shift in sound for them and, once they had caught up, everyone else as well.

smart, literate and pioneering pop that the band made their own, it managed to rhyme 'thirst for knowledge' with 'St Martin's College', a feat that should win a medal on its own.

2 OASIS – 'LIVE FOREVER'

There's no shortage of iconic singalongs in Oasis' back catalogue, but their first album was by some distance their best, and this is, arguably, the best moment on there. No simile, no subtlety, just a life-affirming classic with tears of joy in its eyes.

1 PULP – 'COMMON PEOPLE'

For many people, this is the defining Britpop anthem. Perhaps the pinnacle of the

	ARTIST	SONG	ALBUM	YEAR
10	Supergrass	'Caught by the Fuzz '	*I Should Coco*	*1995*
9	Boo Radleys	'Barney and Me'	*Giant Steps*	*1993*
8	Bluetones	'Slight Return'	*Expecting to Fly*	*1996*
7	Elastica	'Waking Up'	*Elastica*	*1995*
6	The Verve	'Bittersweet Symphony'	*Urban Hymns*	*1997*
5	Suede	'Animal Nitrate'	*Suede*	*1993*
4	Radiohead	'Just'	*The Bends*	*1995*
3	Blur	'Popscene'	*N/A*	*1992*
2	Oasis	'Live Forever'	*Definitely Maybe*	*1994*
1	Pulp	'Common People'	*Different Class*	*1995*

TOP
10

The musician and, these days, the DJ, are habitually nocturnal creatures, coming into their own when nearly everything else is being tucked up in bed. Night time is when all the good stuff happens, but what best soundtracks a night of wining and dining or dancing and prancing? We've given it some thought and come up with the following.

GREAT NIGHTS

10 GEORGE BENSON – 'GIVE ME THE NIGHT'

If George wants the night, it seems like a fair exchange for this smooth slice of disco funk. Having said that, Mr Benson shouldn't get all the credit as the song was actually written by Heatwave keyboards man Rod Temperton.

9 DEODATO – 'NIGHT CRUISER'

Another disco-funk instrumental, this one's all about the feel. And the feel here is one of driving home at the end of the night with the roof down and feeling warm air on your face courtesy of sometime Kool & The Gang producer Eumir Deodato.

8 T-CONNECTION – 'SATURDAY NIGHT'

As the stuttering bass intro makes room for the backbeat and waka-waka guitar, you know that Saturday night is

going to be alright as long as it has this as a theme tune. And by the time the Arp Odyssey synth signals its arrival, everyone's already lost in music.

7 ELTON JOHN – 'SATURDAY NIGHT'S ALRIGHT FOR FIGHTING'

Not wanting to condone violence, but never has the prospect of a punch-up sounded quite so entertaining. Elton's single, off the *Goodbye*

Yellow Brick Road album, was a big departure for him at the time and a much harder sound, musically and lyrically.

6 HEATWAVE – 'BOOGIE NIGHTS'

'Boogie nights are always the best in town' sang Heatwave in this 1982 gem and they may well have a point. A classic of its time, this up-tempo pop disco hit is guaranteed to get people dancing and, crucially, smiling.

5 LIONEL RICHIE – 'ALL NIGHT LONG'

There's no such thing as a guilty pleasure, either you like something or not and, be honest, we all love this a little bit don't we? Why? Because it's fun, ridiculous, a bit over the top and makes everyone very happy. The essence of a good night out.

4 AC/DC – 'YOU SHOOK ME ALL NIGHT LONG'

Not known for subtext in

their lyrics, this single from AC/DC, the first to feature Brian Johnson, is no exception. What they are known for however is good-time blues-based rock 'n' roll, and this excels on all those counts.

3 THE BEE GEES – 'NIGHT FEVER'
OK, so it's cheesy, we've all heard it a million times, and it's far from being the Bee Gees finest moment, but it's frivolous, familiar and fun to be around when you've had a few drinks. That sounds like a winning recipe for a night on the town.

2 ROLLING STONES – 'LET'S SPEND THE NIGHT TOGETHER'
While the Beatles wanted to 'hold your hand' the Rolling Stones wanted to... well, they were more direct. This plea to a young lady from Mick Jagger has all the subtely of a house brick, but when the case is this persuasive, 'no' is hardly likely to be the answer.

1 INDEEP – 'LAST NIGHT A DJ SAVED MY LIFE'
An ode to the disc jockey, Indeep's hit presents the DJ as an heroic, almost superhuman figure. While some may question that assessment (apart from DJs themselves one assumes), the slow, rolling post-disco funk is practically faultless.

	ARTIST	SONG	YEAR
10	George Benson	'Give Me the Night'	1980
9	Deodato	'Night Cruiser'	1980
8	T-Connection	'Saturday Night'	1979
7	Elton John	'Saturday Night's Alright For Fighting'	1973
6	Heatwave	'Boogie Nights'	1977
5	Lionel Richie	'All Night Long'	1983
4	AC/DC	'You Shook Me All Night Long'	1980
3	The Bee Gees	'Night Fever'	1977
2	The Rolling Stones	'Let's Spend the Night Together'	1967
1	Indeep	'Last Night A DJ Saved My Life'	1983

TOP
10

What is it that makes a great club? Obviously there's the music – the DJs – and the location... plus the crowd, you need a good audience. When all of these things come together, it can create something special and unique that's much greater than the sum of its parts. While not an exhaustive list – the world's just too big – here are 10 of the best.

CLUBS

10 MINISTRY OF SOUND

While many are turned off by the big-business, mass-marketing sheen of the UK's best-known club, there's no doubting its influence and significance. And there's not many that can boast Tony Humphries and Harvey among its previous residents.

9 HACIENDA

The only club on the list with a catalogue number, Factory records' folly (it famously cost a huge amount of money to run) was one of the most important clubs in England when the burgeoning house scene was breaking.

8 BERGHAIN

Berlin has long been a destination for the discerning clubber and Berghain a key attraction. Considered by many to be the best techno club in the world, it boasts fantastic sound, a strict door policy and an intriguing reputation for hedonism.

7 SHOOM

Unable to forget their experience at Amnesia, a group of British DJs came back to England where one of them, Danny Rampling, opened up Shoom in 1987, in an attempt to replicate the feel of Ibiza in London's Southwark Street. Unbelievably, it worked.

6 AMNESIA

Sometimes a club just captures a moment in time perfectly. So it is with the 1980s and Amnesia in Ibiza. Boasting DJ Alfredo, the mix of European pop, funk and disco was to launch Balearic Beat, open minds and broaden outlooks.

5 THE WAREHOUSE

The Chicago club boasted Frankie Knuckles as its resident DJ and musical director. While the musical policy was open and broadminded, it became – literally – synonymous with the club itself as Knuckles pioneered a style that was to become known as 'house'.

4 THE LOFT

Pioneering a not-for-profit model in the Seventies that many modern clubs would do well to emulate, for David Mancuso, the party was all. Invite only, anyone who attended heard, in Mancuso, a DJ who revered and respected the records he played.

3 WIGAN CASINO

Known by many as the home of Northern Soul, the Casino may not have had the musical exclusivity of its rival in Blackpool, The Mecca, but the huge club did have its legendary all-nighters, which saw people coming from far and wide to share in the atmosphere.

2 PARADISE GARAGE

Two words that elevate New York City's Paradise Garage - Larry Levan. Often credited with giving birth to the whole aesthetic of the modern club, the nights, with the focus on Levan's legendary DJ sets, were dedicated to dancing and hedonism.

1 STUDIO 54

The inspiration for the Chic song 'Le Freak', after Nile Rogers and co. fell foul of the NYC club's stringent door policy. Possibly the most famous nightclub of all time, while Nicky Siano played records, exclusivity was the key and celebrity the common currency.

	NAME	CITY	COUNTY
10	Ministry of Sound	London	England
9	Hacienda	Manchester	England
8	Berghain	Berlin	Germany
7	Shoom	London	England
6	Amnesia	San Rafael, Ibiza	Spain
5	The Warehouse	Chicago	USA
4	The Loft	New York	USA
3	Wigan Casino	Wigan	England
2	Paradise Garage	New York	USA
1	Studio 54	New York	USA

CHAPTER 3
ON THE DANCEFLOOR

TOP
10

If ever there was a music so perfectly engineered for making people move, it's the funk. So insistent is its command that you dance, it's a bit like having a well-meaning but slightly pushy friend urging you ever nearer the dancefloor where, before you know it, you're having the time of your life. Here are a perfect 10 to get up to get down to...

FUNK FLOORFILLERS

8 CURTIS MAYFIELD – 'MOVE ON UP'

Mayfield's falsetto and inimitable, pioneering style would be enough on its own to set him apart from the pack. However when you tie it in with his ability to write songs as consistently good as this, it elevates him to another level entirely.

7 EDDIE BO – 'HOOK AND SLING PARTS 1 & 2'

'Are you ready? Yeah!" The introduction to this loose-yet-tight funk jam could not be more perfect. Based around a simple refrain, played with expertise and style (particularly by drummer James Black) it's like a party to which we're all invited.

10 RICK JAMES – 'SUPER FREAK'

Even if you don't know this, you know this. Instantly identifiable as the main hook from MC Hammer's 1990 hit 'U Can't Touch This', Rick James's original was a huge hit in its own right - flamboyant, fun funk that was his trademark.

9 THE ISLEY BROTHERS – 'IT'S YOUR THING'

Recorded after the band had left the tight grip of Berry Gordy's Motown label, this was a response to their former boss. A slick and multi-layered sound take nothing away from the power and energy driving the song.

6 FUNK INC – 'KOOL IS BACK'

A 1971 cover of Kool and the Gang's 'Kool's Back Again', this version manages to be

rawer, tighter, bigger and, *adopts hushed tone*, better. Formed in 1969 by organist Bobby Watley, the band found the funk and proceeded to keep it on a very tight leash.

5 FUNKADELIC — 'STANDING ON THE VERGE OF GETTING IT ON'

Is it rock? Is it psychedelia? Who knows? One thing is for sure - it's got the funk. With characteristic humour and a 'waste nothing, use everything' approach, George Clinton's collective created a sound and a universe all their own.

4 SLY & THE FAMILY STONE – 'THANK YOU (FALLETINME BE MICE ELF AGIN)'

Another artist who embraced rock without sacrificing the funk, Sly Stone and his band helped to push the music into new territory. The gritty, gnarly edges that they left unpolished along with Larry Graham's anchored bass make for thrilling listening.

3 STEVIE WONDER – 'SUPERSTITION'

While in the studio with Tonto's Expanding Headband, Stevie Wonder expanded his mind and produced the best work of his career. From those sessions came this, in which

Stevie manages to drape the funk all over a deceptively simple beat.

2 JAMES BROWN – 'HOT PANTS'

You can't have a funk top 10 without James Brown featuring. Of the Godfather of Funk's many genre-defining classics, we've plumped for this ode to the female wardrobe. From his screaming intro to the end, this remains locked on and loaded with funk.

1 METERS – 'I NEED MORE TIME'

Funk's founding fathers sell us a bit of a dummy with the mellow introduction and crooning vocal of this song. Just as the low bass notes tail off and leave us hanging, the band resolves the tension with a funk groove so deep, it's virtually molten.

	ARTIST	SONG	YEAR
10	Rick James	'Super Freak'	1981
9	The Isley Brothers	'It's Your Thing'	1969
8	Curtis Mayfield	'Move On Up'	1970
7	Eddie Bo	'Hook and Sling Parts 1 & 2'	1969
6	Funk Inc	'Kool Is Back'	1971
5	Funkadelic	'Standing on the Verge of Getting it On'	1974
4	Sly & The Family Stone	'Thank You (Falletinme Be Mice Elf Agin)'	1969
3	Stevie Wonder	'Superstition'	1972
2	James Brown	'Hot Pants'	1971
1	The Meters	'I Need More Time'	1970

TOP
10

The 'Disco Sucks' campaign, waged by US DJ Steve Dahl in 1979 successfully whipped up enough prejudice to ensure that thousands of records were destroyed – including a mass burning at a White Sox baseball game. Now, this most joyous of genres is seen as the genuine antecedent of modern dance music and is spoken about with hushed reverence. Balance redressed, bigots repelled.

DISCO DANCEFLOOR BOMBS

10 CERRONE – 'SUPERNATURE'

Abandoning his trademark lush, orchestrated sound, French drummer and composer Cerrone looked to electronics to give him the futuristic sound he needed for this track about mutant creatures rising up against their mankind masters. As you do.

9 SALSOUL ORCHESTRA – 'YOU'RE JUST THE RIGHT SIZE'

Vincent Montana, Jr's Orchestra brought the funk to the disco and got the balance just right as soaring strings and extended vibraphone chords provide a perfect mellow counterpoint for the urgent drums and upfront bass.

8 GINO SOCCIO – 'DANCER'

The Canadian producer scored a huge hit on US dance charts when this was released in 1979, but the big sound was the result of just one man, lots of synths and primitive editing techniques carried out after hours and on a limited budget.

7 MACHINE – 'THERE BUT FOR THE GRACE OF GOD'

There isn't a huge number of 'message songs' in the disco canon, but this gem, from Jay Stovall's disco funk outfit, is a stern cautionary tale about the dangers of leaving the city in pursuit of a better life.

6 DINOSAUR L – 'GO BANG *(FRANCOIS K MIX)*'

Composer and cellist Arthur Russell was a unique and awe-inspiring talent and this is a spaced-out disco classic. It boasts a remix from Francois Kervorkian that tightened things up, smoothed off the rough edges and saw it become a crowd favourite at the Paradise Garage.

5 LOLEATTA HOLLOWAY – 'LOVE SENSATION'

Instantly recognizable from the 'because you're right on time' line nicked by cloth-eared Italian house merchants Black Box for their single 'Ride on Time', this 1980 hit, with backing ably provided by the Salsoul orchestra, is disco gold.

4 **ATMOSFEAR –
'DANCING IN OUTER
SPACE'**
A Brit-jazz funk anthem,
this underground track is
as powerful today as ever.
It begins full of stuttering
energy before settling into a
supremely confident, horn-led
groove and then, from out of
nowhere, comes a perfect,
outer-space skank.

3 **CHIC – 'GOOD TIMES'**
Nile Rogers and
Bernard Edwards' disco outfit
has to make the list, but which
song to choose? 'Le Freak'
has the better story behind
its creation, true, but 'Good
Times' wins out on account of
having the best bassline ever
recorded.

2 LOOSE JOINTS – 'IS IT ALL OVER MY FACE? (MALE VERSION)'

Another Arthur Russell production, another forward-looking masterpiece. On this track, produced with DJ Steve D'Acquisto, he was so concerned with getting the 'energy levels' right that, legend has it, he chose to record during a full moon.

1 DONNA SUMMER – 'I FEEL LOVE'

Over Giorgio Moroder's synth backing, Donna Summer sang her way into disco history with this visionary and game-changing track. It also boasts an inspired remix from Patrick Cowley that lasts longer than some geological periods.

	ARTIST	SONG	YEAR
10	Cerrone	'Supernature'	1977
9	Salsoul Orchestra	'You're Just the Right Size'	1976
8	Gino Soccio	'Dancer'	1979
7	Machine	'There But For the Grace of God'	1979
6	Dinosaur L	'Go Bang' (Francois K mix)	1982
5	Loleatta Holloway	'Love Sensation'	1980
4	Atmosfear	'Dancing in Outer Space'	1979
3	Chic	'Good Times'	1979
2	Loose Joints	'Is It All Over My Face? (Male version)'	1980
1	Donna Summer	'I Feel Love'	1982

TOP 10

Jazz-funk – basically fusion dressed up to the nines and on the lookout for a good party – is what happens when jazz musicians lock in to a groove. Giving the Seventies a great big smile on its face, there's a joy to these songs that sees even those people who claim to hate jazz nodding their head and shuffling their shoes.

JAZZ FINDS THE FUNK

10 MULATU ASTATKE – 'YEGELLE TEZETA'
Is this jazz-funk? Well, it's jazz, it's funky and it's sublime, so we're putting it in. Egyptian maestro Mulatu recently enjoyed a resurgence of interest in his career after collaborating with psychedelic funk band The Heliocentrics, the results of which are well-worth hunting down.

9 RAMSEY LEWIS – 'SLIPPIN' INTO DARKNESS'
The Ramsay Lewis Trio's version of the War song makes it on to the list as it takes the tight funk of the original and proceeds to spread out the chords and give it more width, more scope and an absolutely irresistible groove.

8 GRANT GREEN – 'SOOKIE SOOKIE'
From the Blue Note album Alive!, the jazz guitarist's funk offering is instantly recognizable – largely due to the number of times it's been sampled. With a backing that acts largely as a canvas for the lead players, the bigger picture is very impressive.

7 ROY AYRES – 'RUNNING AWAY'
There are some tunes that just have it. That unidentifiable, inexplicable thing that makes them work perfectly. Roy Ayres has written more than his fair share of those tunes and this is a 1979 example straight from the top drawer.

6 PLACEBO – 'TEMSE'
Listening to this track begin, it feels as if you've wandered into the middle of something, with a backing of unrelenting, unresolved tension asking questions of the listener and players alike. It's worth it though, as the whole is hugely satisfying.

5 MARVIN GAYE – 'INNER CITY BLUES'
Taken from the landmark album What's Going On, on which Marvin Gaye managed to soundtrack desolation and despair with a plangent beauty. He also managed to sneak in an understated bassline that gives a perfect groove-led structure on which to hang the emotion.

4 LONNIE LISTON SMITH – 'EXPANSIONS'
Has a triangle ever played a more significant part in a song? If it has, we're not aware of it. The unmistakable opening of this track sets the tone before the upfront bass, galloping drums or space-funk keys have even had a chance to shine.

3 JOHNNY HAMMOND – 'LOS CONQUISTADORES CHOCOLATES'
Given the uncanny similarity

of Jamiroquai's 'Emergency on Planet Earth' to this, Johnny Hammond must be feeling very, very flattered indeed, although credit for the extended masterpieces on the *Shifting Gears* album must be shared with producers, the Mizell brothers.

2 DONALD BYRD' – 'FALLIN' LIKE DOMINOS'

With the Mizell brothers, Larry and Fonce, on playing and production duties, Donald Byrd was off to a good start. There's a string-led, cinematic feel to the record, full of soaring ambition – and trumpet lines – gently tethered by the rolling rhythms.

1 HERBIE HANCOCK – CHAMELION

A bit like a jazz-funk 'A Day in the Life', this song, from Herbie's *Head Hunters* album is really two for the price of one. Precise funk is neatly joined to a smoother groove by a bridge of drums and bass to give the listener 15 minutes of bliss.

	ARTIST	SONG	YEAR
10	Mulatu Astatke	'Yegelle Tezeta'	1972
9	Ramsey Lewis	'Slippin' into Darkness'	1972
8	Grant Green	'Sookie Sookie'	1970
7	Roy Ayres	'Running Away'	1977
6	Placebo	'Temse'	1973
5	Marvin Gaye	'Inner City Blues'	1971
4	Lonnie Liston Smith	'Expansions'	1974
3	Johnny Hammond	'Los Conquistadores Chocolates'	1975
2	Donald Byrd	'Fallin' Like Dominos'	1975
1	Herbie Hancock	'Chameleon'	1973

TOP
10

Born and raised in Philadelphia... and that's thankfully where the similarities to *The Fresh Prince of Bel Air* end. The lush, orchestrated funk and extended arrangements of Philly soul were really disco by another name, and the Philadelphia International label, set up by Kenneth Gamble and Leon Huff to showcase this sound, deserves to be as well known as Motown or Stax. So, with that in mind...

THE PHILLY SOUND

10 HAROLD MELVIN & THE BLUENOTES – 'THE LOVE I LOST'

The gentle, mellow introduction of this upfront disco track does slightly belie its origins as a ballad. However, whatever the tempo, the rich emotion of Harold Melvin's voice covers this track like tears on a cheek.

9 MCFADDEN & WHITEHEAD – 'AIN'T NO STOPPING US NOW'

Apparently a slight dig at the heavy guiding hands of Gamble and Huff, this song is classic Philly. The surprisingly busy bass still manages to sound laid back, while the strings help to hold the celebratory sentiment of the song aloft and keep it there.

8 THE O'JAYS – 'BACK STABBERS'

This cautionary tale about trusting your fellow man was the title track of the band's 1972 album and exhibits a slower, more plaintive sound.

The tremulous glissando of the strings is matched perfectly by the emotive counsel of the vocals throughout.

7 MONTANA SEXTET – 'HEAVY VIBES'

By taking the best bit of MSFB's 'Love Is the Message' and spreading it out for more than five minutes, Salsoul orchestra leader and composer Vincent Montana Jr created something that was clearly more than the sum of its parts.

6 THE JACKSONS – 'SHOW YOU THE WAY TO GO'

After leaving Motown, the Jacksons decided to take refuge under the welcoming wing of Philadelphia International. This slinky, understated number was one of the good things to come of it. Their stage outfits, on the other hand, were definitely not.

5 BILLY PAUL – 'EAST'

The (sort of) title track from Billy Paul's *Going East* album, this finds him in a contemplative, almost philosophical mood. Not typical of the sound, it is nevertheless an absolutely sublime song, that defies any categorization other than 'beautiful'.

4 MFSB – 'TSOP (THE SOUND OF PHILADELPHIA)'

We'll stick to the story that says MFSB stands for Mothers Fathers Sisters Brothers! This song, featuring the voices of The Three Degrees, was the theme to the TV show Soul Train and perfectly captures the unbridled joy of the Philly sound.

3 INSTANT FUNK – 'I GOT MY MIND MADE UP'

The backing band of choice for stars including Loleatte Holloway, The O'Jays and Curtis Mayfield, Instant Funk could do it on their own too. Boasting a majestic remix from Larry Levan, this hit the clubs and left them stunned, but very happy.

2 THE PEOPLE'S CHOICE – 'DO IT ANY WAY YOU WANNA'

With a bass, piano, synth and at least two guitars playing the same part, the song almost instantly locks onto a forceful groove that could start a line dance in a morgue. As you might imagine, this 1975 single was an enormous hit for the band.

1 THE O'JAYS – 'I LOVE MUSIC'

The band sing this Gamble and Huff composition with the sort of conviction that would make anyone think it was a political manifesto rather than a song. It's also a sentiment that anyone hearing the song would struggle to disagree with.

	ARTIST	SONG	YEAR
10	Harold Melvin & The Bluenotes	'The Love I Lost'	1973
9	McFadden & Whitehead	'Ain't No Stopping Us Now'	1979
8	The O'Jays	'Back Stabbers'	1972
7	Montana Sextet	'Heavy Vibes'	1982
6	The Jacksons	'Show You the Way to Go'	1976
5	Billy Paul	'East'	1971
4	MFSB	'TSOP (The Sound of Philadelphia)'	1973
3	Instant Funk	'I Got My Mind Made Up'	1979
2	The People's Choice	'Do It Any Way You Wanna'	1975
1	The O'Jays	'I Love Music'	1975

TOP 10

With an output as great as Motown's, there are bound to be a few tunes that slip under most people's radar. In fact, there are hundreds. While the public, quite rightly, were dancing to the beat of Stevie Wonder, Diana Ross, The Temptations and The Four Tops, records were still being released at an industrial rate. Here are ten lesser-known gems.

LESSER-KNOWN MOTOWN MOMENTS

10 COMMODORES – 'BRICK HOUSE'
This brash slice of funk was recorded in 1977 and sounds about as much like classic Motown as it does death metal. Make sure to head to the mellower and more inventive extended mix rather than the synthetic bass slap of the single version though.

9 MARY WELLS – 'BEAT ME TO THE PUNCH'
Smokey Robinson's song might not be as lesser-known as some here, mainly on account of it having been a fairly big hit when it was released and earning Mary Wells a Grammy nomination. Still, not as well known as it should be!

8 TERRY JOHNSON – 'SUZIE'
The B-side to his single 'Whatcha Gonna Do' on Gordy records (another Motown subsidiary), this song has a feel and melody that's not unlike the best moments of Franki Valli. Which, if you're wondering, is a very good thing indeed.

7 THE SUPREMES – 'BUTTERED POPCORN'
Notable as the only Supremes single on which Florence Ballard takes lead duties and the group's last for Tamla before moving to Motown, it was beset by problems after its release - not least the shock discovery of a double entendre in the song's title.

6 THE ELGINS – 'HEAVEN MUST HAVE SENT YOU'
Far from sinking without trace on its release, this had some minor success and it's something of a crime that it's not better known. A sweet and naïve love song in the best tradition, it has more than a little in common with 'Baby Love'.

5 EDWIN STARR – 'S.O.S. (STOP HER ON SIGHT)'
The morse code piano intro gives way to a Motown dancer that screams 'Northern Soul' much louder than 'chart hit'. Not that this is a bad thing by any means, this is a song to fill dancefloors full of people and faces full of smiles.

4 THE VELVELETTES – 'LET LOVE LIVE (A LITTLE BIT LONGER)'
A track destined for Motown's V.I.P. label that didn't quite make it, this has since gained fans far and wide on 'Best of' compilations and at live shows, as the Velvelettes are still touring in their original line-up, having reformed in 1985.

3 THE MONITORS – 'NUMBER ONE IN YOUR HEART'
Motown does rock 'n' roll? Well yes... sort of. This B-side to the band's single 'Greetings (This Is Uncle Sam)' was released on the Motown subsidiary label V.I.P. and everything it needed to be a hit. If only they'd stuck it on the A-side.

2 BARBARA RANDOLPH – 'I GOT A FEELING'

With the unmistakable Motown production in full flourish, it's tempting to wonder why this wasn't a hit - particularly when Randolph herself was considered by the label a talent big enough to share the stage with Marvin Gaye.

1 THE MARVELETTES – 'FINDERS KEEPERS, LOSERS WEEPERS'

Another beautifully crafted pop stomper, this was recorded in 1964 but, criminally, didn't get a release until 1980 with Kim Weston's 'Do Like I Do' on the flip. To think that Motown had enough quality to leave stuff like this on the shelf is staggering.

	ARTIST	SONG	YEAR
10	Commodores	'Brick House'	1977
9	Mary Wells	'Beat Me to The Punch'	1962
8	Terry Johnson	'Suzie'	1969
7	The Supremes	'Buttered Popcorn'	1961
6	The Elgins	'Heaven Must Have Sent You'	1966
5	Edwin Starr	'S.O.S. (Stop Her On Sight)'	1966
4	The Velvelettes	'Let Love Live (A Little Bit Longer)'	1965 (recorded) 1999 (released)
3	The Monitors	'Number One in Your Heart'	1966
2	Barbara Randolph	'I Got A Feeling'	1967
1	The Marvelettes	'Finders Keepers, Losers Weepers'	1964 (recorded) 1980 (released)

TOP
10

Controversial? Perhaps. Difficult? Just a bit. To come up with a top 10 for a musical genre that is quite so obsessed with rarity, quality and musical archaeology is a daunting task and one to be greatly sweated over. Thankfully, beer towels and talc were in plentiful supply to combat the perspiration while compiling the following list.

NORTHERN SOUL

10 BOBBY SHEEN – 'DR LOVE'

Taking on the role of 'Dr Love' himself, Bobby Sheen has an answer for broken hearts everywhere with his 'PHd in Loveology'. Not that this will be of great concern to those dancing to this groove-led dancefloor bomb, who'll be too busy to care.

9 FRANKIE VALLI – 'THE NIGHT'

Along with 'Beggin'' this has to be Frankie Valli's best moment ever committed to vinyl. The bass leads in solo before being joined by each element until suddenly it bursts into its joyous whole, leaving spines everywhere tingling.

8 DOBIE GRAY – 'OUT ON THE FLOOR'

A hit almost 10 years after it was recorded, even the most cursory of listens is enough to tell you exactly why this was a hit in the Northern clubs. A celebration of going out dancing, this was an affirmation not just of a night, but of a lifestyle.

7 FRANK WILSON – 'DO I LOVE YOU (INDEED I DO)'

Notorious for its rarity (there are thought to be only two copies of this Motown single left in existence), it's best not to get hung up on price (nearly £26,000) and instead concentrate on the music – which is every bit as good as you would expect.

6 TONY CLARKE – 'LANDSLIDE'

A great example of a simple song executed with flair and subtle authority, this has an air of assured restraint throughout. In fact, far from being a forceful landslide, this tune is all about persuasion, and within two-and-a-half minutes the argument is won.

5 PATTI AUSTIN – 'MUSIC TO MY HEART'

The Motown sound is stamped all over this slice of pop perfection. The music and vocals are absolutely hand in hand throughout this 1968 B-side (which was in fact, released on the abc label) and the huge, sweeping emotion is utterly infectious.

4 AL WILSON – 'THE SNAKE'

This is exactly the sort of song that Tom Jones would have massively oversung, but Al Wilson concentrates on storytelling and emotion rather than belting it out to the back of the room, and we're all better off for that.

3 THE PARISIANS – 'TWINKLE LITTLE STAR'

A world away from the delicate shimmer that the title might suggest, this is a tune that gives you a slap around the face and a swift kick up the arse in its bid to remind you how utterly, immediately affecting and all-consuming music can be.

2 STEVE KARMEN BIG BAND – 'BREAKAWAY'

A big band sound so big that you half expect to find out that it lives at the top of a beanstalk. That the voice of Jimmy Radcliffe manages to be heard over the wondrous clatter and drums of this is a feat in itself.

1 GLORIA JONES – 'TAINTED LOVE'

If it's good enough for Marc Almond to cover, it's good enough for us. In truth, though Soft Cell made this their own, the original still takes the honours with an urgent, galloping tempo that turns from mournful self pity to bitter statement of intent.

	ARTIST	SONG	YEAR
10	Bobby Sheen	'Dr Love'	1966
9	Frankie Valli	'The Night'	1972
8	Dobie Gray	'Out on the Floor'	1966
7	Frank Wilson	'Do I Love You (Indeed I Do)'	1965
6	Tony Clarke	'Landslide'	1965
5	Patti Austin	'Music to my Heart'	1968
4	Al Wilson	'The Snake'	1968
3	The Parisians	'Twinkle Little Star'	1964
2	Steve Karmen Big Band	'Breakaway'	1968
1	Gloria Jones	'Tainted Love'	1965

TOP 10

There are always those in music whose inquisitive nature goes beyond writing a great tune and, instead, takes a step back to consider before taking a closer look at what's going on. The following people weren't content to simply harness the potential of technology, they wanted to test its breaking point and see what was beyond.

ELECTRONIC PIONEERS

10 JEAN MICHELLE JARRE
The Frenchman scored a hit with 'Oxygene (Part IV)', a tune recorded in a home studio. This was far removed from the massive outdoor gigs that he was to end up playing, concerts that mixed synthesisers with lasers and record-breaking crowds.

9 PATRICK COWLEY
In his short life, Patrick Cowley recorded some of the most innovative dance music ever produced. Albums like 1981's *Megatron Man*, containing the otherworldly space funk of 'Sea Hunt', or the recently released *School Daze* LP still sound jaw-droppingly fresh today.

8 MORTON SUBOTNICK
Subonnick's 'Silver Apples of the Moon', was a landmark release and the first piece of its type to be commissioned by a record

label. Although recorded 50 years ago, it is seen as a precursor of modern techno and remains light years ahead of its time.

7 TANGERINE DREAM
After growing out of the burgeoning Krautrock scene, Edgar Froese's band became forerunners in the development of electronic music. Their often dreamy, sometimes tense sonic soundscapes are unmistakeable, as is their effect on modern music.

6 ENO
With a 'head first' approach, Eno is a musician, composer and producer who puts theory over practise. As a result, his series of groundbreaking ambient albums have proved as much of an inspiration as his work with avant-garde rock and pop.

5 ALEXANDER ROBOTNICK
A legend for fans of analogue synth music everywhere, Italian jazz keyboardist Maurizio Dami was responsible for the groundbreaking

1983 single 'Problemes D'Amour', which was instrumental in influencing American dance music.

4 DELIA DERBYSHIRE

Best known for her work putting the musical flesh onto the bare bones of Ron Grainer's score for *Doctor Who*, Delia Derbyshire was also one third of White Noise, whose debut album, *An Electric Storm*, is a masterpiece of its type.

3 DAPHNE ORAM

One of the founders of the BBC Radiophonic Workshop, Oram's vision was as dynamic as her scores. Not content with simply producing music, she built the 'Oramics' machine, which, in the mid Sixties, could convert drawn symbols into music.

2 GIORGIO MORODER

His arpeggiated synth lines became the defining sound of disco, yet when he first recorded them, it was almost unthinkable that a popular dance tune should be made entirely using machines. His singular vision gave birth to electronic dance music.

1 KRAFTWERK

After a beginning based in free-form rock, the strict, sparse and more disciplined Krafwerk sound that was to become their trademark saw the band abandon traditional instruments and strike out on a path that countless others were to follow.

	ARTIST	LISTEN TO...	YEAR
10	Jean Michelle Jarre	*Zoolook*	1984
9	Patrick Cowley	*Megatron Man*	1981
8	Morton Subotnick	*Silver Apples of the Moon*	1967
7	Tangerine Dream	*Phaedra*	1974
6	Eno	*Ambient 1 Music for Airports*	1977
5	Alexander Robotnick	*Ce N'est Q'un Début*	1984
4	Delia Derbyshire	*An Electric Storm – White Noise*	1969
3	Daphne Oram	*Oramics*	2010
2	Giorgio Moroder	*I Feel Love*	1977
1	Kraftwerk	*Autobahn*	1974

TOP 10

As the disco beat faded into the background, several new forms of funk-infused music came to the fore as producers looked for new inspiration. Like the techno scene that was to follow, many of these music makers latched on to sounds coming from Europe and created something heavier, weirder and not unlike a disco populated and staffed entirely by robots.

ELECTRO

10 TELEX – 'MOSKOW DISCO'

Jazz musician Marc Moulin's electronic outfit were an influential act who came with a sound that was fully-formed electro. The computerized voices, train-like percussion (complete with whistle blast) and cold synth lines picked up passengers around the world.

9 WEST STREET MOB – 'BREAK DANCE – ELECTRIC BOOGIE'

While the use of The Incredible Bongo Band's Apache gifts West Street Mob's single a traditional hip hop feel, that soon gives way as a robot barks out instructions on how to breakdance and you know that you're firmly in electro territory.

8 JONZUN CREW – 'WE ARE THE JONZUN CREW'

Relying on live playing of synthesizers rather than the programmed approach favoured by many of their better-known peers, there was a looser, human feel to much of the Jonzun Crew's *Lost in Space* album that should have seen more success.

7 TYRONE BRUNSON – 'THE SMURF'

This instrumental was the only one of Brunson's to make such an impact, but nonetheless, its distinctive percussion, which has since been sampled to death, married to the incredible musicality, ensured that it was a huge club hit in 1983.

6 CYBOTRON – 'CLEAR'

The brainchild of Juan Atkins and Richard Davis, this track is seen as a 'clear' forerunner to the later, techno sound. With a much more driving, linear sound and the synths pared back to create space for the song to breathe, this is a very different electro prospect.

5 MAN PARRISH – 'HIP HOP BE BOP (DON'T STOP)'

Reference to this 1982 classic in the black comedy horror *Shaun of the Dead* left audiences in no doubt that this is not hip hop, but electro. In fact, Man Parrish's debut is so electro that it helped to define the parameters of the genre.

4 HERBIE HANCOCK – 'ROCKIT'

Is there anything that Herbie Hancock can't turn his hand

to? Not judging by this absolute monster of an electro tune. One of the first to feature recorded scratching courtesy of Grand Mixer D.ST, it was a brave and inspiring move for the jazz musician.

3 HASHIM – 'AL NAAFIYSH: THE SOUL'

That the string line in this 1983 electro masterpiece sounds uncannily similar to a Duran Duran song recorded a year earlier ('New Religion'), makes it even better in our eyes. A cornerstone of modern music, it still sounds futuristic 30 years later.

2 KRAFTWERK – 'THE ROBOTS'

A huge influence on the sound along with Yellow Magic Orchestra and synthpop acts like Gary Numan, it's difficult to imagine electro without Kraftwerk. This, off their Man Machine LP, is like the perfect distillation of all the requisite elements.

1 AFRIKA BAMBAATAA & THE SOUL SONIC FORCE – 'PLANET ROCK'

Taking its core melody from Kraftwerk's 'Trans Europe Express' while a synth plays an Ennio Morricone refrain over a Roland TR-808 beat might sound like madness, what it is, is revolutionary and paved the way for hip-hop to flourish.

	ARTIST	SONG	YEAR
10	Telex	'Moskow Disco'	1979
9	West Street Mob	'Break Dance – Electric Boogie'	1983
8	Jonzun Crew	'We Are The Jonzun Crew'	1983
7	Tyrone Brunson	'The Smurf'	1983
6	Cybotron	'Clear'	1983
5	Man Parrish	'Hip Hop Be Bop (Don't Stop)'	1982
4	Herbie Hancock	'Rockit'	1983
3	Hashim	'Al Naafiysh: The Soul'	1983
2	Kraftwerk	'The Robots'	1978
1	Afrika Bambaataa & The Soul Sonic Force	'Planet Rock'	1982

TOP 10

Hip-hop is all about reputation, and they don't come much bigger than Def Jam's. Formed by producer Rick Rubin and Russell Simmons (brother of Run DMC's Rev Run) the record label was one of the first to successfully stamp its size nine trainer all over popular culture and has since gained near-mythical status. This chart aims to show why.

HIP-HOP'S DEF JAMS

10 REDMAN – 'HOW TO ROLL A BLUNT'

Part song, part crazed instruction manual, this track really is a lesson on how to roll an illegal cigar. Despite the NSFW content, the track is funny, irreverent and funky as hell, bringing to mind the best work of forerunners EPMD.

9 BEASTIE BOYS – 'NO SLEEP TIL BROOKLYN'

To parents, teachers and owners of Volkswagens, the Beastie Boys were an affront to common decency. To their fans, they were the best thing to happen to music in years and brought hip-hop to a whole new audience without sacrificing their punk attitude.

8 EPMD – 'BROTHERS ON MY JOCK'

Having signed to Def Jam for their third LP, the New York duo lost none of their trademark funk or dense sample soundscapes and this album opener (which featured guest Redman), with its sample of Bob James's 'Nautilus', is no exception.

7 SLICK RICK – *THE GREAT ADVENTURES OF SLICK RICK* (LP)

It's impossible to choose one track, so we won't. Having set the pace on 'La Di Da Di', the B-side to Doug E Fresh's 'The Show', Rick's 1988 debut shows why he's one of the most influential MCs of all time with Snoop Dogg and Nas among his fans.

6 GHOSTFACE KILLAH – 'THE CHAMP'

Another decade, another success story, this time courtesy of another Wu-Tang Clan member - Ghostface Killah. The album *Fishscale* was heralded as a return to form for Ghostface and this track had the heads of everyone who heard it nodding in agreement.

5 3RD BASS FEATURING ZEV LOVE X – 'THE GAS FACE'

Funny, intelligent and possessed of an almost superhuman talent for creating grooves, 3rd Bass were the perfect fit for Def Jam during the late Eighties. This track, a minor hit at the time, also boasts the lyrical talents of Zev Love X aka MF Doom.

4 METHOD MAN – 'BRING THE PAIN'

During the Nineties, the label continued the quality control with releases including this, from the Wu-Tang Clan man. Which is easier to write than to say. The track's haunting backdrop is courtesy of an inspired sample from Jerry Butler's 'I'm Your Mechanical Man'.

3 NAS – 'HIP HOP IS DEAD'

Not just a triumph for Def Jam but for hip-hop itself,

Nas's declaration pretty much disproved his theory from the off. Both musically and lyrically inventive and eloquent, it showed that artists can have power, self-determination and success.

2 PUBLIC ENEMY – 'REBEL WITHOUT A PAUSE'

It's difficult to imagine a hip hop act with a bigger musical and cultural impact than Public Enemy. The first single from their *It Takes a Nation of Millions to Hold Us Back* album still possesses enough power and life to reanimate the dead.

1 LL COOL J – 'ROCK THE BELLS'

A truly revolutionary record, Def Jam scored a hit with LL Cool J's debut album and pioneered a new sound in hip hop. Sparse production, with scratching and staccato samples stabbed throughout the songs, it was, perhaps, realized best on this single.

	ARTIST	SONG	YEAR
10	Redman	'How To Roll a Blunt'	1992
9	Beastie Boys	'No Sleep til Brooklyn'	1986
8	EPMD	'Brothers on My Jock'	1990
7	Slick Rick	*The Great Adventures of Slick Rick* (LP)	1988
6	Ghostface Killah	'The Champ'	2006
5	3rd Bass *(feat Zev Love X)*	'The Gas Face'	1989
4	Method Man	'Bring the Pain'	1994
3	Nas	'Hip Hop Is Dead'	2006
2	Public Enemy	'Rebel Without a Pause'	1988
1	LL Cool J	'Rock the Bells'	1985

TOP 10

Time to put pen to paper and create your own top 10 list of songs about dancing...

10 ....

9 ....

8 ....

7 ....

6 ....

5 ....

4 ....

3 ....

2 ....

1 ....

TOP 10

Built upon a solid layer of disco, electro funk, Italo and electronic pop, house music's pulsing, 4/4 beat has proved a more lasting structure than many might have expected and has influenced the musical landscape in a profound way. This top 10 looks at some of the architects of that sound with a couple of personal favourites thrown in for good measure.

FOUNDATIONS OF GOOD HOUSE

10 PEPE BRADOCK – 'DEEP BURNT'

If many of the tracks here provide the foundations, this one is more like the first floor - it comes afterwards but is no less essential. This 1999 release is a warm, enveloping cuddle of a track that works equally well in the confines of a club or as house for the home.

9 GLENN UNDERGROUND – 'SOUND STRUCK'

Such is the sheer melodic force of the bassline, it's as if Glenn Underground took all of the notes in existence and crammed them into this song. Add stuttering hi-hats that are nearly tripping over themselves, and you get beautifully orchestrated chaos.

8 CRISPIN J GLOVER – 'NORTHERN LIGHTS (PRIME KUTZ MIX)'

While the invention of acid house may have been down to the Americans, you won't find many better examples of the form than this, from British producer Crispin J Glover. Simultaneously uplifting, piercing, mellow and soothing, this takes some beating.

7 XPRESS 2 – 'MUSIK XPRESS'

As the house sound travelled the globe, British producers, not content to be dancing spectators, came up with their own take on this new genre. Some phenomenal tracks resulted, including the express train chug of Rocky, Diesel and Ashley Beadle's 1992 release.

6 STERLING VOID & PARIS BRIGHTLEDGE – 'IT'S ALL RIGHT'

Feeling down? Don't know which way to turn? Don't worry, as this collaborative effort from Sterling Void and singer Paris Brightledge never tires of telling us, 'It's gonna be alright'. That they do it with such believable authority is this song's genius.

5 PHUTURE – 'ACID TRACKS'

To some, it sounded like a computer game gone into spasm, to others, acid house remains a welcome revolution. While Charanjit Singh appears to have been the first to use a Roland 303 in this way on *Ten Ragas to a Disco Beat*, Phuture were the first to make it sound like it was being punished.

4 MARSHALL JEFFERSON – 'MOVE YOUR BODY'

Purported to be first use of piano on a house record, this sounds so current it's amazing to think that it was released in 1986. Featuring a lyrical theme familiar to the genre - house music itself, this is, however, self-celebration without a hint of hubris.

3 JESSE SAUNDERS – 'ON AND ON'
1984 saw the release of what many believe to be the world's first house record. Using a loop from Mach's disco re-edit (also called 'On and On'), Jesse Saunders created something that was to prove instrumental in the building of a whole new genre.

1 JAMIE PRINCIPLE – 'YOUR LOVE'
Often credited to Frankie Knuckles, the collaboration between the producer and musician Principle was to lead to other tracks, including 'Baby Wants to Ride'. This song once and for all, rubbishes the claim that electronic music lacks soul or emotion.

2 MR FINGERS – 'CAN U FEEL IT?'
Hushed and revered tones are usually reserved for discussion of Larry Heard, such is his legacy. A sublime bassline, perfectly wrapped in sweeping sheets of synthesizer with spoken word history of house make this track a lesson in more ways than one.

	ARTIST	SONG	YEAR
10	Pepe Bradock	'Deep Burnt'	1999
9	Glenn Underground	'Sound Struck'	1996
8	Crispin J Glover	'Northern Lights (Prime Kutz mix)'	1993
7	Xpress 2	'Musik Xpress'	1992
6	Sterling Void & Paris Brightledge	'It's Alright'	1987
5	Phuture	'Acid Tracks'	1987
4	Marshall Jefferson	'Move your Body'	1986
3	Jesse Saunders	'On and On'	1984
2	Mr Fingers	'Can U Feel It?'	1986
1	Jamie Principle	'Your Love'	1986

TOP 10

A bloodless coup, the march of the machines into the British charts during the Eighties was not without controversy however. Accused by some embittered souls to be lacking in creativity, ability and emotion, it not only stood its ground, but set about annexing great swathes of Chartland and influencing pretty much everything that came after. That's a victory in anyone's book.

THE SYNTH-POP REVOLUTION

10 ULTRAVOX
Vienna means nothing to us either, but the band's earlier releases are phenomenal examples of what happens when you take a new wave band with ambition and put them in a room with one of the best Krautrock producers in the world, Conny Plank.

9 PET SHOP BOYS
As unashamedly pop as you might expect from a band including a former Smash Hits journalist, Pet Shop Boys' debut, 'West End Girls', fused perfectly pop songwriting sass with synth savvy – a combination that has never really deserted them.

8 SOFT CELL
The band's first album, *Non-Stop Erotic Cabaret*, could not have been better titled. Marc Almond was always more an accomplished cabaret singer than a pop star, while David Ball's sleazy electronic backing provided the perfect counterpoint for artistic and chart success.

7 EURYTHMICS
For a while, it seemed as if Annie Lennox just needed to be breathing to receive a Brit award, such was the influence of the Eurythmics. But behind the hits and the headlines there remain some genuinely breathtaking examples of experimental synth pop genius.

6 BLANCMANGE
A string of phenomenal pop singles would be enough to secure Blancmange's position on this list but, like the Eurythmics, it's to the B-sides and songs like 'The Game Above My Head' we must turn for a glimpse of their true genius.

5 DEPECHE MODE
Who'd have thought that a bunch of boys from Basildon armed with youthful confidence and a bunch of synthesisers could create perfect pop that would capture the imagination of a generation and influence dance music for decades to come?

4 NEW ORDER
After the death of singer Ian Curtis, it would have been understandable for the rest of Joy Divsion to call it a day. Instead they formed New Order, embraced club culture and electronic music and became one of the most innovative bands in the world.

3 THE HUMAN LEAGUE
After The Human League mk 1 split, singer Phil Oakey had to build a new band. He hired singers Anne Sulley and Joanne Catherill, and then turned to veteran producer Martin Rushent. The pop stardom he dreamed of was to follow in spades...

2 GARY NUMAN

As part of Tubeway Army, Gary Numan was one of the first to achieve real success with the synthpop sound. It was something he then capitalised on with solo singles including 'Cars' and a cold stage persona that fitted perfectly with his machine music.

1 HEAVEN 17

Formed after Martyn Ware and Ian Marsh left new-wave synth pioneers The Human League, Heaven 17 responded to their former band's immediate chart success by producing a contender for the best album of the Eighties in *Penthouse and Pavement*.

	ARTIST	LISTEN TO...	YEAR
10	Ultravox	'Systems of Romance'	1978
9	Pet Shop Boys	'Please'	1986
8	Soft Cell	'Non-Stop Erotic Cabaret'	1981
7	Eurythmics	'Touch'	1983
6	Blancmange	'Mange Tout'	1984
5	Depeche Mode	'Speak and Spell'	1981
4	New Order	*Substance* (compilation)	1987
3	The Human League	'Dare'	1981
2	Gary Numan	'The Pleasure Principle'	1979
1	Heaven 17	'Penthouse and Pavement'	1980

TOP 10

Detroit's starker, more futuristic take on dance music took its cue in equal measure from the science-fiction funk of Funkadelic, European bands like Kraftwerk and the hard steel backdrop of the city's automobile industry. The resulting metal machine music has proved just as lasting as its Chicago-based, disco-dipped cousin and every bit as influential.

TOWERING TECHNO

10 UNDERWORLD – 'COWGIRL'
They may be famous for the shouty stomp of Born Slippy, but the disorientating shifting vocals of this track against the harsh, buzzing background notes and subtle flourishes hiding between the punishing beats is a far more interesting proposition.

9 E-DANCER – 'BANJO (FUNK D'VOID MIX)'
Kevin Saunderson gets a makeover courtesy of Funk D'Void, aka Lars Sandberg, in this end-of-the-millennium belter, so drenched in reverb that it sound like it's permanently breathing in. Full of tense energy and spiky distortion, it's a near-perfect remix.

8 THE AZTEC MYSTIC – 'JAGUAR'
When Sony, unable to license the track from the uncompromising Underground Resistance man, tried to release a tone-by-tone copy on to the market, they started a fight they couldn't win. They've got good taste mind - this is a truly fantastic tune.

7 GALAXY 2 GALAXY – 'JOURNEY OF THE DRAGONS'
Conceived by Mike Banks, of Underground Resistance, this 1993 release has an altogether different feel to much of what had gone before. Musically more ambitious and encompassing, it had a warmer, jazzier sound that involved the listener in a very different way.

6 CYBOTRON – 'ALLEYS OF YOUR MIND'
Proving that the line separating electro from techno is as thin as that which divides soup and stew, is this 1981 release from Juan Atkins and Richard Davis. A lighter, more heady record than its peer, Sharevari, it too helped kickstart the genre.

5 PAPERCLIP PEOPLE – 'THE CLIMAX'
Carl Craig is an anomaly, people just aren't supposed to be as consistent - or make music sound as effortless. While it's tempting to plump for the linear, heads-down approach of Throw here, it's the raw disco-finish of The Climax that takes the honours.

4 MODEL 500 – 'NO UFOS'
Juan Atkins first single under the Model 500 moniker was a calling card that was stark, uncompromising and full of surprises. Snatches of vocal, fighting with delayed drums for space to be heard while an eight bar bass loop keeps everything in check.

3 RHYTHIM IS RHYTHIM – 'STRINGS OF LIFE'
In the same way that Dennis

Law played for United and City, this track is claimed as a classic by both the techno and house camps. It's easy to see why - it straddles both like a colossus, but Derek May's 1987 tune is techno as far as we're concerned.

2 RON TRENT – 'ALTERED STATES'

No build up, no easy in, just bam! Pounding drums softened slightly by faint bells with the pendulum swing of the main melodic motif. Then the handclaps that precede the drifting, distorted strings, which leave you... elsewhere. So good it should be taught in schools.

1 A NUMBER OF NAMES – 'SHAREVARI'

It's got the kick drum, it's got the trembling, mesmerizing bass, a tough snare shackled to reverbed handclaps and sounds like it should be playing in clubs with sweat dripping off the wall. Yep, it's a techno record. And in 1981 too.

	ARTIST	SONG	YEAR
10	Underworld	'Cowgirl'	1993
9	E-Dancer	'Banjo (Funk D'Void mix)'	1999
8	The Aztec Mystic	'Jaguar'	1999
7	Galaxy 2 Galaxy	'Journey of the Dragons'	1993
6	Cybotron	'Alleys of Your Mind'	1981
5	Paperclip People	'The Climax'	1995
4	Model 500	'No UFOs'	1985
3	Rhythim is Rhythim	'Strings of Life'	1987
2	Ron Trent	'Altered States'	1992
1	A Number of Names	'Sharevari'	1981

TOP 10

After the angry assault of punk's stripped-down, back-to-basics approach, post-punk started layering sounds back on to the palette. The ambition in doing so was huge and wide-ranging, but the most welcome development was the renewed interest in making music that you could dance to, leading us to ask, 'Who were the most successful movers on the scene?'

POST-PUNK

10 YELLO – 'I LOVE YOU'
Quite what Swiss musicians Boris Blank and Carlos Peron saw in billionaire Dieter Meier when looking for a singer is unclear, but we're guessing they never had to pay for studio time again. The mix was perfect, as is this single off their third album.

9 CABARET VOLTAIRE – 'SENSORIA'
Sheffield's Cabaret Voltaire had been pursuing an experimental agenda with their music up until about 1983. A conscious decision to try to write hits resulted first in their *Crackdown* album, and then this, from the following year's *Micro-Phonies*. Job done.

8 PIL – 'DEATH DISCO'
Asked by his mother, on her deathbed, to write a disco song for her funeral, John Lydon came up with this. It's an amazing achievement, epic and angry, that nevertheless still manages to be the disco song that Mrs Lydon had asked for.

7 THE UNITS – 'HIGH PRESSURE DAYS'
Recently rediscovered, remixed and re-released, the 1979 original from US synth-punks The Units is still the best as far as this chart is concerned. Imagine a punk band playing the Chemical Brother's back catalogue and you're pretty much there.

6 GANG OF FOUR – 'DAMAGED GOODS'
Not a trace of electronics here, or funk – just drums, voice, scratchy guitar and a hyperactive bassline. Yet this post-punk delight from Leeds band Gang of Four is full of nervous, infectious energy that demands you move to it.

5 MAGAZINE – 'THANK YOU (FALETTINME BE MICE ELF AGIN)'
This breathtaking Sly and the Family Stone cover has a thundering bassline, but that's about all it shares with the original. This slowed-down, multi-layered version takes the song into almost filmic territory, full of taught strings, jagged guitar and reverbed release.

4 GLAXO BABIES – 'SHAKE THE FOUNDATIONS'
Boasting an impressive arsenal of styles, from free jazz improvisation to odd electro and off-kilter krautrock, Glaxo Babies were a difficult band to pin down. Having said that, this is basically incredibly well conceived, brilliantly played, propulsive punk-funk.

3 SEVERED HEADS – 'DEAD EYES OPENED'
The Australian band's obsession for grisly stories and ghastly detail served them

well on this groundbreaking release that saw them marry industrial beats, pulsating bass and floating strings with a spoken word narrative detailing the 1924 murder of a pregnant woman.

2 TALKING HEADS – 'BORN UNDER PUNCHES'

Given his fascination with afrobeat, it's fair to assume it was producer Eno who helped bring the African influence to the Talking Heads party. It was certainly better than a cheap bottle of wine, as this track remains one of their very best.

1 SHRIEKBACK – 'MY SPINE IS THE BASSLINE'

When XTC's Barry Andrews got together with former Gang of Four member Dave Allen, they soon found themselves with a band capable of confidently stripping everything extraneous away and finding considerable room to move in the process.

	ARTIST	SONG	YEAR
10	Yello	'I Love You'	1983
9	Cabaret Voltaire	'Sensoria'	1984
8	PIL	'Death Disco'	1979
7	The Units	'High Pressure Days'	1980
6	Gang of Four	'Damaged Goods'	1979
5	Magazine	'Thank You (Falettinme Be Mice Elf Agin)'	1980
4	Glaxo Babies	'Shake the Foundations'	1980
3	Severed Heads	'Dead Eyes Opened'	1983
2	Talking Heads	'Born Under Punches'	1980
1	Shriekback	'My Spine Is the Bassline'	1983

TOP 10

The broad appeal and cultural shift that acid house brought with it soon trickled down and permeated other areas of music too. Not content to stand in the corner any longer, a generation of shy, retiring, guitar-loving indie kids suddenly found themselves in bellbottoms and gaudy hoodies and dancing to the beat of a different drum. Indie dance was born.

INDIE DANCE

10 BLUR – 'THERE'S NO OTHER WAY'

Before the Doc Martens and dust-ups with Oasis, Blur had a distinctly baggier beat to their drum. This, their second single, shows their talent for a melody fully formed despite tender years and a song that holds its own with their best.

9 FLOWERED UP – 'WEEKENDER'

To many, Flowered Up were to London what the Happy Mondays were to Manchester. It's an easy comparison to make, and unfair to Flowered Up's distinctive sound, best captured on this 13-minute long epic which also boasted an epoch-defining video.

8 CHARLATANS – 'THE ONLY ONE I KNOW'

The 1990 single had the Hammond swirls and loose, groove inflected drums that came to typify much of indie dance, but what it also had up its baggy sleeve was the intro from Deep Purple's 'Hush' and a huge drum break.

7 NEW FAST AUTOMATIC DAFFODILS – 'BIG (BAKA)'

Taking just the vocal line from the Manchester band's bass-heavy indie dance stomper, DJ and producer John Dasliva

stuck it over the top of an acid house tune he had already recorded – a move that resulted in musical alchemy.

6 THAT PETROL EMOTION – 'ABANDON (BOYS OWN MIX)'

Andrew Weatherall on remix duties, this time joined by Terry Farley for a radical rework. Sacrificing none of the incendiary guitar blast of the original, the pair married it to dub-infused bass and hip hop drums so big they need a post code.

5 SPACEMEN 3 – 'BIG CITY'

Although a band more readily associated with passing out rather than dancing, the blessed-out drone-rock of Spacemen 3 was married to an undulating acid line to great effect on this single, effectively a solo outing by band member Sonic Boom.

4 MY BLOODY VALENTINE – 'SOON'
After seeing all of their money being spent on the recording of My Bloody Valentine's second album, it must have been some solace to Creation records that *Loveless* contained the closest the band ever got to a pop single.

3 STONE ROSES – 'FOOL'S GOLD'
With a bass line inspired by Flea's contribution to Young MC's 'Know How', this single abandoned the Sixties' shimmer of the Roses' debut LP, and got kids with fringes everywhere dancing. Often quite badly, but you can't have everything.

2 PRIMAL SCREAM – 'LOADED'
Most of the band's Mercury prize-winning LP *Screamedelica* could have made this list, but it's to Andrew Weatherall's inspired destruction of their song 'I'm Losing More than I'll Ever Have' we turn for a lesson in just how far you can push a remix.

1 HAPPY MONDAYS – 'WFL (VINCE CLARK REMIX)'
One of the best indie dance bands to ever pick up a guitar and stumble onstage, the Mondays remain a shambolic, shamanic, ramshackle joy. This 1989 track managed to straddle the genres with more authority than any before or since.

	ARTIST	SONG	YEAR
10	Blur	'There's No Other Way'	1991
9	Flowered Up	'Weekender'	1992
8	Charlatans	'The Only One I Know'	1990
7	New Fast Automatic Daffodils	'Big (Baka)'	1990
6	That Petrol Emotion	'Abandon (Boys Own Mix)'	1990
5	Spacemen 3	'Big City'	1991
4	My Bloody Valentine	'Soon'	1991
3	The Stone Roses	'Fool's Gold'	1990
2	Primal Scream	'Loaded'	1990
1	Happy Mondays	'WFL (Vince Clark remix)'	1989

Despite concern from some quarters, rock wasn't impervious to the dancefloor influence – it was, after all, a huge and very profitable market. Inevitably when the disco rainbow was mixed with the primary colours of rock, a new hue was created, one that, at certain times, proved to be positively luminous. Here's our ten that shine like stars.

ROCK COMES TO THE DISCO

10 MARTIN CIRCUS – 'DISCO CIRCUS'

From theatric psych-rock through nondescript pop to delirious disco, the career of French band Martin Circus was wide-ranging to say the least. While the middle of these periods is best avoided, this out-and-out disco track from 1979 is an absolute must.

9 BLONDIE – 'HEART OF GLASS'

Early demos of this song listed it as 'The Disco Song' – something of an oddity for a band at the forefront of New York's new wave scene. Add producer Mike Chapman, a touch of Moroder-esque synths and you have a career-defining track.

8 THE CLASH - 'ROCK THE CASBAH'

'The Sharif don't like it', sang the Clash on their biggest hit. We can only assume then, that the Sharif is the kind of cloth-eared poltroon that wouldn't recognize the sublime boogie of this punk-funk classic if it came with a name badge.

7 YOKO ONO – 'WALKING ON THIN ICE'

It was a tape of this song that Lennon was carrying on the fateful day he was shot. It's a song that shows a radical, exciting change of direction for Yoko as an artist and Lennon as a producer, but one that was tragically short-lived.

6 PINK FLOYD – 'ANOTHER BRICK IN THE WALL (PART II)'

With attention generally focusing on the double negative of the uneducated children's choir, Pink Floyd sneaked a perfectly formed, slow disco delight under the radar. Sadly, they then left the dancefloor, never to return.

5 BEE GEES – 'JIVE TALKIN''

Having been through as many styles as most bands have outfits, the brothers Gibb took to dance with characteristic aplomb. It was a transformation that started on 1975's *Main Course* album, and the unbeatable disco peacock strut of 'Jive Talkin''.

4 QUEEN – 'ANOTHER ONE BITES THE DUST'

Unsurprisingly, given the prominence of the bassline, this was written by Queen's bassist, John Deacon. Inspired by hanging out with Chic (and the song 'Good Times' in particular), it manages to be funk, rock and disco all at the same time.

3 SUPERTRAMP – 'CANNONBALL'

With a simple piano refrain, and a beat and bassline so tight that sound like they're handcuffed together, this isn't

just a case of a rock band trying their hand at disco, it's a band trying to fuse the elements with style and succeeding.

2 THE ROLLING STONES – 'MISS YOU'
Apparently the result of a jam session with session player and right hand man Billy Preston, (who doesn't get a writer's credit) this is as smooth, sleek and successful as you'd imagine the Stones to be and also heralded their first dance remix.

1 CHICAGO – 'STREET PLAYER'
Used as the sample source for Kenny Gonzalez's1995 house smash The Bomb, the truly surprising thing is how little he actually had to do to this 1979 single by US rock stalwarts Chicago. A perfect example of how to rock the disco.

	ARTIST	SONG	YEAR
10	Martin Circus	'Disco Circus'	1978
9	Blondie	'Heart of Glass'	1978
8	The Clash	'Rock the Casbah'	1982
7	Yoko Ono	'Walking on Thin Ice'	1981
6	Pink Floyd	'Another Brick in the Wall (Part II)'	1979
5	Bee Gees	'Jive Talkin''	1975
4	Queen	'Another One Bites the Dust'	1980
3	Supertramp	'Cannonball'	1985
2	The Rolling Stones	'Miss You'	1978
1	Chicago	'Street Player'	1979

TOP
10

On the island of Jamaica in the 1950s, a musical movement was to send shockwaves around the world - and not just because of the bass levels. The rise of the soundsystem was a social revolution, as DJs and selectors loaded up vans with turntables and speakers big enough to have their own gravitational field and took the party to the people.

SOUNDSYSTEMS

9 THE HERCULORDS
Having grown up in Jamaica, Clive Campbell - aka DJ Kool Herc - was familiar with big sound systems. This stayed with him and, after moving to New York, he held huge outdoor parties on his own system, the Herculords, and pretty much invented hip hop.

8 SAXON STUDIO SOUND SYSTEM
Lewisham might not seem like the obvious birthplace of an internationally renowned sound system but, in 1976, that's exactly what happened. With MCs including Tippa Irie and Smiley Culture passing through their ranks, they also count Maxi Priest among their alumni.

10 AFRIKA BAMBAATAA
Throwing parties since the tender age of 11, Afrika Bambaataa started small in more ways than one.

Progressing from what was basically a home stereo system to louder equipment over time, his progressive attitude - and impressive record collection - proved the key to his success.

7 JAH SHAKA
Running his roots sound system since the 1970s in South East London, Jah Shaka

is also a musician, composer and record label owner. Having consistently eschewed fashion trends and stuck to a roots sound, his reputation as one of the best is richly deserved.

6 TOM THE GREAT SEBASTIAN

The first big sound system in Jamaica, this was formed by Tom Wong. Having created the leading system of his day, once others started to muscle in on his territory, he seemed to step aside, having succeeded in inspiring a new generation.

5 KING EDWARDS THE GIANT

One of 'the big three' along with Coxsone and Trojan, King Edwards The Giant was formed after a a trip to America in 1954, when Vincent – at his brother's request – brought back some 45s to capitalise on the sudden boom in sound systems in Jamaica.

4 VOICE OF THE PEOPLE

After working on Sir Coxsone's Downbeat, Cecil Bustamente Campbell used the invaluable knowledge he had gained to set up his own sound system. Before long, it was considered one of the best on the island and led to his incredible recording career.

3 SIR COXONE'S DOWNBEAT

Invoking another great Jamaican love, Clement Seymour Dodd was nicknamed Coxsone after the Yorkshire cricketer, Alex Coxon. The name stuck for his soundsystem, which he ran before setting up the groundbreaking Studio One recording studio.

2 DUKE REID'S THE TROJAN

Named after the trucks they used to transport the system to dance halls around Jamaica, Duke Reid's 1950s system comprised large speakers, a record playing deck and a powerful amplifier, often used to battle Coxsone Downbeat.

1 TUBBY'S HOMETOWN HI-FI

Formed in 1958, this was one of the great sound systems in Jamaica. King Tubby's understanding not just of music, but the mechanics of the sound system itself meant he had an important edge when it came to the quality of his equipment.

	ARTIST	COUNTRY
10	Afrika Bambaataa	USA
9	The Herculords	USA
8	Saxon Studio Sound System	UK
7	Jah Shaka	UK
6	Tom the Great Sebastian	Jamaica
5	King Edwards The Giant	Jamaica
4	Voice of the People	Jamaica
3	Sir Coxone's Downbeat	Jamaica
2	Duke Reid's the Trojan	Jamaica
1	Tubby's Hometown Hi-Fi	Jamaica

TOP 10

The trickiest gig for any DJ is the wedding: so many people to please, all with different tastes and opinions, all in the same venue and all desperate to have a good time. While no list can guarantee ballroom bliss in these situations, here is our top ten songs aiming to bridge the gap between old and young, happy and sad, drunk and sober.

SONGS FOR A WEDDING DANCEFLOOR

10 THOMPSON TWINS – 'IN THE NAME OF LOVE'

A perfect singalong chorus, which, at the right time of the evening will even get men of a certain age on the dancefloor, even if it is to badly air drum along to the amazing percussion break, before seeing if the bar's still free.

9 CHIC – 'I WANT YOUR LOVE'

After the bridal waltz, everyone needs to be encouraged to take to the floor, partly to save the blushes of the bride and groom, who may be feeling a little self-conscious while everyone looks on. Only 'I Want Your Love' can save the day!

8 JOHN PAUL YOUNG – 'LOVE IS IN THE AIR'

What better sentiment for the most sentimental of occasions than the Australian singer's claim that love is everywhere you look. The lyrics could have come out of the cards on display on the present table, but a wedding's no place for cynicism.

7 THE SONICS – 'HAVE LOVE WILL TRAVEL'

There are several versions of this ode to the power of attraction that one person can hold over another that you could chose for the post-nuptial shindig. Thee Headcoatees cover is great, but The Sonics edge it with their timeless take.

6 SISTER SLEDGE – 'WE ARE FAMILY'

One for the bridesmaids, this. By the end of the night they can be arm-in-arm, singing along to this, while a tearful bride tells them all that she feels like they're all her sisters before bursting into tears. That's the power of music! And double vodka tonics.

5 CANDI STATON – 'YOUNG HEARTS RUN FREE'

While Candi's message may be that men will ultimately let you down and leave you high and try, the unbridled optimism of the somgs chorus is enough to have people dancing and singing and agreeing that, yes, love is all there is.

4 BANBARRA – 'SHACK UP'

Unmarried couples can nod sagely while the lyrics of this manifesto for eschewing marriage will go over the heads of most (and probably just as well), but this taut funk monster leads to dancing like weddings lead to tears.

3 JACKIE WILSON – 'I GET THE SWEETEST FEELING'

'The greater your love, The stronger you hold me, baby.' People dancing at a wedding is great, but ideally you want

them dancing with each other! Jackie Wilson's beautiful song has the beat, the melody and the lyrics to deliver on that score.

2 CHAKA KHAN – 'I FEEL FOR YOU'

On the big day, sentiment is everything. Chaka Khan's bold and direct song about the unmistakable onset of burgeoning love and feeling all warm and tingly is guaranteed to hit the right note and get people dancing into the bargain.

1 THE FACES – 'STAY WITH ME'

Most people will hear what they want to in a song, so wedding guests will happily chug around the floor to the 'Stay with me' of the chorus, happily lending the song a very different meaning to the one that Rod Stewart intended.

	ARTIST	SONG	YEAR
10	Thompson Twins	'In the Name of Love'	1982
9	Chic	'I Want Your Love'	1978
8	John Paul Young	'Love Is in the Air'	1978
7	The Sonics	'Have Love Will Travel '	1965
6	Sister Sledge	'We Are Family'	1979
5	Candi Staton	'Young Hearts Run Free'	1976
4	Banbarra	'Shack Up'	1975
3	Jackie Wilson	'I Get the Sweetest Feeling'	1968
2	Chaka Khan	'I Feel For You'	1984
1	The Faces	'Stay With Me'	1971

TOP
10

The best DJs don't just play records, they use music to dictate the emotional curve of the night. It's not about carefully pre-planning a set to show off skills, it's a responsive talent, one that involves watching the crowd, reading the situation and responding with the right record. Even when it's something people might not know they want.

DJs

10 **DJ HARVEY**
Harvey Bassett's now legendary nights at London's Gardening Club (Moist) and Blue Note (New Hard Left) were followed by his Stateside Sarcastic Disco venture, which has seen his star, and legend, rise. As unafraid to play the well-known as the obscure, he dances to the beat of his own drum.

9 **IAN LEVINE**
One of the most important and progressive DJs on the Northern Soul scene, it was all about the records for Ian Levine - and he had tunes that others could only dream of, bought in the blistering Miami heat while on holiday in America - a luxury few could afford.

8 **NORMAN JAY**
The only royally endorsed DJ on the list, Norman Jay (MBE) set up the

Good Times sound system with his brother Joey after inspiring trips to New York. It has since become a Notting Hill Carnival staple and Norman an international star.

7 ALFREDO
When he started DJing on the terrace at Ibiza's Amnesia club in 1976, Argentinian born Alfredo Fiorito's eclectic mix of disco and European pop was not an immediate hit. Given time

though, it was to define the Balearic sound and have huge influence.

6 GRANDMASTER FLASH
His recording career has pulled focus away from his DJing, but it's worthwhile taking a closer look as he was the first to really use turntables as an instrument. Think of pretty much any DJ technique - Flash either invented it or perfected it.

5 DJ KOOL HERC
As well as having the Herculords sound system, DJ Kool Herc had incredible vision and creativity. He was the first to switch between the funky, drum-led passages in funk records - the breaks - to create an entirely new piece of continuous music.

4 FRANCIS GRASSO
It was New York DJ Grasso, legend has it, who invented the idea of

beatmatching to create a continuous flow of music. His uncompromising approach and rich array of (often unknown) records kept the crowd on its toes both literally and metaphorically.

3 FRANKIE KNUCKLES
Simply put, Frankie Knuckles invented house music. The Chicago club at which he was resident, the Warehouse, even lent its name to the new, underground style and his productions with artists including Jamie Principle are some of the best examples of the genre.

2 LARRY LEVAN
Finding a home - and fame - at New York's Paradise Garage club at the height of disco, Larry Levan had an eclectic palette and a talent for incorporating live elements and high drama into his sets that helped to inspire awe and devotion in his fans.

1 DAVID MANCUSO
With a complete respect for the music he was playing, Mancuso was famous for letting records play in their entirety, just as they had been produced. This reverence, along with an ability to use music to provide a narrative to the night is a rare skill indeed.

	NAME	ASSOCIATED CLUBS/ NIGHTS
10	Harvey	Moist/New Hard Left/Sarcastic Disco
9	Ian Levine	The Blackpool Mecca
8	Norman Jay	Good Times
7	Alfredo	Amnesia
6	Grandmaster Flash	Various locations, New York
5	DJ Kool Herc	Various locations, New York
4	Francis Grasso	Sanctuary
3	Frankie Knuckles	The Warehouse
2	Larry Levan	Paradise Garage
1	David Mancuso	The Loft

CHAPTER 4
ON TOUR

TOP 10

A change is as good as a rest they say, and certainly a shift in surroundings has been an inspiration to countless musicians as they trek around the globe playing to audiences far and wide. The cosmopolitan charge of a city's streets has provided the perfect backdrop to some of music's finest moments, and the following have been practically paved with gold.

CITIES

8 SUFJAN STEVENS – 'CHICAGO'

While his plan of an album for every US state hasn't quite panned out, this track, off the Illinois album (naturally), is a two-for-one as it also stops off in New York while telling its tale of youth, fragile idealism, road trips and tears.

7 ELVIS PRESLEY – 'VIVA LAS VEGAS'

Probably best to remember Elvis from the film *Viva Las Vegas* than when he was in his latter years in Vegas. Although, like a bloated, booze-soaked George Best, caberet Elvis is still better than 95% of whatever else was on offer at the time.

10 FRANK SINATRA – 'NEW YORK, NEW YORK'

So good they named it twice – although they did the same with Washington, but that doesn't scan quite as well. Ol' Blue Eyes' take on this track makes the top 10 simply for ubiquity, but there's also passion in that delivery that goes a long, long way.

9 GIL SCOTT-HERON – 'JOHANNESBURG'

If all political broadcasts sounded this good, there'd be no problem with turnout. Gil Scott-Heron confronted the problems in South Africa with a politically charged, unifying piece of music that spoke more eloquently than most politicians could ever hope to.

6 BOBBY WOMACK – 'ACROSS 110TH STREET'

The iconic song from not one, but three films: Barry Shear's 1972 thriller of the same name, Quentin Tarantino's

blaxploitation homage *Jackie Brown* and Ridley Scott's 2007 *American Gangster*. Harlem , it seems, can shake it with the best of them.

5 SIMPLE MINDS — 'THEME FOR GREAT CITIES'

Simple Minds really understood how to marry the rock aesthetic with dance music. At first, this is all haunting dread, like a post-apocalyptic vision – then the bass kicks in and you remember it's actually just Sunday and you're on your way home from a club.

4 LOU REED – 'BERLIN'

While the version on the former Velvet Underground frontman's album of the same name may get the plaudits, it's the rough and ready Berlin of his debut LP to which we turn here. Not to be difficult you understand, just because it's much, much better.

3 STEVE MILLER BAND – 'MACHO CITY'

If Frank Zappa were to deliver a TV news bulletin over a backing of beats, random noises and cut-up snippets of stuff, it might sound a fraction as weird as this marvellous and riotously odd quarter of an hour from the Steve Miller Band.

2 BLOSSOM DEARIE – 'I LIKE LONDON IN THE RAIN'

Adding colour to the grey, wet pavements of London town, Blossom Dearie sees beauty where others would see the need for a sturdy umbrella. She also feels compelled to express this over a thunderous drum break, which is fine by us.

1 THE CLASH – 'LONDON CALLING'

The Clash's contention that, 'London is drowning and I, I live by the river', may yet mark them out as the environmental Nostrodamuses of punk. In the meantime, this song cements their reputation as some of the genre's best songwriters.

	ARTIST	SONG	YEAR
10	Frank Sinatra	'New York, New York'	1980
9	Gil Scott-Heron	'Johannesburg'	1975
8	Sufjan Stevens	'Chicago'	2005
7	Elvis Presley	'Viva Las Vegas'	1965
6	Bobby Womack	'Across 110th Street'	1972
5	Simple Minds	'Theme For Great Cities'	1981
4	Lou Reed	'Berlin'	1973
3	Steve Miller Band	'Macho City'	1981
2	Blossom Dearie	'I Like London in the Rain'	1970
1	The Clash	'London Calling'	1979

TOP
10

What is it about cars and pop music that makes them such perfect companions? Could it be the sense of freedom and abandon associated with them? The ability to dictate your surroundings that they both allow? Whichever, cars and driving are themes as prevailing as love, death and heartbreak in popular music. Here are 10 for the road...

CARS

10 IDES OF MARCH – 'VEHICLE'

Possessing a blistering horn riff that pushed this Vehicle firmly into the fast-lane and heading for the big time, the cautionary tale of stranger-danger was, in-part, inspired by anti-drug pamphlets that had been distributed at singer Jim Peterik's school.

9 IGGY POP – 'THE PASSENGER'

Written from the privileged point of view of someone who's just along for the ride, the instantly recognizable riff and singalong chorus (featuring guest vocals from Iggy's Berlin buddy, David Bowie), make this an irresistible choice.

8 CHUCK BERRY – 'NO PARTICULAR PLACE TO GO'

The ultimate ode to carefree cruising, this 1964 single screams the virtues of teenage abandon as the privileges of adulthood blend with a childish sense of inconsequence and herald 'the best years of your life.' Cracking guitar work, too...

7 THE BEACH BOYS – 'FUN, FUN, FUN'

With Brian Wilson's ear for a melody and Mike Love's ear to the ground when it came to what the kids wanted, this story of one girl's freedom and rebellion (until her daddy took the T-bird away at least) became one of their most enduring songs.

6 JANIS JOPLIN – 'MERCEDES BENZ'

Among the last recordings that Joplin ever made, this a cappella song – a rejection of consumerism dripping

with irony (or, as she puts it 'a song of great social and political import'), has since been co-opted by advertising companies to flog cars.

5 PRINCE – 'LITTLE RED CORVETTE'

Despite the image of Prince as a rich American Noddy that this throws up (particularly with the Raspberry Beret), this is the singer's bid to convince a woman to settle down with him. Perhaps not likening her to a car might be a start Prince?

4 CANNED HEAT – 'ON THE ROAD AGAIN'

Although originally recorded by blues great Floyd Jones, the Canned Heat version is the one that's going on this car stereo as the distinctive falsetto vocal sits comfortably on the gentle engine murmur of the band's rolling accompaniment.

3 THE BEATLES – 'DRIVE MY CAR'

In the same way that The Beatles may well have wanted to do more than hold hands, it sounds like something awfully euphemistic's going on here, too. It's from *Rubber Soul*, where the band went groovy and revved up their career in earnest.

2 GARY NUMAN – 'CARS'

A song written after having to take refuge in his car to avoid a beating during a road-rage incident, this certainly explains the claustrophobic feel of Gary Numan's insular pop classic, full of stalagmite synth lines that stab their way through the speakers.

1 KRAFTWERK – 'AUTOBAHN'

The ultimate driving song, with electronic, motorik rhythms propelling the track ever further forward without once feeling the need to check in the rear-view mirror. There's no point really, as nothing stands a chance of catching it.

	ARTIST	SONG	YEAR
10	Ides of March	'Vehicle'	1970
9	Iggy Pop	'The Passenger'	1977
8	Chuck Berry	'No Particular Place to Go'	1964
7	The Beach Boys	'Fun, Fun, Fun'	1964
6	Janis Joplin	'Mercedes Benz'	1970
5	Prince	'Little Red Corvette'	1982
4	Canned Heat	'On the Road Again'	1967
3	The Beatles	'Drive My Car'	1965
2	Gary Numan	'Cars'	1979
1	Kraftwerk	'Autobahn'	1974

TOP 10

Primarily associated with France, the distinctive, early Sixties Yé-yé European pop sound is unmistakable – as is the look. Although deeply rooted in its time, the almost overpowering allure of this simple and direct music never strays too far from popular culture, and still turns up today on film soundtracks and television series.

YEAH YEAH TO YÉ-YÉ

10 FRANCE GALL – 'POUPÉE DE CIRE, POUPÉE DE SON'
One of the many Gainsbourg-penned hits for France Gall. A thematic twin perhaps with 'Puppet on a String', the title translates as 'Wax Doll, Rag Doll' and the upbeat, cheery backing proved a hit at Eurovision, where it took the top spot in 1965.

9 PETULA CLARK – 'VA TOUJOURS PLUS LOIN'
It was released in England as 'Around Every Corner', but the French version of Tony Hatch's relentlessly optimistic song is about a million times better, with production that gives it a harder, almost mod edge in between the soft, lush, string-led lulls.

8 SYLVIE VARTAN – 'CETTE LETTRE LA'
With a work ethic like few other pop stars, Sylvie Vartan also had a less shiny, polished sound. This is a very good example of immediate pop that manages to get the killer hooks in you without sacrificing class or quality.

7 JACQUES DUTRONC – 'J'AI MIS UN TIGRE DANS MA GUITARE'
Yé-yé wasn't just a girls' monopoly... OK, it was, but that didn't mean the boys couldn't occasionally play, too. The best of the bunch and, possibly, the coolest man on the planet, was Jacques Dutronc (Msr Francoise Hardy), who put a tiger in his guitar, apparently.

6 FRANÇOISE HARDY – 'LE TEMPS DE L'AMOUR'
With a more mature sound, Hardy brought a grown-up glamour to Yé-yé as well as a whole lot of sophistication. This song, in part written by her husband, Jacques Dutronc, is all smoky haze and lingering, longing looks.

5 CHRISTIE LAUME – 'LA MUSIQUE ET LA DANCE'
Original copies of this 45 can set you back a few quid but, thankfully, other formats exist. This is a great example of the carefree, youthful exuberance that all truly great pop music has as its hallmark. Agathe Ou Christie, on the same EP, is great, too.

4 ANNA KARINA – 'ROLLERGIRL'
Abandoning the saccharine strings for a fuzzy blast of guitar, Anna Karina's 1967 song from the French TV movie *Anna* is bit late to be considered classic Yé-yé, but it still has that unmistakable pop nous and a killer, Wild Thing-esque hook.

3 JACQUELINE TAÏEB – '7 HEURES DU MATIN'
Sounding like a Yé-ye version of The Who's 'My Generation', this spiky and punky slab of

pop has stood the test of time better than most. Best of all, there's an English version on the flip for those who didn't study hard enough at school.

2 GILLIAN HILLS – 'ZOU BISOU BISOU'
Once again on nodding terms with the zeitgeist courtesy of an appearance in HBO's hit series Mad Men, there's some disagreement as to who was first to record the song – Hills or Sophia Loren. Either way, this is as sweet as a song can get.

1 FRANCE GALL – 'LAISSE TOMBER LES FILLES'
The spy-theme twang of this 1964 single gives it a distinctive edge, as does the perfectly judged lyrical cadence. Tarantino recognised this when he used the English-language version ('Chick Habit') to add an air of insouciant cool to 2007's *Death Proof*.

	ARTIST	SONG	YEAR
10	France Gall	'Poupée de Cire, Poupée de Son'	1965
9	Petula Clark	'Va Toujours Plus Loin'	1966
8	Sylvie Vartan	'Cette Lettre La'	1966
7	Jacques Dutronc	'J'ai Mis un Tigre Dans Ma Guitare'	1966
6	Francoise Hardy	'Le Temps de L'Amour'	1962
5	Christie Laume	'La Musique et la Dance'	1967
4	Anna Karina	'Rollergirl'	1967
3	Jacqueline Taïeb	'7 Heures du Matin'	1967
2	Gillian Hills	'Zou Bisou Bisou'	1960
1	France Gall	'Laisse Tomber les Filles'	1965

TOP
10

Time to put pen to paper and create your own top 10 list of songs from different countries...

10

9

8

7

6

5

4

3

2

1

TOP 10

While all eyes – and ears – were on Britain and America in the Sixties, there was something happening over in Holland. Taking their inspiration from the sounds heard on pirate stations like Radio Veronica, a generation of Dutch kids picked up guitars and quietly got on with starting their own noisy scene – Nederbeat.

DUTCH BEAT GROUPS

10 SHOCKING BLUE
A result of Nederbeat rather than practitioners of the sound, 'Send Me a Postcard' and 'Hot Sand' suggest that the legacy was in safe hands. Better known is the huge hit 'Venus' and the song 'Love Buzz' – which was covered by Nirvana.

9 DRAGONFLY
How do a band who only released two 45s make it in to the top 10? By making them as wonderfully inventive and weird as the 1968 offerings from Dragonfly. In truth, their sound is too late and psychedelic to be considered proper Nederbeat, but it's wonderful nonetheless.

8 THE ZIPPS
After forming in 1965, Zipps released a few singles with a heavy US influence, including 'Roll the Cotton Down' and the fantastic 'Kicks and Chicks', all raw melodies

and confident swagger. Their next, 'Marie Juana' saw them embrace psychedelia but, sadly, lose the tunes.

7 DE MASKERS
Perhaps surprisingly, De Maskers collaborated with king of the twist Chubby Checker. They did, and the results aren't great to be honest. Turn instead to blistering 1966 single 'Three's a Crowd', or the pop hooks of 'Play the Game Now'.

6 BINTANGS
If Golden Earrings were the Dutch Beatles then Bintangs were Holland's answer to the Rolling Stones. With a much more R&B sound to tracks including 'Groovin'' and 'Splendid Sight', they got progressively heavier as the decade wore on.

5 GOLDEN EARRINGS
Although Golden Earring are known around the

world for the 1973 hit Radar Love, the band were previously plural and had a penchant for writing Sixties guitar pop, which, although indebted to the Beatles and the Kinks, was none the worse for it.

4 THE HUNTERS
Featuring Jan Ackerman, before prog rock and fusion had taken hold of him, this band released a handful of great singles between '66 and '68. Of these, 'Russian Spy and I', is perhaps the best and lent its name to a mid-Eighties compilation.

3 THE MOTIONS
One of the biggest bands on the Dutch scene, they released two killer albums, 1965's *Introduction to the Motions* and *Their Own Way* in '66 as well as a slew of great singles. Guitarist Robbie Van Leeuwen eventually left to form Shocking Blue.

2 Q65

With a harder sound than many of their peers - they took their cue from the Pretty Things rather than the Beatles - Q65 were purveyors of sharp-edged tunes including the awesome 'The Life I Live', which was backed with the equally potent 'I Cry in the Night'.

1 THE OUTSIDERS

Favouring original material over cover versions, The Outsiders had a distinctive style right from the get-go. A crunching, violent blast - but never at the expense of melody - their 1968 album *C.Q.* is an absolute classic of the genre.

	ARTIST	LISTEN TO...	YEAR
10	Shocking Blue	'Send Me a Postcard'	1970
9	Dragonfly	'Celestial Empire'	1968
8	The Zipps	'Kicks and Chicks'	1966
7	De Maskers	'Three's a Crowd'	1966
6	Bintangs	'Groovin''	1966
5	Golden Earrings	*Just Ear-rings* (album)	1965
4	The Hunters	'Russian Spy and I'	1966
3	The Motions	'I'll Follow the Sun'	1965
2	Q65	'I Cry in the Night'	1966
1	The Outsiders	'Misfit'	1968

TOP 10

There's a huge amount of debate as to what constitutes a Balearic tune, never mind what the best examples may be. Eclectic pop oddities that sound great in the right setting is as good a definition as any, so, with that in mind, this list attempts to pinpoint the very best of the inimitable island sound.

BALEARIC BEATS

10 IZIT – 'STORIES'
'Feel the rhythm of the beat, it's time to move your feet, Feel the rhythm move around it's time for getting down...' the best rolling vocal line in popular music, introduces an improbably funky journey into an aural montage of flute, acoustic guitar, layered vocals and drum breaks.

9 SIMPLE MINDS – 'THIS FEAR OF GODS'
Balearic is, if nothing else, a broad church – if it's good, it's in. Simple Minds, of all the new wave bands, had big ambitions and an even bigger sound – one that translates perfectly to blissed-out balconies and sun-kissed terraces.

8 SEBASTIEN TELLIER – 'LA RITOURNELLE'
Some records are engineered to make you weep tears of joy. This is one of those records. The sweeping emotion of the introduction (which is, to be fair, half the song) gives way to a glorious release and a declaration of love steeped in honesty and integrity.

7 RICHIE HAVENS – 'GOING BACK TO MY ROOTS'
A disco hit for Odyssey, Richie Havens wakes the song up the morning after and takes it down the beach to show it that, in fact, the open air, sun-kissed setting works much better as a backdrop than the cramped confines of a club.

6 REY DE COPAS – 'FRONTERA DEL ENSUENO'
If there's one song on this list that's capable of making you feel like you're on holiday when you're actually unable to leave the house such is the ferocity of the rain outside, it's this. Flamenco guitar with dubbed-out piano and mariachi horns against a disco beat. That'll do nicely.

5 BELOVED – 'SUN RISING'
Surprisingly fast for a track that is so blissfully on the edge of sleep, 'Sun Rising' is an exceptionally onomatopoeic achievement. If House legend Larry Heard had grown up in the Home Counties, he'd probably have written something like this.

4 THE BLOW MONKEYS – 'LA PASSIONARA'
Take one part Michael Viner's Apache, one part flamenco flamboyance and one part pop

smarts. Stir them – don't shake – and then stand well back as smiles start to appear all round. Leave to rise for just under five minutes for best results.

3 BOCCA JUNIORS – 'RAISE'

A beefed-up version of the Thrashing Doves' 'Jesus on the Payroll' piano part opens this jolly Boys' Own outing. Andrew Weatherall, Terry Farley, Pete Heller and Hugo Nicholson set out to write a Balearic anthem and did so with apparent ease.

2 TULLIO DE PISCOPO – 'PRIMAVERA'

The simple, route-one approach taken by this gem of a song sees the bass and drums locked into a functional, metronomic task and provides a core from which the song unfolds, like petals on a flower that thrives in extremely sunny conditions. And very sandy soil.

1 MANUEL GOTTSCHING – 'E2-E4'

The former Ash-Ra Tempel guitarist released this hour-long track in 1984. Spread across two sides of a 12" single, it was a phenomenal achievement, not least because it holds the attention of the listener for every minute of its glistening, shimmering life.

	ARTIST	SONG	YEAR
10	Izit	'Stories'	1989
9	Simple Minds	'This Fear of Gods'	1980
8	Sebastien Tellier	'La Ritournelle'	2004
7	Richie Havens	'Going Back to My Roots'	1980
6	Rey de Copas	'Frontera del Ensueno'	1989
5	Beloved	'Sun Rising'	1990
4	The Blow Monkeys	'La Passionara'	1990
3	Bocca Juniors	'Raise'	1990
2	Tullio de Piscopo	'Primavera'	1983
1	Manuel Göttsching	'E2-E4'	1984

10

Perhaps it's something in the fjords, but bearing in mind that Sweden is a country populated by fewer than 10 million people, it punches well above its weight when it comes to rock music. And not just any old rock, either – this is rock with the words 'progressive' and 'psychedelic' stamped all the way through it. Which beats 'Greetings from Bognor' any day.

PSYCHEDELIC SWEDEN

10 THE AMAZING
Counting Dungen guitarist Reine Fiske among their number, The Amazing's 2009 self-titled debut was released, as most Swedish records seem to be, on Subliminal Sounds. It's an impressive record that highlights their knack for making songs shimmer and spines shiver.

9 S.T. MIKAEL
During the mid Eighties and Nineties, the mysterious and reclusive figure of S.T. Mikael released five albums of incredible psych before going off radar for more than a decade. His return, with 2007's *Mind of Fire*, confirmed the missing years hadn't been wasted.

8 GOAT
Imagine if Doctor John, rather than Kid Creole, had been backed by the coconuts... Part Fela Kuti, part Funkadelic with heavy, psychedelic, voodoo guitars over infectious, polyrhythmic drums, their 2012 debut LP is great – live, they're even better.

7 DUNGEN
Singer/composer Gustav Ejstes' gained international acclaim with 2004's *Ta Det Lungt*, despite the album being sung in Swedish (as all their songs are). It raised the bar for psychedelic rock so high that, at times, only Dungen themselves seem capable of reaching it.

6 PUGH ROGEFELDT
As Mary Poppins observed, the beginning is a very good place to start, and so it is with singer Pugh Rogefeldt. His debut, 'Ja, dä Ä dä!', recorded with drummer Janne Carlsson is full of big ideas and playful production, including the awesome 'Love, Love, Love'.

5 PÄRSON SOUND
Although they didn't release any records at the time, the influence of Pärson sound was huge. They created extended pieces of music that left audiences agog, like the near half an hour of the eastern-infused Skrubba, none of which were released until 2001.

4 HANSSON & KARLSSON
Formed of keyboard player Bo Hansson (of whom more later) and drummer Janne Carlsson (the band's name was the result of a misprint), their fusion sound was to develop into something altogether heavier, including the track 'Tax Free', covered by Jimi Hendrix.

3 BO HANSSON
When Janne Carlson moved on, Bo Hansson released his fantasy prog opus

'Lord of the Rings', which managed to chart in the UK. He followed this with the astounding *Attic Thoughts*, which sounds, in parts, like a later offering from DJ Shadow.

2 BABY GRANDMOTHERS

The band that (with the addition of Mecki Bodemark) were to become Mecki Mark Men, had a relatively short existence that saw the release of one incendiary single, 'Somebody Keeps Calling My Name'. It's dramatic hard rock, but laced with acid experimentation.

1 MECKI MARK MEN

One of Sweden's first big psychedelic bands, Mecki Bodemark's band made the kind of music you'd expect for a band at the tail-end of the Sixties – part Hendrix, part Iron Butterfly, part prog tendencies. What stood them apart was how well they did it.

	ARTIST	LISTEN TO...	YEAR
10	The Amazing	'The Amazing'	2009
9	S.T. Mikael	'The Unknown'	1991
8	Goat	'World Music'	2012
7	Dungen	'Ta Det Lugnt'	2004
6	Pugh Rogefeldt	'Ja, Dä Ä Dä!'	1969
5	Pärson Sound	'Pärson Sound'	2001
4	Hansson & Karlsson	*Hansson & Karlsson (compilation)*	1998
3	Bo Hansson	'Lord of the Rings'	1972
2	Baby Grandmothers	*Baby Grandmothers (compilation)*	2007
1	Mecki Mark Men	'Mecki Mark Men'	1967

TOP
10

The mid-20th century was a time of great political turmoil with many Eastern European countries under the authoritarian rule of Russia. It's tempting to think that lives were played out in monochrome or, at best, sepia, however, the music on this list shows that there were dashes of colour and creativity as people got on with the business of living life and making music.

EASTERN BLOC PARTY

but it's a killer version.

9 NOVI SINGERS – 'TORPEDO'

All parties need to warm up – you can't just go from 0-60. Just as well, then, that we've got the close harmonies and groovy lounge arrangements of Poland's Novi Singers to count on. This, from their 1970 album of the same name, oozes quiet cool.

8 ALI BABKI – 'SŁOŃCE W CHMURACH ŁAZI'

Brilliant girl-band action from Ali Babki's 1969 debut album, this denotes the point in the evening when the nibbles are dispensed with and the coffee tables moved out of the way to make room for all of the dancing that will inevitably follow.

10 THE FLAMINGO GROUP -- 'BIG CHAIN'

Proving that our Eastern European cousins can do English-language pop are Czech band Flamingo (not to be confused with Czech beat-group-turned-prog-pioneers Flamengo) and their cover of Aretha's 'A Change'. They might have misheard slightly,

7 LOCOMOTIV GT – 'RINGASD EL MAGAD'

With almost as many versions

of this song as there are stars in our galaxy, we're spoilt for choice. We'll put aside, for now, the guitar-heavy version in LGT main man Gabor Presser's rock opera and go for the funk-filled breaks of their 1974 disco(ish) remake.

6 ALLA PUGACHEVA – 'TIREDNESS'

The Russian singer has had a huge number of hits in her career, but this relatively unknown track on her 1983 album, *How Disturbing Is This Way*, has the disco beat, squelchy bass and oddball electronics to get any party started in style.

5 MARTA KUBISOVÁ – *TAK DEJ SE K NÁM A PROJDEM SVET*

Kubisova's *Songy a Balady* album was banned by occupying forces in Czechoslovakia, lending it the iconic status that she already enjoyed. Presumably they were worried about the enormity of the bass line, which is big enough to stop tanks in their tracks.

4 MONDIAL UND DAS ELECTRECORD-ORCHESTER – *OMULE*

Their name may be bit of a mouthful, but the psych leanings of this meaty, beaty, big and bouncy Romanian band are very easy to swallow.

The self-titled album that this is taken off is no one-hit wonder either – an impressive feat after more than 40 years.

3 KATI KOVÁCS - *ADD MÁR URAM AZ ESÖT*

Hungarian funky rock that hits the right notes and the solar plexus at roughly the same time. Kati Kovacs is a huge star in both Hungary and Germany and hidden away in her back catalogue are a number of sleeper hits like this.

2 CZERWONE GITARY – *RYTM ZIEMI*
The solo drum break that opens this song by Poland's all-time greats Czerwone Gitary (Red Guitars) pretty much sets the pace in more ways than one. What follows is heavy, slightly psychedelic and as funky as a rock band is ever likely to get.

1 ILLÉS - *A BOLOND LÁNY*
Hungary's Illes had recorded this psychedelic monster of a record earlier in their career, but it's 1973 version, from their album *Ne Sirjatok, Lanyok!* that gets a place on this list for being more propulsive than a space shuttle engine at take off.

	ARTIST	SONG	YEAR
10	The Flamingo Group	'Big Chain'	1971
9	Novi Singers	'Torpedo'	1970
8	Ali Babki	'Słońce W Chmurach Łazi'	1969
7	Locomotiv GT	'Ringasd el magad'	1974
6	Alla Pugacheva	'Tiredness'	1983
5	Marta Kubisova	'Tak Dej Se K Nám A Projdem Svet'	1969
4	Mondial Und Das Electrecord-Orchester	'Omule'	1972
3	Kati Kovacs	'Add Már Uram Az Esöt'	1972
2	Czerwone Gitary	'Rytm Ziemi'	1974
1	Illes	'A Bolond Lány'	1973

TOP 10

The name 'Krautrock' is far from the best describer that this strand of experimental music from Germany could hope for. Kosmische perhaps? Whatever your preferred terminology, one thing is for certain – the lasting legacy of the industrious, industrial and inventive music is assured, with bands over the last 30 years plundering the canon for ideas and inspiration. They wouldn't go far wrong with these...

KRAUTROCK

10 CLUSTER – *ZUCKERZEIT*
Cluster were the second incarnation of avant-garde pioneers Kluster, and Zuckerzeit represents a massive change in direction. At heart a pop album – albeit one with oddball electronics and off-kilter rhythms – it's both accessible and satisfying.

9 ASH RA TEMPEL – *S/T*
Often seen as purveyors of wonky space-rock, there were more strings to Ash Ra Tempel's bow than that. This album veers from barely-there vapour trails blending back into the void and the deafening, earthy sound of a band coming in to land.

8 EMBRYO – *FATHER, SON & HOLY GHOSTS*
Embracing styles and influences from around the world, Embryo are, in essence, a fusion band. This album sees them blend their more high-minded jazz tendencies into a compelling, coherent whole, with 'Free' being, ironically, the most contained and restrained example.

7 TANGERINE DREAM – *PHAEDRA*
Although, for some, their first album marked the beginning of the end for Tangerine Dream's creative peak, they may be conflating a cynical bid for commercial acceptance with musical coherence. This album is where all the drifting space debris forms a heavenly body of work.

6 KRAFTWERK – *S/T*
Before the robots took control, Kraftwerk mixed elements of music concréte, the avant garde and Krautrock to come up with a sound that, though largely disowned by the band now, remains compelling listening. 'Ruckzuck' and 'Stratovarius' are the key tracks here.

5 AMON DUUL II – *YETI*
Following the improvised wig-out of debut LP Phallus Dei, *Yeti* is a much more considered record, with the unusually conformist heavy rock of 'Archangel Thunderbird' making sure you're paying attention by repeatedly smacking you round the head.

4 FAUST – *SO FAR*
Faust's first album may have been hailed as revolutionary – and with good reason – but it was, as their label Polydor was acutely aware, a bit light on songs. Not so 'So Far', which boasts the pounding (relative) pop of 'It's a Rainy Day, Sunshine Girl'.

3 HARMONIA – *MUSIK VON HARMONIA*
Formed when Cluster's Dieter Moebius and Hans-Joachim Roedelius were joined by Michael Rother of Neu!, Harmonia was a name heavy with irony as the musical

differences surfaced. That tension, however, was to produce extraordinary, improvised kosmiche pop.

2 NEU! – *NEU! 75*

Having met while playing in Kraftwerk, Klaus Dinger and Michael Rother left to form NEU! With producer Conny Plank on board, theirs was to become a defining Krautrock sound and also, with one side of this magnificent last-gasp LP, pretty much invent punk rock.

1 CAN – *TAGO MAGO*

Tempting though it is to go for the back-to-basics of Delay 68, as the group began to play with primitivism, it is Tago Mago, recorded three years later that is essential. Fresh textures were layered onto their sound and new directions taken.

	ARTIST	ALBUM	YEAR
10	Cluster	*Zuckerzeit*	1974
9	Ash Ra Tempel	*S/T*	1971
8	Embryo	*Father, Son & Holy Ghosts*	1972
7	Tangerine Dream	*Phaedra*	1974
6	Kraftwerk	*S/T*	1970
5	Amon Duul II	*Yeti*	1970
4	Faust	*So Far*	1972
3	Harmonia	*Musik von Harmonia*	1974
2	NEU!	*NEU! 75*	1975
1	Can	*Tago Mago*	19/1

TOP
10

Few genres have had as profound effect on modern pop culture and sounds as Italo disco. The late Seventies and early Eighties proved a fertile time for budding producers, spurred on by the success of luminaries such as Giorgio Moroder. Synths, sequencers and singing (usually in English) were the key elements, as was a good ear for an irresistibly upbeat tune.

ITALO DISCO

10 MOONBASE – 'WAITING FOR A TRAIN'

There was something of a trend in Italo disco for covering tracks by other artists and then not crediting them. This is one such example, although Moonbase take the Flash and the Pan song, and beef it up with better, more richly textured instrumentation.

9 HYPNOSIS – 'END TITLE (BLADE RUNNER)'

The B-side to 'Pulstar' (another Vangelis over version), there's a distinctly electro feel to this track. It's slower than many and has more space for all the elements to breathe – but the tell-tale professionalism in the huge sounding production is Italo all the way.

8 CAPRICORN – 'I NEED LOVE'

Most emphatically nothing to do with the LL CoolJ

track of the same name, this dancefloor monster could get even the most reluctant souls dancing as spiky, funky guitar cuts through the bass-heavy backing and twitching beats.

7 KIRLIAN CAMERA – 'COMMUNICATE (INSTRUMENTAL VERSION)'

One of the pioneers of the Italian synthpop scene, Kirilian Camera's sound took a much darker path as the Eighties progressed. This 1983 release, however, remains as one of the pinnacles of their career and of Italo disco as a genre.

6 GAZNEVADA – 'SECRET AGENT MAN'

With both male and female vocal mixes on this record, we really are spoiled for choice. Having said that, it's the lolloping, live bass of the female version that really gets the head moving on this 1983 mid-paced tale of voyeurism and espionage.

5 WET – 'THAT'S THE GAME (INSTRUMENTAL VERSION)'

If the game in question is creating a proto-house monster in 1983 Belgium then

Wet seemed to have secured an impressive away win (beware though, the vocal version still remains an acquired taste for some). So far ahead of its time, we're still catching up.

4 STEEL MIND – 'BAD PASSION'
Bringing the boogie back to the Italo disco, this release from 1982 has more swing than many others in its class and little funk flourishes. It still sounds like it was made by a robot, but that robot was probably Twiki from Buck Rogers.

3 ALEXANDER ROBOTNICK – 'PROBLEMS D'AMOUR'
After someone suggested there was money to be made in dance music, Robotnick took them at their word and effortlessly came up with this

seminal disco track, although many at the time – including the producer himself – couldn't see its genius.

2 CHARLIE – 'SPACER WOMAN'
When it comes to the themes of Italo disco, y'know, the big, metaphysical stuff that keeps people awake at night – there's love, obviously... then, probably, space and robots. This carefully combines all three, using arpeggiated synth as a bonding agent.

1 MR FLAGIO – 'TAKE A CHANCE'
If you do take a chance on this wonderful cover version of Material's 1982 song, you'll be rewarded with a disco track that sparkles and shines, squelches and beeps and has a melody that always stays just the right side of cheesy.

	ARTIST	SONG	YEAR
10	Moonbase	'Waiting For a Train'	1983
9	Hypnosis	'End Title (Blade Runner)'	1983
8	Capricorn	'I Need Love'	1982
7	Kirlian Camera	'Communicate (Instrumental version)'	1983
6	Gaznevada	'Secret Agent Man'	1983
5	Wet	'That's the Game (Instrumental version)'	1983
4	Steel Mind	'Bad Passion'	1982
3	Alexander Robotnick	'Problems D'Amour'	1983
2	Charlie	'Spacer Woman'	1983
1	Mr Flagio	'Take a Chance'	1983

TOP 10

Singer, songwriter, composer, writer actor, director... there were many strings to the bow of French visionary Serge Gainsbourg. One of his chief talents – aside from smoking, drinking, womanising and courting scandal wherever he went – was to compose timeless songs at the drop of a hat. And quite possibly other items of clothing too.

GAINSBOURG'S GALLIC GREATS

10 'JE T'AIME... MOI NON PLUS'
Originally recorded with Brigitte Bardot, Gainsbourg re-recorded it with lover Jane Birkin. The explicit nature of the song (rumours abounded that they'd got 'carried away') ended up overshadowing the fact that it's actually a very direct, honest love song.

9 'INITIALS BB'
No prizes for guessing which impossibly beautiful French actress provides the inspiration for this release. Intertwining horn lines and string parts mesh as the song progresses to its climax. All entirely incidental, we're sure.

8 'NO NO, YES YES'
Taken from the score for the 1969 film *Mr Freedom* about an American nationalist who travels to France to help the fight against the Communist 'threat'. Gainsbourg worked on this with another outstanding French producer, Michel Colombier.

7 'FLASH FORWARD'
The 1976 album *L'homme A Tete de Chou* came five years after *Histoire*...and certainly shows a more reflective approach. Painting from a similar musical palette, there is a more considered and restrained feel, though not to the detriment of the songs.

6 'CANNABIS'
A collaboration with long-time arranger Jean Claude Vannier, this song was from the film score for the 1970 movie of the same name. As with all Vannier/Gainsbourg productions, it sounds lush, elaborate and extravagant but, in truth, nothing here is wasted.

5 'BONNIE AND CLYDE'
With Brigitte Bardot as a singing partner, you're not going to go far wrong – especially when there's not actually a lot of singing to do. The acoustic guitar strum of this ballad carries both tune and voices to a satisfying, if rather final, conclusion.

4 'AUX ARMES ET CAETERA'
It takes a special kind of bravado to record a new version of your country's national anthem, especially when that recording leads to death threats. Still, haters gonna hate... and if you've got top reggae men Sly and Robbie on board, the ship will be seaworthy.

3 'EN MELODY'
This is the penultimate track on what is probably Gainsbourg's most complete album - and certainly his most well known - *Histoire De Melody Nelson*. Gainsbourg's session band for this recording could have good claim to be the best ever of its kind.

2 'LA HORSE'

A keyboard sound that could have been bussed in from the middle ages introduces some unlikely stablemates – including galloping drums and a banjo. Amazingly, it all works on this unbelievably rare instrumental that isn't really about a horse at all.

1 'CONTACT'

A zither strums away while a bass picks out a Sixties sci-fi funk groove and the actress tries to communicate with extraterrestrials by Spea. King. One. Syll. A. Ble. At. A. Time. In truth, some might find this song a little... odd. It's not, it's amazing.

	SONG	WAS RELEASED ON...	YEAR
10	'Je T'aime... Moi Non Plus'	*Jane Birkin/Serge Gainsbourg*	1969
9	'Initials BB'	*Initials BB*	1968
8	'No No, Yes Yes'	*Mr Freedom (soundtrack EP)*	1968
7	'Flash Forward'	*L'homme à Tête de Chou*	1976
6	'Cannabis'	*Cannabis (soundtrack)*	1970
5	'Bonnie and Clyde'	*Initials BB* and *Bonnie and Clyde*	Both 1968
4	'Aux Armes Et Caetera'	*Aux Armes Et Caetera*	1979
3	'En Melody'	*Histoire de Melody Nelson*	1971
2	'La Horse'	*La Horse (soundtrack 7" single)*	1969
1	'Contact'	*Show (Brigitte Bardot album)*	1968

TOP 10

As we continue on our world tour, we turn to the good old reliable train, whose rattling rhythms and percussive propulsion has ended up gaining it a special place in the popular music songbook. Whether it's as a narrative or directly musical device, the number of potential passengers lining up to ride this express makes for one hell of a rush hour.

TRAINS

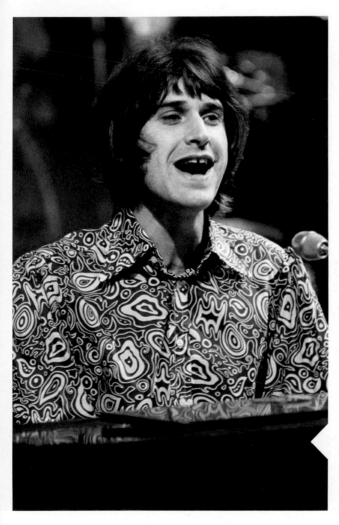

10 LITTLE JUNIOR'S BLUE FLAMES — 'MYSTERY TRAIN'

A blues standard in which the singer is waiting for a train to arrive - on board one of the 16 coaches is the woman he loves. Its gentle, sophisticated approach (the song's not the train's) lays clear tracks for the rockabilly sound that was to follow.

9 PENTANGLE — 'TRAIN SONG'

Another song that manages to be successfully onomatopoeic and provide a real sense of movement - although, given the band's folk roots, in a suitably gentle and bucolic fashion. It also gave the parent album, *Basket of Light*, its title.

8 THE KINKS — 'LAST OF THE STEAM-POWERED TRAINS'

Despite appearing on the

bands' homage to English country life, *The Kinks Are the Village Green Preservation Society,* this track has a particularly American blues feel to it. Taking inspiration from 'Smokestack Lightnin'', it's a very welcome homage.

7 GARY ATKINSON – 'WANDERIN' SOUL'

'I hear a train whistle blow, In the night and I feel so low, And I know I have to go, 'Cause I've got a wanderin' soul.'

So begins the story of one man's battle with the Devil for his soul. Simply magnificent country funk.

6 JAMES BROWN – 'NIGHT TRAIN'

If you're the Godfather of Funk, does that mean you have to remember its birthdays? You certainly have to give it advice as it grows up, help it steer a certain course. James Brown did that superbly, and this

1961 recording of the blues standard is no exception.

5 THE JAM – 'DOWN IN THE TUBE STATION AT MIDNIGHT'

There are dark songs, horrific songs and then there's this. More unsettling than anything of its time (or possibly since), this story of a man left for dead after being attacked in an underground station makes the blood run cold and the heart beat faster.

4 THE CLASH – 'TRAIN IN VAIN'
Like a defective departure board at a station, the sleeve to The Clash's *London's Calling* album didn't list this track. It came than, as a very welcome surprise when, Paul Simenon's distinctive bass introduced one of the band's most instant and emotive songs.

3 CROSBY, STILLS AND NASH – 'MARRAKESH EXPRESS'
The chipper, bright and bouncy feel of Graham Nash's song, as he and his bandmates travel in perfect harmony, gives the impression of a breezy journey, pootling along while smiling at friendly locals rather than delays, unscheduled stops and congestion.

2 THE MONKEES – 'LAST TRAIN TO CLARKSVILLE'
What do you get when you cross Paperback Writer with... Paperback Writer? Still, if you're going to ape something, may as well make it something amazing. And despite the obvious similarities, this is still glorious pop done with panache, style and wit.

1 KRAFTWERK – 'TRANS-EUROPE EXPRESS'
Dispensing with both destination and journey, Kraftwerk turn their attention to the mode of transport itself for this sonic model of a train. From the mechanical drum rhythms to the hard steel sound of the synthesizers, it urges us to jump on board.

	ARTIST	LISTEN TO...	YEAR
10	Little Junior's Blue Flames	'Mystery Train'	1953
9	Pentangle	'Train Song'	1969
8	The Kinks	'Last of the Steam-Powered Trains'	1968
7	Gary Atkinson	'Wanderin' Soul'	1975
6	James Brown	'Night Train'	1963
5	The Jam	'Down in the Tube Station at Midnight'	1978
4	The Clash	Train in Vain	1979
3	Crosby, Stills and Nash	'Marrakesh Express'	1969
2	The Monkees	'Last Train to Clarksville'	1966
1	Kraftwerk	'Trans-Europe Express'	1977

TOP 10

As producers and record diggers traveled further and further afield looking for the perfect beat, India proved very fertile ground. Rich in offbeat breaks and soundtrack curiosities, the musical heritage of the country was far more varied than the big-hitting Bollywood soundtracks would have you believe. With a huge volume of releases, a definitive list is impossible, but you won't go far wrong with these...

DIGGING INDIA'S FUNKY SIDE

10 ASHA BHOSLE – 'DUM MARO DUM'
Another RD Burman composition, this was a huge hit when it was released. It's from the 1971 film *Hare Rama Hare Krishna*, and its appeal has proved lasting, having been sampled by many, including Method Man for his 2004 single 'What's Happenin''.

9 KALYANJI ANANDJI – 'PYAR ZINDAGI HAI'
Complete with choppy, wah-wah scratch and propulsive bass, this is perfect cop show territory. Part of the soundtrack to 1978's box-office smash *Muqaddar Ka Sikandar*, it also boasts Asha Bhonsle's impossibly beautiful vocals and startling, but welcome, keyboard intrusions.

8 RD BURMAN – 'THE BURNING TRAIN'
Despite a big budget and high hopes, 1980's *The Burning Train* wasn't the cinematic smash that everyone had hoped for. The soundtrack however, by the legendary composer RD Burman, contains this inventive - and slightly bonkers - masterpiece.

7 SAPAN JAGMOHAN – 'SOTE SOTE ADHI RAT'
Not one person, but a composer duo wrote this infectious funk floorfiller from the soundtrack to the horror/thriller film *Siskeyan*. A rough and ready riff introduces the bouncing funk that just gets bigger and better as the perfectly formed song progresses.

6 HEMANT BHOSLE – 'SANSANI KHEZ KOI BAAT (FT. ASHA BHOSLE)'
With a beat that wouldn't sound out of place on a house record and ethereal, drifting synths providing a gentle background wash, the vocals are all important here. What luck then, that Hemant Bhosle could ask his mum, Asha, to oblige...

5 ASHA BHOSLE – 'TUM JAISON KO TOH PAAYAL MEIN BAANDH'
One of the greatest singers in Bollywood history, Ashaji has sung on more than a thousand films. In this, from 1972's *Garam Masala*, she trills over a delightfully delicate bass groove while synthesizers and strings wrap themselves around her.

4 ANANDA SHANKAR – 'DANCING DRUMS'

Nephew of sitar hero Ravi Shankar, Ananda had previous form with mixing western styles and released versions of 'Jumpin' Jack Flash' and 'Light My Fire'. However, on this, he blends frantic drums, electric guitar, moog and boundless energy to thrilling effect.

3 ATOMIC FOREST – 'OBSESSION '77'

With the number of potential opponents next to zero, it's probably safe to call Atomic Forest India's best psychedelic rock band. This track, off their almost impossible to find album, is a sprawling beast of a song in the best possible sense.

2 KALYANJI ANANDJI – 'STREETS OF CALCUTTA'

Ananda again, this time with a more traditionally Western feel. Having said that, the sitar and flute melodies bring the flavours of India with them, while the tabla doesn't flag at all from its impressively optimistic early pace setting.

1 KALYANJI ANANDJI – 'DHARMATMA THEME MUSIC (SAD)'

Possessing the funk like Donald Trump possesses money, the drum break and bass hold the mariachi-style horns and fuzz guitar in check before the piercing voice comes in and makes a bid for being precisely the best thing you've ever heard.

	ARTIST	SONG	YEAR*
10	Asha Bhosle	'Dum Maro Dum'	1971
9	Kalyanji Anandji	'Pyar Zindagi Hai'	1978
8	RD Burman	'Burning Train'	1979
7	Sapan Jagmohan	'Sote Sote Adhi Rat'	1984
6	Hemant Bhosle	'Sansani Khez Koi Baat (ft Asha Bhosle)'	1981
5	Asha Bhonsle	'Tum Jaison Ko Toh Paayal Mein Baandh'	1972
4	Ananda Shankar	'Dancing Drums'	1975
3	Atomic Forest	'Obsession '77'	1982
2	Ananda Shankar	'Streets of Calcutta'	1975
1	Kalyanji Anandji	'Dharmatma Theme Music (sad)'	1975

* Some of these songs appeared initially in films, in which case the dates refer to the film release

TOP 10

In 1962, a nation was born as Jamaica gained its independence. That wasn't the only new arrival however; 1962 also heralded the birth of a whole new genre of music, ska. The exact circumstances surrounding this landmark delivery are unclear, but its name seems to stem from the trademark guitar scratch. Huge thanks go to DJ Sir Merrick, of the Dub Bunnies collective, whose chart this is.

SKA

give him the first of many hits.

9 LAUREL AITKEN – 'SKINHEAD'

Also known as the Godfather of Ska, self-proclaimed Boss Skinhead Laurel Aitken was revered by mods, skinheads, the West Indian community and, well... pretty much anyone with ears. He was also a huge influence on the 2 Tone movement.

8 PRINCE BUSTER – 'ENJOY YOURSELF'

Of all the people who have sung versions of this song over the years, none has managed to stamp their personality on it with quite the authority that Prince Buster did. It was later covered by ska revivalists The Specials in 1980.

7 DERRICK & PATSY – 'NATIONAL DANCE'

Singing the praises of the genre itself, Derrick Morgan and Millicent Todd's love song to

10 DESMOND DEKKER – 'HONOUR YOUR MOTHER AND FATHER'

1963 saw the release of this, the first single from the soon to be legendary Desmond Dekker. His distinctive, powerful, high register and the song's heartfelt message combined to

ska was released on the Island label in 1965 and references its popularity not just in Jamaica, but also in London, as the music took hold of the world.

6 PRINCE BUSTER - 'WASH WASH'

A track that drinks deep from music's redemptive and spiritually cleansing waters, this 1962 release has the trademark rhythms, yet against the ska stroke is a vocal delivery with a distinctly African influence, giving it a beautiful, expansive feel.

5 MILLIE – 'MY BOY LOLLIPOP'

Originally recorded in the mid-Fifties by Barbie Gayle with, interestingly, the distinctive ska upstroke much in evidence, it took Jamaican teen Millie Small to make this a smash hit nearly a decade later, and establish Island records in the process.

4 BOB MARLEY & THE WAILERS – 'SIMMER DOWN'

Reading like a fantasy team of Jamaican music, The Skatalites, the Wailers (including Bunny Wailer and Peter Tosh) plus producer Clement 'Coxsone' Dodd all contributed to this plea for calm among the more 'excitable' members of the Jamaican community.

3 DERRICK MORGAN – 'BE STILL'

Released on Prince Buster's legendary label before the friends' feud over claims of intellectual theft and copying, this 1962 record marked a golden period of across-the-board success for Morgan and helped to usher in the shuffle of ska.

2 ROBERT MARLEY – 'JUDGE NOT'

The first single Robert 'Bob' Marley ever released. The danger in listening to it from the privileged position of knowing what was to come is that it can be mistaken for a curiosity, rather than the wiser-than-its-years success it should have been at the time.

1 PRINCE BUSTER AND THE VOICE OF THE PEOPLE – 'THEY GOT TO COME'

A defiant roar of resilience from Prince Buster as he refuses to be brought down by 'bad-minded people'. And the 'grudgeful' ones as well. He responds in the best way he knows, by releasing a record that lifts the spirits and steels resolve.

	ARTIST	SONG	YEAR
10	Desmond Dekker	'Honour your Mother and Father'	1963
9	Laurel Aitken	'Skinhead'	unknown
8	Prince Buster	'Enjoy Yourself'	1968
7	Derrick & Patsy	'National Dance'	1965
6	Prince Buster	'Wash Wash'	1963
5	Millie	'My Boy Lollipop'	1964
4	Bob Marley & the Wailers	'Simmer Down'	1964
3	Derrick Morgan	'Be Still'	1962
2	Robert Marley	'Judge Not'	1962
1	Prince Buster and the Voice of the People	'They Got to Come'	1962

TOP 10

As the Sixties drew on, something new was stirring in Jamaica. While giving a nod to both ska and rocksteady, heads began to move in a new direction. Reggae. Faster than rocksteady, more complex than ska, it was a new and persuasive beat. Once again, we doff our cap and nod our head in the direction of DJ Sir Merrick for this list.

REGGAE

10 THE MELODIANS – 'RIVERS OF BABYLON'

Taking its lyrics from Psalm 137: 1-4, and its melody from the traditional song, 'How Dry I Am', this is literally a mash-up of Biblical proportions. Thankfully they chose to avoid the final verses of the psalm, which are altogether less in keeping with the tone.

9 THE STARLITES – 'SOME A WEH A BAWL'

The heavy, dubbed out feel of this 1975 track from Stanley Beckford's band sits surprisingly well against the hints of mento (Jamaican folk music) that come through his voice – a style to which he was to turn later in his career.

8 GREGORY ISAACS – 'BUMPING AND BORING'

While Isaacs' beautiful, crystal clear tones sit perfectly on top of the gently bobbing backing, the flip side's absolutely killer 'version' sees the reverb turned up to dangerous levels and the bass attempt to eat the vocal whole.

7 ERIC DONALDSON – 'CHERRY OH BABY'

Donaldson found himself suddenly famous after this song exploded in 1971. Along with the hook-filled melody and his falsetto, the unusual but compelling stop/start rhythm marks this track out as something a bit special.

6 BIG YOUTH – 'NOTTY NO JESTER'

Starting with lyrical echoes of Derrick Morgan's 'Be Still' (don't wake a sleeping lion), this 1975 song showcases Big Youth's considerable linguistic ability and highlights the production skills of Clive Chin, whose backing is so fat it could fall through the floor at any moment.

5 BUNNY WAILER – 'BLACKHEART MAN'

Wailer's debut album is regarded to be his finest work. This track tells the story of the Blackheart Man, a sinister, mythical figure that children came to fear. There's nothing to be afraid of in the understated melodic genius of

the song however...

4 DENNIS BROWN – 'MONEY IN MY POCKET'

If Bob Marley says you're his favourite singer, you know that you must be doing something right! Dennis Brown's career was profilic in much the same way that water is wet and this track shows why his popularity is so enduring.

3 JOHN HOLT – 'TRIBAL WAR'

This version of the Little Roy-penned appeal for calm was released on the legendary Channel One label in 1974. Despite its slow, dubby feel, it is actually a considerably faster and brighter take than the original and all the better for it.

2 BOB MARLEY – 'ONE LOVE (PEOPLE GET READY)'

Originally recorded by the Wailers as a ska song, Bob Marley took some of the pace out of it, and re-recorded it for 1977's *Exodus* album. There's an additional writing credit for Curtis Mayfield on this version, recognizing the use of his 'Impressions' song.

1 JUNIOR MURVIN – 'POLICE AND THIEVES'

With a social message delivered in Murvin's beautiful falsetto, this song wasn't just a hit with the reggae audience. Huge crossover appeal, helped by the Clash's cover on their debut album, saw this become an anthem for disaffected youth everywhere.

	ARTIST	SONG	YEAR
10	The Melodians	'Rivers of Babylon'	1970
9	The Starlites	'Some A Weh a Bawl'	1975
8	Gregory Isaacs	'Bumping and Boring'	1979
7	Eric Donaldson	'Cherry Oh Baby'	1971
6	Big Youth	'Notty no Jester'	1975
5	Bunny Wailer	'Blackheart Man'	1976
4	Dennis Brown	'Money in My Pocket'	1979
3	John Holt	'Tribal War'	1978
2	Bob Marley	'One Love (People Get Ready)'	1977
1	Junior Murvin	'Police and Thieves'	1977

TOP
10

We've had planes, trains and automobiles, so now we're searching for a soundtrack to sail the seven seas. Music's rarely about the destination, it's all about the journey, and what better way to get from A to B than in the laid-back glamour of a private yacht? Not all the songs featured here are lying in the lap of luxury, but they're all seaworthy.

SAILING

10 ROD STEWART – 'SAILING'

It would seem a pointed snub to have a top 10 of songs about sailing without including Rod's 1975 chart topper and, tempting though that was, we couldn't really bring ourselves to. Especially after all the effort he went to dressing up in the video...

9 BEACH BOYS – 'SLOOP JOHN B'

Taking a West Indian folk song, Brian Wilson managed to transform it from a simple three-chord affair to an expansive pop song that provided a convenient stepping stone between the lowbrow frug of Barbara Ann and pop sophistication of 'Wouldn't it Be Nice'.

8 FAIRPORT CONVENTION – 'A SAILOR'S LIFE'

While not actually as long as a sailor's life, 11 minutes is still going some for a folk song. Thankfully, the unstoppable groove that the folk-rock pioneers lock into halfway through is more than capable of carrying the listener safely to shore.

7 MADNESS – 'NIGHT BOAT TO CAIRO'

The Nutty Boys were renowned for infectious pop and silly videos and this is a prime example of both. As catchy as malaria, the song's reputation as a carefree classic was further cemented by the happy-go-lucky, karaoke feel of their last-minute video.

6 THE DOORS – 'LAND HO!'

A high point of the *Morrison Hotel* album, this rock shanty was one of the songs that saw Jim Morrison and co. rescue their reputations and get back on course after the critical failure of their fourth album, *The Soft Parade* threatened to

sink their career.

5 NICK CAVE – 'THE SHIP SONG'

Whether it's with the brutal rock of 'Birthday Party' or beguiling ballads like this, Nick Cave always manages to connect with devastating simplicity. It's a modern classic of the Great Australian Songbook (and if there isn't one, there should be).

4 WINGS – 'MORSE MOOSE AND THE GREY GOOSE'

This documents the attempts of a person - the 'Morse

Moose' – to contact the Grey Goose – a ship in distress. Obviously, the best way to do this is by veering between disco-soaked rock and a traditional sea shanty. McCartney's grand ambition wins again.

3 THE O'JAYS – 'SHIP AHOY'

Starting with the sound of creaking wood and crashing waves, a whip's crack and the heave-ho rhythm of the bass, this heavyweight song addresses the dark subject matter of slave transportation. Crucially, the theme never dominates at the expense of the music.

2 ROBERT WYATT – 'SHIPBUILDING'

Written by Elvis Costello, this beautiful song addresses the difficulty in marrying the newfound prosperity of the UK's shipyards during the Falklands War, with the loss of life that resulted. Robert Wyatt's fragile, emotive delivery expresses all this and more.

1 CROSBY STILLS AND NASH – 'WOODEN SHIPS'

This may well be the only song on this list to actually have been composed on a boat (for which double points). David Crosby's light touch and gorgeous textures ensure calm waters before the swell of the chorus lifts the listener to new heights.

	ARTIST	SONG	YEAR
10	Rod Stewart	'Sailing'	1975
9	The Beach Boys	'Sloop John B'	1966
8	Fairport Convention	'A Sailor's Life'	1969
7	Madness	'Night Boat to Cairo'	1979
6	The Doors	'Land Ho!'	1970
5	Nick Cave	'The Ship Song'	1990
4	Wings	'Morse Moose and the Grey Goose'	1978
3	The O'Jays	'Ship Ahoy'	1973
2	Robert Wyatt	'Shipbuilding'	1982
1	Crosby Stills and Nash	'Wooden Ships'	1969

TOP 10

In equal parts traditional Nigerian music, jazz, funk and righteous political anger, there's a spirit to Afrobeat that is identifiable yet indescribable. Heading up the vanguard in Sixties' Africa was Fela Anikulapo Kuti. Following behind him big, big bands – the size of which was rarely seen outside of jazz – ready to confront leaders, play music, dance with abandon and entertain with ease.

AFROBEAT

10 ANTIBALAS – 'DIRTY MONEY'
Afrobeat is a style that still resonates today, and this is best illustrated by the bands currently playing it. Of these, Brooklyn-based 12-piece Antibalas are the top of the pile and have got everything right without resorting to copying. They just get it.

9 ASSAGAI – 'AKASA'
A band of South African and Nigerian musicians who recorded in London, there's a truly international background to Assagai. This track is from their 1971 album Zimbabwe and has grand ambition in its musical aims, encompassing rock, jazz and funk into the polyrhythms.

8 SEUN KUTI & EGYPT 80 – 'MR BIG THIEF'
Seun started singing for Africa 80, his late father Fela's band, aged just 14. There is then, a continuation of sound and feel from the classic canon that few could manage, leading many to proclaim Seun the true inheritor of his father's crown.

7 FEMI KUTI - 'TRUTH DON DIE'
You can hear much of Fela's phrasing in his eldest son's sound, as you might expect from a musician who played in his father's band. Femi has also inherited Fela's sense of righteous indignation and ear for a good groove, both of which feature here.

6 JONI HAASTRUP – 'WAKE UP YOUR MIND'
A one-time keys player for Ginger Baker's Airforce, former Modern Aces singer Haastrup got to tour the UK and returned there in the late Seventies to record this solo record - basically a funk album, but one with Haastrup's African influence all over it.

5 TONY ALLEN PLAYS WITH AFRIKA 70 - 'AFRO DISCO BEAT'
Perhaps the single most important figure when it comes to the development of the Afrobeat sound, drummer Tony Allen, here with the legendary Africa 70 from the 1976 album Progress, shows exactly why he's held in such high regard.

4 OSCAR SULLEY & THE UHURU DANCE BAND – 'OLUFEME!'
With a flute in one hand and a bag full of jazz and funk in the other, Ghanaian flautist Oscar Sulley strode forward looking for new paths for African music to take. On this track, he was ably followed by the Uhuru Dance Band.

3 ORLANDO JULIUS & HIS MODERN ACES – 'ISE OWO'
One of the formative albums in Afrobeat history, the 1966

album, *Super Afro Soul*, blended American funk and jazz influences with traditional African rhythms and, in doing so, laid the flagstones which would later become an international stage.

2 MANU DIBANGO – 'SOUL MAKOSSA'

The influence of Cameroon-born saxophonist and vibraphonist Dibango on America's burgeoning hip hop scene is well-documented. Listen closely to the 'Mama-say, mama-sa, ma-ma-ko-sa' vocal line and it becomes apparent that Michael Jackson was a fan, too.

1 FELA KUTI – 'WATER GET NO ENEMY'

Arguably Fela's strongest album, *Expensive Shit* boasted the jazzy, earthy feel of this 11-minute song on the B-side. Featuring some blistering brass and comparatively languid piano, this nonetheless builds a tight, hypnotic groove that finds release in the magnificent horn arrangement.

	ARTIST	SONG	YEAR
10	Antibalas	*Dirty Money*	2012
9	Assagai	*Akasa*	1971
8	Seun Kuti & Egypt 80	*Mr Big Thief*	2011
7	Femi Kuti	*Truth Don Die*	1998
6	Joni Haastrup	*Wake up Your Mind*	1978
5	Tony Allen Plays with Afrika 70	*Afro Disco Beat*	1976
4	Oscar Sulley & the Uhuru Dance Band	*Olufeme!*	2005 (reissue)
3	Orlando Julius & His Modern Aces	*Ise Owo*	1966
2	Manu Dibango	*Soul Makossa*	1972
1	Fela Kuti	*Water Get No Enemy*	1975

TOP
10

1968 saw worldwide political upheaval including, in Brazil, the birth of Tropilcalia, an arts-based movement vocal in its opposition of a repressive and brutal dictatorship. Fusing funk and psychedelic rock with avant-garde experimentation, the movement lasted just a year, yet the impact was felt profoundly – not least by the dictatorship, which exiled two of its leading figures, Caetano Veloso and Giberto Gil.

TROPICALIA

10 OS MUTANTES – 'ALGO MAIS'

From their second album, this track shows Os Mutantes on absolutely scorching form. Regarded generally as a more polished offering, this track shows the band running at music with their arms wide open and using any and every influence that came their way.

9 GAL COSTA – 'TUAREG'

Taking its lead from Oswald de Andrade's 1928 Cannibal Manifesto which claimed that Brazillian culture was best when it took from others, Tuareg, off psychedelic 1969 masterpiece, *Gal*, is full of Eastern promise and Western hooks.

8 JORGE BEN JOR – 'TAKE IT EASY MY BROTHER CHARLES'

The acoustic strum, jazzy horns and reassuring, optimistic sentiment of the lyrics lend this an easy-going charm and mark it

out as a Tropicalia release devoid of dense, crowded experimentation and allows all of us - not just Charlie - to take it easy.

7 RITA LEE – 'VAMOS TRATAR DA SAUDE'

While enjoying success with Os Mutantes, Rita Lee tried her hand at a solo career. The first album didn't end well, but her second effort, from which this funk-filled song is taken, is really an Os Mutantes album in all but name and, as such, is great.

6 GAL COSTA – 'RELANCE'

Another Gal Costa track, this time from 1974's *India* album. While the introductory percussion and accordion line - descending notes all gasping for breath - can make you wonder where the song is going, the assured funk of the drums soon makes this crystal clear.

5 GILBERTO GIL – 'GELÉIA GERAL'

The screaming statement of intent of the Tropicalia movement, this is manifesto as music. The parody and satire of the song, which takes aim at supposedly high culture and the established elite, is delivered against an elaborate backdrop that sounds not unlike a Brazilian Sgt Pepper's.

4 OS MUTANTES – 'A MINHA MENINA'

If the 13th Floor Elevators had ever tried their hand at upbeat, sunshine pop instead of eating LSD like other people eat toast, there's a strong chance that it would have sounded like this - fuzzy, warm and twirling around, arms outstretched, in a sun-kissed park.

3 CAETANO VELOSO – 'TROPICALIA'

Showing the way in which art, literature and music fed into each other in the Tropilcalia movement, this song, from

Caetano Veloso's 1968 debut album, takes its name from an art installation by Hélio Oiticicia, and mixes styles with joyful abandon.

2 TOM ZE – 'JIMMY, RENDA-SE'

Sampled, remixed, borrowed... this song has proved something of an underground hit since it resurfaced in the 1990s - along with its creator - after a spell in relative obscurity, though it's difficult to see how anyone could forget this after hearing it.

1 GILBERTO GIL – 'BAT MACUMBA'

While Os Mutantes recorded a great cover version, it's Gilberto Gil's original (the song was written by Gil and Caetano Veloso) that has the looser feel, the Byrds-esque guitar shimmer and the massive congas to mark it out as the one to make the top 10.

	ARTIST	SONG	YEAR
10	Os Mutantes	'Algo Mais'	1969
9	Gal Costa	'Tuareg'	1969
8	Jorge Ben Jor	'Take It Easy My Brother Charles'	1969
7	Rita Lee Vamos	'Tratar Da Saude'	1972
6	Gal Costa	'Relance'	1973
5	Gilberto Gil	'Geleia Geral'	1969
4	Os Mutantes	'A Minha Menina'	1968
3	Caetano Veloso	'Tropicalia'	1968
2	Tom Ze	'Jimmy, Renda-Se'	1970
1	Gilberto Gil	'Bat Macumba'	1968

TOP 10

Perhaps it's the sense of awe in seeing the world laid out in front of you - perhaps it's the feeling of mortality that presents itself when you're 30,000 feet up in a really heavy metal tube. Either way, flying has inspired more songs than budget airliners could cram on to a single flight. These have all made the upgrade from economy in first-class style.

FLYING

10 FRANK SINATRA – 'FLY ME TO THE MOON'
The number of people who have covered this song is enormous, but the combination of Quincy Jones, Count Basie and Frank Sinatra gave this classic the nearest anyone will ever get to a definitive version, exploding with energy and verve.

9 FOO FIGHTERS – 'LEARN TO FLY'
It may be one of Dave Grohl's least favourite songs from Foo Fighters' third album, *There Is Nothing Left to Lose*, but the anthemic power pop had wings as far as everyone else was concerned and gave the band their first major hit.

8 STEVE MILLER BAND – 'FLY LIKE AN EAGLE'
There's a definite sense of flight in the rising keyboard lines that drift in and out of this epic track and, while there may be a sniff of cod philosophy about the lyrics, it's never jarring enough to bring everything crashing back to Earth.

7 THE BEATLES – 'BACK IN THE USSR'
The sound of a plane landing is the point at which this tune takes off. It's a fantastic rock 'n' roll song, though strangely orthodox compared to the rest of its White Album peers, even down to the Beach Boys-esque middle eight.

6 PEAKING LIGHTS – 'HEY SPARROW'
This will be a new one to most, taken from the critically acclaimed 2011 debut album *936*. It's a lo-fi affair - imagine trying to record a band in the next room using a dictaphone - but also a breathtaking celebration of beauty in the everyday.

5 SMOKIE – 'WE'RE FLYING HIGH'
There's barely a charity shop in the land that doesn't have at least one record by Bradford's Smokie available for pennies. Sadly, it's unlikely to be this uplifting anthem, in which the soaring melodies are much closer to America than the north of England.

4 THE CREATION — 'NO SILVER BIRD'

Not to be confused with the English psych band of the same name, this Creation hailed from Albuquerque, New Mexico. From the opening, delayed chords it's quite clear that this band didn't need an aeroplane to achieve optimum altitude.

3 JUDY HENSKE - 'HIGH FLYING BIRD'

Predating the soon-to-be-massive folk rock boom in America by a good year at least, Judy Henske's husky vibrato was backed by a full band for this mournful, human imagining of a bird's idea of flight and showed the shape of things to come.

2 THE BYRDS — 'EIGHT MILES HIGH'

Despite raised eyebrows at the song's overtly psychedelic nature, Roger McGuinn maintains that it was simply about a plane journey. This is, however, a claim dismissed by David Crosby and Gene Clark who, ironically enough, was a Byrd who hated flying.

1 BUFFALO SPRINGFIELD — 'EXPECTING TO FLY'

The expansive sound and elaborate arrangement of this Neil Young song from the band's second album are enough to make you think they'd just teamed up with the Walker brothers. As such, it remains one of the album's high points.

	ARTIST	SONG	YEAR
10	Frank Sinatra	'Fly Me to the Moon'	1964
9	Foo Fighters	'Learn to Fly'	1999
8	Steve Miller Band	'Fly Like an Eagle'	1976
7	The Beatles	'Back in the USSR'	1968
6	Peaking Lights	'Hey Sparrow	2011
5	Smokie	We're Flying High	1975
4	The Creation	No Silver Bird	1967
3	Judy Henske	High Flying Bird	1964
2	The Byrds	Eight Miles High	1966
1	Buffalo Springfield	Expecting to Fly	1967

CHAPTER 5
IN THE STUDIO

TOP 10

Producers have to tease the best from musicians and songs alike, while working out what will work and, crucially, which ones are likely to be the commercial big hitters for the record company. In short, in a room full of children and toys, they have to be the grown up. They may as well try to herd cats.

PRODUCERS

10 PHIL SPECTOR
Taking charge of the whole process of production, Spector achieved exactly the results he wanted. He created the famous 'Wall of Sound' and, in doing so, gave rise to new and endless aesthetic possibilities. He's currently serving 19 years to life for murder.

9 TONY VISCONTI
Marsha Hunt, Osibasa and T.Rex were all lucky enough to work with Tony Visconti, but it's his groundbreaking work creating the fragile, isolated soundscape of Berlin-era David Bowie (and we'll chuck in Iggy Pop's *The Idiot* here, too) that sets him apart from the pack.

8 DJ PREMIER
For many, it's Dre who nails it when it comes to hip-hop, and certainly he's more famous, but Premier's work for Gang-Starr, M.O.P., Jay-Z and Nas shows his encyclopedic knowledge of music and his ability to incorporate real feeling into his beats.

7 QUINCY JONES
When it comes to music, there's pretty much nothing that Quincy Jones can't do. After a career in jazz and film scores, he met Michael Jackson and went on to produce *Off the Wall*, *Thriller* and *Bad*, and, in doing so, broke records and made history.

6 LEE 'SCRATCH' PERRY
Operating in parallel to ordinary people, but quite clearly in a world all of his own, is the producer for whom the word 'maverick' seems entirely inadequate. Perry's influence over modern music is huge and his productions a delight of dub and delay.

5 NILE RODGERS
Having re-defined disco is Chic's guitarist could have been forgiven for resting on his laurels, which were, presumably, stuffed full of comfy cash. He didn't though and Diana Ross, the B-52s, Grace Jones, Madonna and Duran Duran, to name a few, must be very grateful.

4 ENO
A musical magpie, but with a penchant for more extravagant plumage, Brian Eno introduced Bowie to Krautrock and took African rhythms to *Talking Heads*. He's also released a slew of adventurous albums, and is, if not the father, the affectionate uncle of ambient.

3 BRIAN WILSON
Leaving his contemporaries open-mouthed in his wake as he rode the crest of his own creativity, Beach Boy Brian Wilson continually pushed himself and the boundaries of pop

music. After a string of incredible achievements he eventually had to have a lie-down. For three years.

2 JOE MEEK
Meek's interest lay in sounds rather than tunes, and his pioneering use of home-made equipment to generate delay and reverb gave his productions an unmistakable sonic signature. Sadly in 1967, plagued by debt and depression, he killed his landlady before shooting himself.

1 GEORGE MARTIN
The first name on everyone's lips when the words 'Fifth Beatle' are mentioned, Sir George's legacy is assured. He saw the spark in the Fab Four and was the chief scientist behind successful experiments including *Sgt Pepper's* and *Revolver*.

	NAME	LISTEN TO	YEAR
10	Phil Spector	*Be My Baby* – The Ronettes	1963
9	Tony Visconti	*Low* – David Bowie	1977
8	DJ Premier	'Just to Get a Rep' – Gang Starr	1991
7	Quincy Jones	*Off the Wall & Thriller* – Michael Jackson	1979/1982
6	Lee 'Scratch' Perry	*14 Dub Blackboard Jungle* – Upsetters	1973
5	Nile Rodgers	*C'est Chic* – Chic	1978
4	Eno	*Before and After Science*	1977
3	Brian Wilson	*Pet Sounds*	1966
2	Joe Meek	*Telstar* – The Tornados	1962
1	George Martin	*Revolver* – The Beatles	1966

TOP 10

While music lists are, by their very nature, controversial, the top 10 debut albums is the one that's most likely to provoke a strongly worded email – or a mild nuclear rebuke. Like Sophie's Choice but for music nerds, trimming down the field can be an agonizing process and impossible to get right. Having said that, this is a very strong line-up.

DEBUTS

10 GUNS 'N' ROSES – APPETITE FOR DESTRUCTION
By 1987, heavy metal had stagnated, much of it a poor pastiche. Enter Axl Rose, Slash and co to give it a swift kick up the arse. With the instant impact of 'Welcome to the Jungle' and 'Paradise City', this was the hard rock reboot metal needed.

9 THE CLASH – S/T
While the Pistols screamed and shouted, the Clash tried to start a revolution – although they'd have settled for a riot. From the inspired cover versions ('Police and Thieves', 'I Fought the Law') to their own, incendiary, songs, this was the perfect calling card.

8 NAS – ILLMATIC
The first hip-hop album to boast a team of 'super producers' including DJ Premier, Pete Rock and Q-Tip, Illmatic was musically assured even before a 20-year-old Nas stepped up and delivered his incredible storyboard songs with a facility for language that belied his age.

7 THE RAMONES – S/T
Superficially simple, or simply superficial? The Ramones put their collective foot down and sped through their freshman offering safe in the knowledge that they'd stripped down rock to its bare essentials and created something vital, primal and blindingly good.

6 SEX PISTOLS – NEVER MIND THE BOLLOCKS
Some albums are like old friends – they become part of the furniture. Other albums break into your house, nick the furniture and sell it. Everyone wanted to be on nodding terms with the Pistols' snarling debut, but couldn't be sure whether they were liked in return.

5 THE BEATLES – PLEASE PLEASE ME
The sophisticated pop premiere that changed everything. The Beatles wrote songs every bit as sophisticated and accomplished as their (well chosen) cover versions, they played and sang them with a comfortable confidence, and they recorded this all in a day. One day.

4 JOY DIVISION – UNKNOWN PLEASURES
The stark, uncompromising cover is iconic and a good indicator of the music that lies underneath - a glimpse of despair and pain communicated with supreme melodic and poetic flair. The songs, and Martin Hannett's incredible production, are simply stunning.

3 THE VELVET UNDERGROUND – *THE VELVET UNDERGROUND AND NICO*

If commercial success were directly proportional to the cultural influence of a band, the surviving members of the Velvet Underground would be Bilderberg rich by now. This record continues to colour the musical landscape with its invention, ambition and incredible songs.

2 BEASTIE BOYS – *LICENSED TO ILL*

Not everyone got the joke and, for some, the Beastie Boy's larger-than-life cartoon creations seemed like a genuine threat. In reality, this was a funny, literate and musically sharp album, mixing punk, metal and rap and humour with style.

1 JIMI HENDRIX – *ARE YOU EXPERIENCED*

An album that knocked people backwards, forwards and side to side. The guitar playing, obviously, puts a smile on the face of anyone whose jaw isn't on the floor, but the sheer consistency of the songs makes this debut sound like a greatest hits.

	ARTIST	ALBUM	YEAR
10	Guns 'n' Roses	*Appetite For Destruction*	1987
9	The Clash	*The Clash*	1977
8	Nas	*Illmatic*	1994
7	The Ramones	*The Ramones*	1976
6	Sex Pistols	*Never Mind the Bollocks*	1977
5	The Beatles	*Please Please Me*	1963
4	Joy Division	*Unknown Pleasures*	1979
3	Beastie Boys	*Licensed to Ill*	1986
2	The Velvet Underground	*The Velvet Underground and Nico*	1967
1	The Jimi Hendrix Experience	*Are You Experienced*	1967

TOP
10

While debuts can take years of under-the-radar work to perfect, bands are not afforded the same luxury when it comes to their under-the-spotlight and against-the-clock follow up. With record companies breathing down their necks and fans waiting, breath baited for more of the same, many bands fall at the second hurdle. Here are 10 that, with vaulting ambition, beat their personal best.

'DIFFICULT' SECOND ALBUMS

8 JIMI HENDRIX – *AXIS: BOLD AS LOVE*

In 'Little Miss Lover' and 'You Got Me Floating', *Axis...* has the heavy guitar grooves that made *Are You Experienced* so popular. 'Little Wing' and 'Castles Made of Sand' however, show off the increased subtlety and maturity in both songwriting and playing.

7 CAROLE KING – *TAPESTRY*

One of the most successful albums of all time, Carole King's sophomore effort was certainly no slump. A high watermark in songwriting craft, its genius lies in managing to be confessional and intimate while, at the same time, inclusive and universal.

10 RADIOHEAD – *THE BENDS*

Radiohead's second album marked their first collaboration with engineer and producer Nigel Godrich. Dark and brooding, intense and intriguing, it is a much more coherent collection than Pablo Honey and spawned no fewer than five singles.

9 BLACK SABBATH – *PARANOID*

When your first album is as good as Black Sabbath's debut, there are always going to be question marks as to how you follow it. These concerns were more than answered by the end of side one of Paranoid, leaving no one in any doubt as to the band's credentials.

6 BEASTIE BOYS – *PAUL'S BOUTIQUE*

One of two acts to have an entry in both album top 10s, the Beastie Boys wowed the

world when they came back from the frat-hop of *Licensed to Ill* with a Dust Brothers-produced album that was bigger and bolder in every conceivable way.

5 NIRVANA — *NEVERMIND*
While early songs like 'About a Girl' and 'Spank Thru' had hinted at the band's potential for writing a pop hook, it wasn't until *Nevermind*

that this potential fused with the devastating dynamics of the band's raw sound and created a epoch-defining record.

4 NEIL YOUNG – *EVERYONE KNOWS THIS IS NOWHERE*

Neil Young's second album was a debut in some respects as it was his first outing with backing band Crazy Horse. It's a near-faultless collection and contains songs that to this day form the backbone of Young's searing live shows.

3 PUBLIC ENEMY – *IT TAKES A NATION OF MILLIONS TO HOLD US BACK*

If 1987's *Yo! Bum Rush the Show* was a warning shot, then Public Enemy's second album was a full-on tactical assault. Chuck D's revolution rhymes and social commentary were perfectly soundtracked by Hank Shocklee's battle-ready productions.

2 VAN MORRISON – *ASTRAL WEEKS*

Unhappy with the presentation of 1967's *Blowin' Your Mind*, *Astral Weeks* was a chance for Van Morrison to start again. Jazz, blues and folk combine to create something extraordinary – and a world away from the light breeze of 'Brown Eyed Girl'.

1 BOB DYLAN – *THE FREEWHEELIN' BOB DYLAN*

The album that marked Bob Dylan out as the best songwriter of his generation also brought folk music out of the clubs and onto the radio. The achievement is all the more remarkable when you consider Dylan was just 22 at the time.

	ARTIST	ALBUM	YEAR
10	Radiohead	*The Bends*	1995
9	Black Sabbath	*Paranoid*	1970
8	The Jimi Hendrix Experience	*Axis: Bold As Love*	1967
7	Carole King	*Tapestry*	1971
6	Beastie Boys	*Paul's Boutique*	1989
5	Nirvana	*Nevermind*	1991
4	Neil Young	*Everybody Knows this Is Nowhere*	1969
3	Public Enemy	*It Takes a Nation of Millions to Hold Us Back*	1988
2	Van Morrison	*Astral Weeks*	1968
1	Bob Dylan	*The Freewheelin' Bob Dylan*	1963

TOP 10

For some bands, releasing albums that were effectively a collection of unconnected short stories wasn't enough. They craved the kudos and creative respect commanded by great art with grand themes – they wanted to write a novel. Inevitably, many bands would stall at the first chapter, but this top 10 is populated by wholly satisfying stories.

CONCEPT ALBUMS

10 THE BEATLES – SGT. PEPPER'S LONELY HEARTS CLUB BAND
Certainly the most famous concept album of all time, even if the concept is a (very) loose one. Adopting the persona of a different band was intended to free them up to experiment more, and it's in that sense, rather than a unified theme, that it works.

9 THE KINKS – THE KINKS ARE THE VILLAGE GREEN PRESERVATION SOCIETY
While the theme of isolation is prevalent in the concept album, so is the theme of loss. On their 1968 release, we find the Kinks in mourning for an England that seems to be lost - one of steam trains and village fêtes - and the echoes are still heard today.

8 SMALL FACES – ODGEN'S NUT GONE FLAKE
Getting gobbledegook king Stanley Unwin to narrate this tale of a young boy's search for the missing half of the moon was the band's first stroke of genius with this album. Writing the best suite of songs of their career to go with it was the other.

7 PINK FLOYD – DARK SIDE OF THE MOON
Dark Side... is perhaps Pink Floyd's most feted album. In some respects, all Floyd records had been conceptual, but this was the first time that we see a structured narrative, one that sensitively addresses death, greed, humanity and mental illness.

6 SERGE GAINSBOURG – HISTOIRE DE MELODY NELSON
Only in the mind of Serge Gainsbourg could a crash

between a Rolls Royce and a
bicycle lead to an obsessive
love affair. His mini drama
in seven parts is set to Jean
Claude Vannier's exceptional
scoring which gives the piece
musical as well as lyrical
continuity.

5 THE PRETTY THINGS –
SF SORROW
The life of the fantastically
named Sebastian F Sorrow
provides the focus for the
Pretty Things' musical
biography. It is a harrowing
and relentlessly downbeat

tale of loss and betrayal, but is
musically brilliant and almost
entirely successful.

4 THE WHO – *TOMMY*
The rock opera was the
perfect vehicle for possibly
rock's most literate songwriter,

Pete Townshend, whose storytelling prowess and musical genius saw deaf, dumb and blind Tommy's journey out of a semi-catatonic state translated on to stage and screen.

3 DAVID BOWIE –
THE RISE AND FALL OF ZIGGY STARDUST AND THE SPIDERS FROM MARS
It's that age-old story... bisexual rock star from another planet comes to Earth to deliver a message of hope to mankind before it consumes itself completely and is ultimately destroyed. Musically amazing, it's actually much less weird than it sounds.

2 THE WHO – *QUADROPHENIA*
Pete Townshend really ran with the form after Tommy, producing probably the most complete and successful story of any concept album before or since. It's a terrific tale of teenage identity and tribalism played out against a Mods and Rockers backdrop.

1 PINK FLOYD – *THE WALL*
This story of rock star isolation, despair and the loss of humanity was Roger Waters' crowning achievement. It's also the last truly great Pink Floyd moment before the band buckled under the increasing weight of middle-eight spread.

	ARTIST	ALBUM	YEAR
10	The Beatles	*Sgt. Pepper's Lonely Hearts Club Band*	1967
9	The Kinks	*The Kinks Are the Village Green Preservation Society*	1968
8	Small Faces	*Odgen's Nut Gone Flake*	1968
7	Pink Floyd	*Dark Side of the Moon*	1973
6	Serge Gainsbourg	*Histoire de Melody Nelson*	1971
5	The Pretty Things	*SF Sorrow*	1968
4	The Who	*Tommy*	1969
3	David Bowie	*The Rise and Fall of Ziggy Stardust and the Spiders from Mars*	1972
2	The Who	*Quadrophenia*	1973
1	Pink Floyd	*The Wall*	1979

TOP 10

'A little less conversation, a little more action' sang Elvis and it's a sentiment that we can all get behind. There are times when we need the brain to be in neutral to really lose ourselves in music, and words can keep us grounded while we're trying to drift away – much like an unwanted conversation at bedtime. Pray silence please, for the top 10 instrumentals.

ROCK AND POP INSTRUMENTALS

10 THE EURYTHMICS – 'I DID IT JUST THE SAME'

Hiding in plain sight, well... on the 1984 album, is this unexpected gem, whose mid-paced chug sounds like it could have been released any time in the last five years. Annie Lennox does feature, but only in a wordless, wailing way.

9 TORNADOS – 'TELSTAR'

For a song inspired by science fiction and recorded in a tiny flat on London's Holloway Road, this space-rock satellite transmission punched well above its weight. A huge hit in America, it also saw Joe Meek's star rise around the world.

8 JOHN BARRY – 'THIS IS HOW YOU DANCE'

A slight cheat as this is from a soundtrack, but the feel is pure pop. John Barry's work on Bond films is widely known, but his talent extends to the sort of dreamy, flighty music more associated with Sixties shindigs than cinemas, and this is a prime example.

7 PINK FLOYD – 'ECHOES'

With so many instrumentals to choose from, you'd think that narrowing down Pink Floyd's oevre to a field of one would be difficult. When the track in question is a sprawling masterpiece that stands in a field of its own, however, it's really easy.

6 MOGWAI – 'MOGWAI FEAR SATAN'

There's absolutely no reason for Scottish rockers to be scared of the Devil - if he ever heard this, he'd duck and cover such is the thunderous, righteous rage of the guitar assault that follows the barely-there, shimmering whisper of the introduction.

5 THE COMMODORES – 'MACHINE GUN'

Hello? Is it Lionel Ritchie you're looking for? It is, but don't expect any schmaltzy balladeering. Or any singing at all in fact. Literally too funky for words, Lionel is in charge of the high-end keyboard lines, but everyone's too busy dancing to notice.

4 INCREDIBLE BONGO BAND – 'APACHE'

Those drums! That guitar! Even if the jury's out on whether this is the best instrumental of all time, it has to be a contender for the most influential. Special mention goes to the Shadows' original, but it's Michael Viner's bongo rhythms all the way.

3 DAVID AXELROD — 'URIZEN'
To some, this is fusion but, for the purposes of this list, it's arty, avant-garde pop. With the same sort of lush, orchestrated feel Alxelrod brought to US rock band The Electric Prunes, this - like the William Blake poems that inspired it - was largely ignored at the time.

2 BOOKER T & THE MGS — 'MELTING POT'
'Green Onions' may be the Booker T default setting, but 'Melting Pot' is the one you want - preferably the album take which, at eight-

minutes long, guarantees utter dancefloor devastation. There's a brilliant Boris Gardener version too, but that's a whole other list...

1 LINK WRAY — 'RUMBLE'
Banned from the airwaves despite being an instrumental (the title was an allusion to a street fight), this delightfully distorted offering from master guitarist Link Wray is aptly titled, given the sound he manages to achieve - he broke amplifiers as well as boundaries.

	ARTIST	SONG	YEAR
10	The Eurythmics	'I Did it Just the Same'	1984
9	The Tornados	'Telstar'	1962
8	John Barry	'This Is How You Dance'	1971
7	Pink Floyd	'Echoes'	1971
6	Mogwai	'Mogwai Fear Satan'	1997
5	The Commodores	'Machine Gun'	1974
4	Incredible Bongo Band	'Apache'	1973
3	David Axelrod	'Urizen'	1968
2	Booker T & The MGs	'Melting Pot'	1971
1	Link Wray	'Rumble'	1958

TOP 10

While they weren't taking barely concealed pot shots at each other from behind the gossamer-thin veneer of lyrical conceit, the post-break-up Fab Four showed the world exactly why they had been the biggest band in it for years. Well, three of them did (sorry Ringo). This top 10 attempts to sort the wheat from the Frog Chorus.

POST-BEATLES TUNES FROM THE FAB FOU

10 PAUL MCCARTNEY – 'UNCLE ALBERT/ ADMIRAL HALSEY'
This is taken from the *Ram* LP, which was, unfairly, panned on its release. Much like medley on side 2 of *Abbey Road*, this is a patchwork quilt of song fragments superbly stitched together to make something beautiful, warm and comforting.

9 PAUL MCCARTNEY – 'CHECK MY MACHINE'
A wonderfully off-the-wall experiment, it was the first thing he recorded on the *McCartney II sessions* (to check his equipment). The satisfyingly dubby results, with dancing, machine melodies show that, even when doodling, he can create an abstract masterpiece.

8 JOHN LENNON – 'WORKING CLASS HERO'
This song was the B-side yang to 'Imagine's' yin. Once again,

it's when Lennon's angry that he's at his best - all acerbic barbs and flippant fury - and this outsider's view of how society controls and demeans is delivered with bitter intent.

7 GEORGE HARRISON – 'ALL THINGS MUST PASS'
While all eyes were on Paul and John, George surprised everyone by sneaking out a triple album of real quality. On the title track, he sounds like he's coming to term with recent events in a beautiful, elegiac song, originally given to Billy Preston to record.

6 JOHN LENNON – 'GIMME SOME TRUTH'
'Imagine' isn't in this top 10, what with it being crippled by saccharine sentiment and sixth-form poetry. This however, off the same album, is superb - a snarling, vicious, angry pot shot at politicians and everything that's wrong with the world.

5 WINGS – 'LIVE AND LET DIE'
There are so many Wings songs to choose from, so why not go straight for the big guns? From the opening moments of the James Bond theme tune, full of wonderfully overblown theatrical bombast, we are taken on a ride as thrilling as any spy movie.

4 GEORGE HARRISON – 'WAH WAH'
Hang on? No 'My Sweet Lord'? No. *Let the All Things Must Pass* album carry on playing for about 10 seconds after George's big hit ends, and you'll end up slap bang in the middle of one of the best moments of his entire career.

3 JOHN LENNON – 'INSTANT KARMA!'
Lennon is on unusually optimistic form on this *Plastic Ono Band* single, which, as he rightly identified himself, is a 'monster'. It really was almost instant, too, being written and

recorded on 27 January 1970 and released just 10 days later.

2 PAUL MCCARTNEY – 'MY SECRET FRIEND'

From the *McCartney II* sessions, this track was originally hidden away on the B-side of a limited-run 12". It's a shame as this proto-house jam is better than almost anything on that album and highlights McCartney's fascination with, and mastery of, technology.

1 PAUL MCCARTNEY – 'MAYBE I'M AMAZED'

Paul McCartney's self-played, self-produced debut solo album had many great moments – many of them surprising those expecting to hear his trademark sound. This however, is a classic, with tell-tale McCartney melodies and an effortless elegance in its lyrical simplicity.

	ARTIST	SONG	YEAR
10	Paul McCartney	'Uncle Albert/ Admiral Halsey'	1971
9	Paul McCartney	'Check My Machine'	1980
8	John Lennon	'Working Class Hero'	1971
7	George Harrison	'All Things Must Pass'	1970
6	John Lennon	'Gimme Some Truth'	1971
5	Wings	'Live and Let Die'	1973
4	George Harrison	'Wah Wah'	1971
3	John Lennon	'Instant Karma!'	1970
2	Paul McCartney	'My Secret Friend'	1980
1	Paul McCartney	'Maybe I'm Amazed'	1970

TOP 10

While most songs follow a basic rhythmic pattern, there are only so many times that four beats can walk into a bar without the set-up getting a little tired. The desire to have a bit of fun with time signatures it perfectly understandable then, but it needs to be done well, otherwise everyone ends up feeling lost in music.

ODD TIME SIGNATURES

10 THE BEATLES – 'ALL YOU NEED IS LOVE'

To be honest, this just stinks of showing off, but it's done so well you can't help but say 'bravo'. The verse is sort of 7/4 (except one single bar of 8/4) and the chorus is mainly 4/4 (apart from the 6/4 bit right at the end). Ringo - all is forgiven!

9 LED ZEPPELIN – 'THE CRUNGE'

Putting to one side Robert Plant's 'crunge'worthy James Brown impression, when Led Zep went funk they did a pretty good job of it. Particularly as landing on 'the one' is a whole lot more difficult when you have no idea where the hell it's supposed to be.

8 JIMI HENDRIX – 'MANIC DEPRESSION'

While the idea of waltzing to Jimi Hendrix is almost too bizarre to contemplate, it can be done - as Manic Depression

shows. It might not feel - or sound - like a classic waltz, but that's mainly thanks to the impossibly dexterous drumming of Mitch Mitchell.

7 NICK DRAKE – 'RIVER MAN'

One of the only times he used a normal tuning and Nick Drake makes it difficult for students of folk everywhere by employing the tricky 5/4 timing. Without percussion to drive the point home, it sounds effortless, despite being anything but.

6 THE STRANGLERS – 'GOLDEN BROWN'

OK. Are you sitting comfortably? There's a waltz-time keyboard with a harpsichord playing in 6/8 time. Which would be fine - if every fourth bar didn't revert to a standard 4/4. Now, take your partners by the hand and... wait for the next song!

5 DAVE BRUBEK – 'TAKE FIVE'

The king of oddball swing, jazz legend Dave Brubeck gave entire albums over to his experiments in rhythm. *Time*

Further Out's 'Unsquare Dance', with its 7/4 beat is amazing, but 'Take Five' is Brubek's best-known song with good reason.

4 DIONNE WARWICK – 'I SAY A LITTLE PRAYER'

With a metre varying between 10/4 and 11/4, this looks more like long division than musical instruction. It's hard to fathom that anything complex is going on when you hear the song, until you realise it sounds like it's trying to catch up with itself.

3 LALO SCHIFRIN – 'MISSION IMPOSSIBLE'

Managing to smuggle an odd timing under the radar (or, more likely, the laser beam alarm), the song's 5/4 beat is perfect for the job in hand - putting people on the edge of their seat and creating subliminal tension.

2 OUTKAST – 'HEY YA!'

It's an odd time signature, veering between 4/4 and 2/4, but it works so well that it begs the question 'why doesn't every song do this?' The fact that almost no one who bought or loves this record realizes there's anything untoward is its genius.

1 PINK FLOYD – 'MONEY'

The song starts like 'Are You Being Served?' on mogadon, and the bass line sounds so natural - so right - that it's a while until you realise odd time trickery is at play. The 7/4 beat is followed with a languid ease that makes it seem much more simple than it is.

	ARTIST	SONG	TIME SIGNATURE	YEAR
10	The Beatles	'All You Need Is Love'	7/4, 8/4, 4/4 and 6/4	1967
9	Led Zeppelin	'The Crunge'	9/8, 5/4	1973
8	Jimi Hendrix	'Manic Depression'	3/4	1967
7	Nick Drake	'River Man'	5/4	1969
6	The Stranglers	'Golden Brown'	3/4, 6/8, 4/4	1981
5	Dave Brubek	'Take Five'	5/4	1959
4	Dionne Warwick	'I Say a Little Prayer'	4/4, 10/4, 11/4	1967
3	Lalo Schifrin	'Mission Impossible'	5/4	1967
2	Outkast	'Hey Ya!'	11/4 (mixing 4/4 and 2/4)	2003
1	Pink Floyd	'Money'	5/4	1973

TOP 10

Although they say that those who play together, stay together, many of the doomed pairings on this list go to show that 'they' may not have a clue what they're on about. That said, there have been some fantastic records – not to mention headlines – made by some of these musical marriages over the years.

COUPLES

10 RONNIE AND PHIL SPECTOR
One look and you could tell the sums didn't work. She was a stunning, stylish singer while he... well, he looked a bit creepy – and it hardly seems likely his winning personality stole Veronica Bennett's heart. Still, she made her hits and then, thankfully, her escape.

9 JACK WHITE AND MEG WHITE
What do you do if you're a recently divorced couple in one of the hottest bands of the moment and reporters are sniffing around? You claim that you're brother and sister of course! Keeping to that story once the marriage certificate surfaced was delightfully contrary.

8 BEYONCÉ AND JAY-Z
Hip-hop's golden couple, it's fair to say that neither married for money. The sound of their newborn daughter, Blue Ivy, crying is audible on Jay Z's single 'Glory', an achievement for which she was credited, making her the youngest billboard chart star ever.

7 IKE AND TINA TURNER
While the much-documented bust-ups and violent arguments during their tempestuous marriage have been given headline space, it's easy to forget just how big Ike and Tina Turner were. Which is, in fairness, not nearly as big as Tina when she went solo.

6 SONNY & CHER
They famously had each other – right up to the point where they divorced. Until then though, they had a string of pop hits in the Sixties and a hugely successful TV career in the early part of the Seventies. So, at least they proved their love could pay the rent.

5 LYNDSEY BUCKINGHAM AND STEVIE NICKS
Anyone who's listened to *Rumours* will, presumably, know that this didn't end well. The childhood sweethearts had recorded an album together before joining Fleetwood Mac and then promptly splitting up. However, awkward studio session's produced some amazing results.

4 JOHNNY CASH AND JUNE CARTER CASH

After Johnny Cash proposed to June Carter during a live performance, the pair married and stayed together for 35 years, until June's death, in 2003. The lived together, recorded together and almost died together – Johnny passed away four months after his wife.

3 ABBA

Four people, two couples, one band. What could possibly go wrong? Fame, world tours, stresses and strains all took their toll and both Agnetha and Bjorn and Benny and Anni-Frid called it a day. All this while having to sing 'One of Us' to crowds of thousands.

2 JOHN LENNON AND YOKO ONO

Seen by some as the relationship that broke up the Beatles, the truth is likely to be some way from the convenient soundbite. The pair collaborated at length, and lived life in the full glare of the media spotlight up until Lennon's murder in 1980.

1 JOHN & BEVERLEY MARTIN

The folk duo met in 1969 and recorded two albums together, the peerless Stormbringer! and The Road to Ruin. John returned to playing solo when domesticity, life and Island records got in the way of their musical partnership.

	ARTIST	LISTEN TO...	YEAR
10	Ronnie and Phil Spector	*Presenting the Fabulous Ronettes (album)*	1964
9	Jack White and Meg White	*Elephant (album)*	2003
8	Beyoncé and Jay-Z	'Crazy in Love'	2003
7	Ike and Tina Turner	'Whole Lotta Love'	1975
6	Sonny & Cher	'I Got You Babe'	1965
5	Lyndsey Buckingham and Stevie Nicks	*Buckingham Nicks (album)*	1973
4	Johnny Cash and June Carter Cash	'Long Legged Guitar Pickin' Man'	1967
3	Abba	'One of Us'	1981
2	John Lennon and Yoko Ono	*Double Fantasy (album)*	1980
1	John & Beverley Martin	*Stormbringer (album)*	1970

TOP 10

On closer inspection, the notion of the tortured artist channeling despair into great art is a convenient myth. It promotes an idealised, iconic image – and icons are easy to market. In reality lives are cut short, talent wasted and the promise of what could have been looms large. Some make it through – others aren't so lucky.

TROUBLED SOULS

9 JOE MEEK
At a time when homosexuality was illegal in Britain, being gay probably didn't help Joe Meek's spiraling paranoia. Prone to violent outburts, the genius descended into rage-fuelled madness that saw him shoot his landlady before turning the gun on himself.

8 ELLIOT SMITH
The death of Elliot Smith who, after struggling with depression and drug addiction, is reported to have killed himself aged 34, was shocking, if not surprising. Despite rumours surrounding the exact nature of his death, the lingering thought is of huge wasted potential.

7 SYD BARRETT
When Pink Floyd's former bandmate turned up at the recording of *Dark Side of the Moon*, no one recognized him, such was the change he had undergone. The excessive drug use and mental illness that had plagued his performances eventually robbed him of his music.

6 IAN CURTIS
A complex character, Ian Curtis inspires, to this day, devotion in fans like few figures can manage. His lyrics paint a picture of a tortured and introspective soul who, frustrated by the limitations of life and himself found it impossible to carry on.

5 BRIAN WILSON
Following the death of Brian Wilson's dominant, bullying father and the huge demands made of his terrific talent, something had to give. Unfortunately, it was Brian and he took to his bed for three years with cake and cocaine. Thankfully, he came through the other side.

10 WHITNEY HOUSTON
The singer's problem with drugs was the subject of intense media scrutiny and constant conjecture. Sadly it came to dominate a career that should have been remarkable for the pure quality and breathtaking range of Houston's voice.

4 MARVIN GAYE
The soul singer's addictions have been well publicised, as has his conflicted personality, that veered between self-loathing and wild confidence in his ability. There was also conflict in the relationship with his fundamentalist father, who shot him dead during an argument.

3 AMY WINEHOUSE
The precocious talent Amy displayed on her first album, *Frank*, was prodigious by the time *Back to Black* was released. Then came headlines rather than hits as she struggled with addiction and fell apart in full view while the world looked on.

2 KURT COBAIN
While the success of Nevermind never sat easily with Kurt Cobain, his troubles were significantly more deep-rooted than an aversion to jocks buying his music. His death was shocking in its self-inflicted violence (he shot himself), but speaks of fragility rather than fame.

1 NICK DRAKE
While rock stars push out their chest and strut, Nick Drake hunched his shoulders and hid. Famously shy, he also battled depression for much of his life. After recording three incandescently beautiful albums he died from an overdose of antidepressants.

	ARTIST	LISTEN TO...	YEAR
10	Whitney Houston	*Whitney Houston*	1985
9	Joe Meek	*Portrait of a Genius: The RGM Legacy (compilation)*	2005
8	Elliot Smith	*From a Basement on the Hill*	2004
7	Syd Barrett	*Piper at the Gates of Dawn* – Pink Floyd	1967
6	Ian Curtis	*Unknown Pleasures*	1979
5	Brian Wilson	*Brian Wilson presents Smile*	2004
4	Marvin Gaye	*What's Going On*	1971
3	Amy Winehouse	*Back to Black*	2006
2	Kurt Cobain	*In Utero*	1993
1	Nick Drake	*Five Leaves Left*	1969

TOP 10

Popular music has a deep and rich history of anti-establishment songs. It has been used as a positive voice for peace, a nihilistic scream into the void and an anarchic call to arms. Over the years it has, in equal parts, empowered, enraged, changed and engaged, but what are the best songs to soundtrack a mutiny?

REVOLUTIONARIES

10 THEE HYPNOTICS – 'REVOLUTION STONE'

The band The Cult could have been had commercial success not come calling. While Thee Hypnotics' sound might not have been revolutionary, the Eighties rock revivalists' live shows were certainly riotous – just listen to this from 1989's *Live'r Than God* album!

9 SUPER FURRY ANIMALS – 'THE MAN DON'T GIVE A FUCK'

This sweary, two-fingered dance of dissent was introduced live with a sample of comedian Bill Hicks's summary of the political elite ('All governments are liars and murderers'). The song laments a generation pacified by media and reminds them what side they're on.

8 FELA KUTI – 'COFFIN FOR THE HEAD OF STATE'

Fela takes down the tempo, but this is no appeal for calm. It's a deeply personal musical missile launched against a government whose troops lay siege to the Kalakuta Republic (Kuti's commune), beating residents – including his mother, who later died from her injuries.

7 T. REX – 'CHILDREN OF THE REVOLUTION'

Very much a teen rebellion, Marc Bolan won't have had figures of authority cowering in the corner, despite some concerns that the song promoted a communist agenda. It did, however, empower a generation of kids who felt that someone was on their side.

6 SPACEMEN 3 – 'REVOLUTION'

A revolution of the mind, rather than one that requires running through the streets - this is, after all, from a band who sat down to play. Rugby's finest deliver a blistering sonic attack however with the sheets of guitar drone so aggressive, they could do the dirty work for us.

5 THE BEATLES – 'REVOLUTION'

Any revolution needs a pause for thought, and this is it. Released in 1968, the year of the student uprising in Paris, Vietnam war demos and anti-government protests in Poland, the Beatles' cautious questioning of the validity of revolution caused outrage on the Left.

4 THE CLASH – 'GUNS OF BRIXTON'

Written and sung by bassist Paul Simonon, the intense and insular feel of this song mirrors perfectly the discontent felt in 1979 south London due to the increasingly heavy-handed tactics of the police. Posing a question rather than offering solutions, its power is enormous.

3 BOB MARLEY – 'GET UP, STAND UP'
With a fair few Bob Marley songs to choose from, this makes the list for its positive, empowering feel. A direct order to the disenfranchised, this is no patronizing platitude, instead telling people to take what's theirs rather than what they're given.

2 WOODY GUTHRIE –
'THIS LAND IS YOUR LAND'
One of the greatest protest songs of all time, Woody Guthrie rails against landowners and the death of the American Dream. While people erected fences and made claims to huge swathes of land, Guthrie's battle cry was a heartfelt tribute to the exploited.

1 GIL SCOTT-HERON –
'THE REVOLUTION WILL NOT BE TELEVISED'
The poet, novelist, novelist, singer and songwriter hits the ground running with this sociopolitical poem set to music. A devastating, stripped-bare attack on the media's coverage of civil unrest, the drums, pounding bass and spoken-word delivery foretold hip hop.

	ARTIST	SONG	YEAR
10	Thee Hypnotics	'Revolution Stone'	1990
9	Super Furry Animals	'The Man Don't Give a Fuck'	1996
8	Fela Kuti	'Coffin for the Head of State '	1981
7	T. Rex	'Children of the Revolution'	1972
6	Spacemen 3	'Revolution'	1988
5	The Beatles	'Revolution'	1968
4	The Clash	'Guns of Brixton'	1979
3	Bob Marley	'Get Up, Stand Up'	1973
2	Woody Guthrie	'This Land Is Your Land'	1945
1	Gil Scott-Heron	'The Revolution Will Not Be Televised'	1970

TOP 10

From the recording studio to the film studio – it's a well-worn path as musicians try to spread their wings, find their feet and chance their arm in the world of acting. It's a fairly safe bet, too, as an established musician is likely to put a few bums on seats, even if it's just people desperate for a fix of schadenfreude.

MUSICIANS-TURNED-FILM STARS

10 MADONNA
After getting a taste for acting opposite Susan Sarandon in *Desperately Seeking Susan*, Madonna has, if we're honest, struggled to replicate the form of her assured debut. Having said that, a Golden Globe for *Evita* isn't to be sniffed at.

9 ELVIS
For Elvis, films seemed to come as just another part of his career rather than an artistic choice. Starting with 1956's *Love Me Tender*, he went on to star in another 30 films. None of them is exactly high art, but they did the business for Elvis and studio alike.

8 CHER
Beginning her film career with husband Sonny in 1967's *Good Times*, there wasn't a sense that anyone was watching a future movie star. Yet the singer was to get three Golden Globe awards (including one for her role in *Silkwood*) as well as an Oscar for *Moonstruck*.

7 FRANK SINATRA
Ol' Blue Eyes may have copped flack for not copping flack during World War Two, but the singer's perforated eardrum – which kept him away from active service – left him free to embark on an Oscar-winning career on the silver screen.

6 MOS DEF
The hip hop star was that rare thing, an underground act who achieved mainstream success by being good rather than selling out. His subsequent film career has followed a similar trajectory with standout roles in *16 Blocks*, *Be Kind, Rewind*, and *The Woodsman*.

5 DAVID BOWIE
David Bowie's been

acting for as long as he's been performing. The reason his stage personae are so successful is because he inhabits them so well, so it's no surprise his typically unshowy roles, including a great turn in Christopher Nolan's *The Prestige*, are so accomplished.

4 MARK WAHLBERG
When he first bounded onto the stage with his Funky Bunch, 'Marky' Mark Wahlberg was better known as New Kid on the Block Danny's younger

brother. It didn't stay that way for long though as a string of hit films proved that acting, not rapping, is his calling.

3 KRIS KRISTOFFERSON
After releasing two albums and enjoying some success, Kristofferson was cast in the Dennis Hopper-directed *The Last Movie*. More followed, including Sam Peckinpah's *Convoy*, before a Golden Globe came his way for his role in *A Star Is Born*, with Barbra Streisand.

2 JENNIFER HUDSON
If TV talent shows are ever prosecuted for crimes against entertainment, Jennifer Hudson will be the case for the defence. Although she

came 7th in *American Idol*, she went on to win a Grammy for her debut album and an Oscar, no less, for her role in the film *Dreamgirls*.

1 WILL SMITH
Having taken the Fresh Prince from records to telly with alarming ease, Will Smith had already proved he had the chops for acting. It's unlikely however, that anyone at that time would have earmarked him as a two-time Academy Award nominee.

	ARTIST	KEY FILM	YEAR
10	Madonna	*Desperately Seeking Susan*	1985
9	Elvis	*King Creole*	1958
8	Cher	*Moonstruck*	1987
7	Frank Sinatra	*The Manchurian Candidate*	1962
6	Mos Def	*Be Kind Rewind*	2008
5	David Bowie	*The Man Who Fell to Earth*	1976
4	Mark Wahlberg	*Boogie Nights*	1997
3	Kris Kristofferson	*Pat Garrett and Billy the Kid*	1973
2	Jennifer Hudson	*Dreamgirls*	2006
1	Will Smith	*I, Robot*	2004

TOP 10

Time to put pen to paper and create your own top 10 list of songs you wish you'd written...

10 ....
_____
....

9 ....
_____
....

8 ....
_____
....

7 ....
_____
....

6 ....
_____
....

5 ....
_____
....

4 ....
_____
....

3 ....
_____
....

2 ....
_____
....

1 ....
_____
....

TOP
10

Not so much ripping up the rule book as just not bothering to find out whether there was one in the first place, Tony Wilson's legendary Manchester label valued high-minded ideals over commercial viability every time. While this ensured a fair deal for bands and some of the most vital music of a generation, it also led to the label going bankrupt in 1992.

FACTORY RECORDS RELEASES

10 VARIOUS – A FACTORY SAMPLE (2X7")

A double 7" single was the first Factory record released and, as opening gambits go, it's a fairly bold one. Joy Division, The Durutti Column, John Downie and Sheffield's Cabaret Voltaire all had a side each on which to shine.

9 QUANDO QUANGO – 'ATOM ROCK (MARK KAMINS MIX)'

Before M People, Hacienda DJ Mike Pickering headed up electro dance band Quando Quango. Produced by Bernard Sumner, this track also includes Johnny Marr on guitar, and sounds like the sort of record Malcolm McLaren would have sold his grandmother to write.

8 DURUTTI COLUMN – THE RETURN OF THE DURUTTI COLUMN (LP)

In an act of conceptual genius, the cover of Durutti Column's debut LP was made out of coarse sandpaper, to ruin the records next to it in the racks. Unfortunately, the sandpaper went inside the cover too, and scratched the hell out of a very fine record.

7 A CERTAIN RATIO – THE GRAVEYARD AND THE BALLROOM (LP)

Only released on cassette in 1980, this is an incredibly accomplished debut, full of direct songwriting and assured musicianship ('The Fox' is a particular stand out). It sounds like Joy Division might have, had they found the funk rather than been in one.

6 HAPPY MONDAYS – BUMMED (LP)

So good that the band dusted it off for a 25-year anniversary tour, Bummed was the sound of a bunch of friends grabbing the zeitgeist firmly round the shoulders and taking it off for a night out to show it what was really going on.

5 SECTION 25 – 'LOOKING FROM A HILLTOP' (12")

If anyone should find themselves looking for the perfect example of what happens when former punks go electro, this is it. The influence of this transcendent, trance-laden masterpiece goes far beyond Manchester – or even the UK – and still resonates today.

4 NEW ORDER – 'BLUE MONDAY' (12")

In true Factory style, the biggest selling 12" single of all time ended up costing them money with its beautifully extravagant packaging – a die cut sleeve with a silver inner. Not a huge problem, had the track not outstripped all expectations.

3 JOY DIVISION – 'SHE'S LOST CONTROL' *(12")*

With this on one side and 'Atmosphere' on the other, this is the best 12" record the label ever released. 'She's Lost Control' was a live favourite, but the heavy, electronic feel that Martin Hannett brought to this version is mesmerising.

2 THE HACIENDA

Factory's great folly, the amount of money poured in to The Hacienda (purportedly £10,000 every month) was paid for largely by New Order's record sales. With the explosion of Acid House the club's fortunes changed and it became one of the best in the world.

1 TONY WILSON'S COFFIN

It seems fitting that the last object to bear a Factory catalogue number (FAC 501) was Anthony H Wilson's coffin. It's an art-prank statement, but also speaks volumes about his commitment to the label, the value of art and of artists themselves.

	ARTIST	PRODUCT	YEAR	CATALOGUE NUMBER
10	Various	*A Factory Sample (2x7")*	1979	FAC 2
9	Quando Quango	'Atom Rock (Mark Kamins Mix)'	1985	FAC 102
8	Durutti Column	*The Return of the Durutti Column (LP)*	1980	FACT 14
7	A Certain Ratio	*The Graveyard and the Ballroom (LP)*	1980	FACT 16
6	Happy Mondays	*Bummed (LP)*	1988	FACT 220
5	Section 25	'Looking From a Hilltop' (12")	1984	FAC 108
4	New Order	'Blue Monday' (12")	1982	FAC 73
3	Joy Division	'She's Lost Control' (12")	1980	FACUS 2
2	The Hacienda	*n/a*	1982-1997	FAC 51
1	Tony Wilson's coffin	*n/a*		FAC 501

TOP
10

With the number of bands formed at art college, it's not surprising to find that many musicians are frustrated artists at heart. Why this marriage of audio and visual? Maybe it's the flighty creative impulse looking for any suitable spot on which to settle, or maybe it's the fact that art was bit of a doss and the homework was easy.

MUSICIANS-CUM-ARTISTS

10 GOLDIE
Goldie's something of an anomaly in that he was an artist first who then went on to find fame as a pivotal figure in drum and bass. His graffiti pieces were featured in the street art bible, *Spraycan Art* and he now exhibits around the world.

9 MILES DAVIS
The jazz musician used painting as therapy, saying 'It keeps my mind occupied when I'm not playing music.' Having been drawing all his life, it wasn't until 1980 that he took it up seriously and produced work that is a riot of colour and shape.

8 PATTI SMITH
Having established herself with classic albums including *Horses and Easter*, poet and songwriter Patti Smith has also earned a reputation as an accomplished visual artist whose photographs and drawings have been exhibited since 1978.

7 JOHN SQUIRE
The Stone Roses' iconic covers were all the work of guitarist John Squire. While his early endeavours were Pollock pastiche pieces, his later work hinted at a confident and clever artist and has certainly been a better use of his time than The Seahorses.

6 PAUL MCCARTNEY
While tragic bandmate Stuart Sutcliffe was an artist who picked up a bass, Paul McCartney has taken the opposite route. Encouraged by Willem de Kooning, Macca picked up a brush, and has proved himself to be an accomplished - and challenging - artist.

5 BOB DYLAN
Having started painting to alleviate the boredom of touring, Bob Dylan has shown work at London's National Portrait Gallery. The collection of pastel portraits, *Face Value*, is no vanity project, however - they're far too unsettling for that.

4 JONI MITCHELL
Not content with simply being one of the most inspiring singer/songwriters of all time, Joni Mitchell is also a talented artist whose work veers between impressionistic studies of colour and movement to reflective self-portraits, as seen on the cover of her album *Clouds*.

3 TONY BENNETT
With his work in the permanent collections of several galleries and the Smithsonian Museum, it's fair to say that Tony Bennett - or Anthony Benedetto - is no amateur. If you want an original, you'd better start saving though; they can cost up to $80,000.

2 RONNIE WOOD

The Stones' guitarist is a student of Ealing Art College and, as such, has actually learnt how to draw – unlike many artists. His paintings, often depicting the Stones themselves, have been displayed around the world and he's even been the subject of a South Bank Show.

1 BILLY CHILDISH

An advocate of amateurism, musician, artist and maverick spirit Billy Childish sees this as a way of preserving the joy he takes in what he does. Artist Peter Doig labeled him 'one of the most outstanding figures on the British art scene'. Which just about covers it.

	ARTIST	LISTEN TO...	YEAR
10	Goldie	*Inner City Life*	1994
9	Miles Davis	*Kind of Blue*	1959
8	Patti Smith	*Easter*	1978
7	John Squire	*The Stone Roses*	1989
6	Paul McCartney	*McCartney II*	1980
5	Bob Dylan	*Blood on the Tracks*	1975
4	Joni Mitchell	*Court and Spark*	1974
3	Tony Bennett	*Bennett Sings, Basie Swings*	1958
2	Ronnie Wood	*I've Got My Own Album to Do*	1974
1	Billy Childish	*25 Years of Being Childish (compilation)*	2002

TOP 10

There's a vivid connection between art and music. In both you start with a basic sketch to which, over time, you give depth by adding new tones and splashes of colour until you step away and decide that it's finished. Then, it's time to unveil it to the world and let people judge your creation. The following 10 are all masterpieces.

SONGS INSPIRED BY ART

10 SHOCKING BLUE – 'VENUS'

The figure of Venus has proved an inspiration for artists throughout time, and the Dutch band were not immune to her charms. It's worth taking another look as the cover versions over the years have tended to blur the fine detail of the original master.

9 DAVE BRUBECK – *TIME FURTHER OUT: MIRÓ REFLECTIONS LP*

Brubek and his band interpret the Catalan Spanish painter Joan Miró through jazz. Well, 12 bar blues at any rate. Like Miró, the band upsets certain elements of their art (the time signatures) but presents them in a way that, though unfamiliar, still makes perfect sense.

8 TEENAGE FANCLUB – 'EVERY PICTURE THAT I PAINT'

Escher, from Teenage Fanclub's album *Thirteen*, may have provided the more obvious link here, but there's an uncomplicated and almost naïve sentiment to this love song from their debut, 'A Catholic Education', that makes it irresistible.

7 THE MODERN LOVERS – 'PABLO PICASSO'

Jonathan Richman's proto-punk rockers recorded this song for their debut album, although it didn't make the cut. Their producer, Velvet Underground's John Cale, obviously saw merit in it, as he released his own version three years later.

6 NANCY PRIDDY – 'CHRISTINA'S WORLD'

This beautiful song, from the singer's sublime 1968 album, *You've Come This Way Before*, was written for the Priddy's daughter, actress Christina Applegate, who was named after Andrew Wyeth's 1948 landscape, also called Christina's World.

5 JAY-Z – 'PICASSO BABY'

A song referencing one of the most famous artists of all time which itself became a work of art through the video *Picasso Baby: A Performance Art Film*, which documents a six-hour interactive performance of the song at a New York art gallery.

4 MANIC STREET PREACHERS – 'INTERIORS (SONG FOR WILLEM DE KOONING)'

One of the lighter moments on the *Everything Must Go* album, that followed the disappearance of guitarist and lyricist Richey Edwards, the verse is virtually note-for note 'Nothing Can Stop Us Now' by St Etienne. Which isn't a criticism in any way...

3 THE BEATLES — 'LUCY IN THE SKY WITH DIAMONDS'

Despite suggestions as to the inspiration for this song, with its seemingly acronymic title, John Lennon always insisted that it was his son's painting, not LSD that was the creative spark. Whichever it is, it remains a lovely, shimmering ditty.

2 STATUS QUO — 'PICTURES OF MATCHSTICK MEN'

From Status Quo's short-lived psychedelic period, the matchstick men of the title refer to the figures in the paintings of L.S. Lowry, whose work was also the subject of the one-hit wonder 'Matchstalk Men and Matchstalk Cats and Dogs', by Brian and Michael.

1 DAVID BOWIE — 'ANDY WARHOL'

No guessing who this song is about! Warhol, whose work is shot through with references to transitional fame and pop icons, was a huge inspiration for Bowie, who penned this song in his honour. The artist was, reportedly, pretty nonplussed by the results.

	ARTIST	SONG	YEAR
10	Shocking Blue	Venus	1970
9	Dave Brubeck	*Time Further Out: Miró Reflections (LP)*	1961
8	Teenage Fanclub	'Every Picture That I Paint'	1990
7	The Modern Lovers	'Pablo Picasso'	1976
6	Nancy Priddy	'Christina's World'	1968
5	Jay-Z	'Picasso Baby'	2013
4	Manic Street Preachers	'Interiors (Song For Willem De Kooning)'	1996
3	The Beatles	'Lucy in the Sky with Diamonds'	1967
2	Status Quo	'Pictures of Matchstick Men'	1968
1	David Bowie	'Andy Warhol'	1971

Songs are rooted in a strong tradition of storytelling and as such it's only natural that books should be a huge source of inspiration for musicians over the years. A picture, as we know, is worth a thousand words, but there's as yet been no count to determine what literary value a piece of music has. The following 10 however, are priceless.

SONGS INSPIRED BY BOOKS

10 NIRVANA – 'SCENTLESS APPRENTICE'

Famously thought of as an 'unfilmable novel' (though that didn't stop them), no one wondered whether you could successfully write a song about *Perfume*, Patrick Süskind's 1985 book. It turns out you can, and it sounds like the end of the world.

9 DEVO – 'WHIP IT'

Musically, American band Devo's 1980 single Whip It was indebted to the sound of Krautrock and its simple, linear beat. Lyrically, songwriter Gerald Casale cites Thomas Pynchon's vast novel, *Gravity's Rainbow*, as the main influence.

8 KATE BUSH – 'WUTHERING HEIGHTS'

Showing a talent that was both prodigious and precocious, this literary number one hit

was written by Kate Bush when she was just 18 in just a few hours. For a generation of schoolchildren, this song proved to be the perfect revision aid for English 'O' level.

7 CREAM – 'TALES OF BRAVE ULYSSES'
While the lyrics were, as the title suggests, inspired by Homer's epic poem *The Odyssey*, the tune itself owes a passing nod to the Lovin

Spoonful's 'Summer in the City'. This 1967 song was featured on the album *Disraeli Gears*.

6 PETE SEEGER – 'TURN! TURN! TURN! (TO EVERYTHING THERE IS A SEASON)'
Many musicians have turned, turned, turned to that biggest of books, *The Bible*, for inspiration, but few with the success of Pete Seeger's plundering of the Book of

Ecclesiastes for this folk classic that was later covered by the Byrds.

5 RADIOHEAD – 'BANANA CO.'
Although not explicitly cited as an influence, *100 Years of Solitude* provides the background for this Radiohead song. Quite what author Gabriel Garcia Marquez would have made of it is unclear, as he seems to have been more a Shakira kind of guy.

4 THE POLICE – 'DON'T STAND SO CLOSE TO ME'

Detailing a girl's crush on her teacher and his nervousness at the situation, this 1980 single from the Police contains the lines, 'It's no use, he sees her/He starts to shake and cough/Just like the old man in/That book by Nabakov', a reference to *Lolita*.

3 VELVET UNDERGROUND – 'VENUS IN FURS'

Launching headlong, almost without warning, into a disorientating, eastern-influenced heady whirl of noise, this song takes its cue from the book of the same name by Leopold von Sacher-Masoch and echoes its sado-masochistic themes.

2 DAVID BOWIE – 'OH! YOU PRETTY THINGS'

Anthem, Ayn Rand's 1938 tale of a dystopian future where individuality has all but been wiped out, isn't a book that screams 'chart hit' at the top of its voice. That didn't stop David Bowie referencing the book in this classic from 1971's *Hunky Dory*.

1 THE CURE – 'KILLING AN ARAB'

Robert Smith's attempt to condense Albert Camus' existentialist masterpiece *L'Étranger* (The Stranger) into a three-minute pop song was not without controversy. The title in particular has been misinterpreted by many, who have taken it at face value.

	ARTIST	SONG	YEAR
10	Nirvana	'Scentless Apprentice'	1993
9	Devo	'Whip It'	1980
8	Kate Bush	'Wuthering Heights'	1978
7	Cream	'Tales of Brave Ulysses'	1967
6	Pete Seeger	'Turn! Turn! Turn! (to Everything There Is a Season)'	1965
5	Radiohead	'Banana co.'	
4	The Police	'Don't Stand So Close to Me'	1980
3	Velvet Underground	'Venus in Furs'	1967
2	David Bowie	'Oh! You Pretty Things'	1971
1	The Cure	'Killing an Arab'	1978

TOP 10

In an age of multi-media platforming and social media marketing, the radio can seem something of an anachronism. Like seeing someone popping the kettle on in the middle of *Star Wars*. At one time the DJ had the power to make or break a record, but the role is a constantly changing one – this list celebrates those who led from the front.

INFLUENTIAL RADIO DJS

10 WOLFMAN JACK
A fan of Alan Freed, Robert Weston Smith, aka Wolfman Jack, became a legendary voice of rock'n'roll during the Sixties. His passion and singular style piqued the interest of listeners and bands alike, with several artists turning the (turn)tables and recording songs about him.

9 KENNY EVERETT
Not known for his championing of music, Kenny Everett pioneered a different kind of DJing altogether. Using effects, skits, invented characters and creating an anarchic atmosphere in the studio, he – rather than the music – became the focus.

8 MIKEY DREAD
A towering figure in Jamaican radio, Michael George Campbell's JBC show, 'Dread at the Controls', was wall-to-wall reggae and proved such a hit with listeners that they started sending cassettes of it to family and friends back in England.

7 RODNEY BINGENHEIMER
Described as one of the most influential kingmakers in American pop, Rodney Bingenheimer hung out with everyone who was anyone in Sixties' LA. He was given a show in 1976 and, against the prevailing tide, pushed punk music day and night.

6 TIM WESTWOOD
Although to some, Westwood's street schtick can be off-putting, there's absolutely no doubting this man's dedication to the cause of hip-hop. An instrumental figure in raising the genre's profile, the list of artists that are indebted to him is endless.

5 ANNIE NIGHTINGALE
Annie Nightingale is a rare thing – a DJ who has broadcast over four decades while maintaining a passion for new music and never getting stuck in the past. From prog to punk, drum and bass to dubstep, Annie Nightingale's boundless love for music is utterly infectious.

4 CHRISTOPHER STONE
When the BBC first went on air, it wasn't apparent to them that there was any value in having a programme that consisted of someone playing records. It took Christopher Stone to convince them, in 1927, and his relaxed, informal manner soon made him a star.

3 JOHN PEEL
Generations of kids – and adults – relied on John Peel to hear the sort of music they simply wouldn't get to hear otherwise. His Perfumed Garden show on Radio London and his subsequent work for the BBC were full of fabulously

eclectic and experimental music.

2 MARTIN BLOCK

An enthusiastic amateur radio operator, Block first found work as an announcer on a New York radio station. Starting by playing records in between announcements, he soon had his own show, Make Believe Ballroom, and revolutionized the role of the DJ.

1 ALAN FREED

Alan Freed invented Rock 'n' Roll. After organizing a wildly popular rhythm and blues concert in 1952 that ended in chaos, the popularity of his radio show soared. Forced to change the name, he came up with The Rock'n'Roll Party and a genre was born.

	NAME	COUNTRY
10	Wolfman Jack	US
9	Kenny Everett	UK
8	Mikey Dread	Jamaica
7	Rodney Bingenheimer	US
6	Tim Westwood	UK
5	Annie Nightingale	UK
4	Christopher Stone	UK
3	John Peel	UK
2	Martin Block	US
1	Alan Freed	US

TOP
10

Video may not have killed the radio star, but it did make them at least put a comb through their hair and have a quick look in the mirror on their way out. As the video age drew on, more musicians realized that their song's shiny, moving advert could be a work of art in itself, at which point creativity – and budgets – took a sharp upturn.

GROUNDBREAKING VIDEOS

9 HERBIE HANCOCK – 'ROCKIT'

Herbie Hancok's video for his foray into electro earned him no fewer than five MTV awards. The Godley & Creme-directed film shows a world without humans, populated instead by dismembered robots. An artistic high point, it also brought dance music to MTV.

8 FATBOY SLIM – 'PRAISE YOU'

Another Spike Jonze creation, this is part music video, part performance art as Jonze employed the help of actor-dancers to create a fictional oddball dance troupe who he then filmed dancing to the song in front of bemused onlookers. It's brilliant and cost about five hundred quid.

7 BEASTIE BOYS – 'SABOTAGE'

Possibly the first Beastie Boys

10 APHEX TWIM – 'WINDOWLICKER'

By far the most powerfully unsettling video on this list, director Chris Cunningham's mind must be a dark, dark place. Starting off as a mockery of an MTV hip hop stereotype, it ends up a disorientating, genuinely disturbing clash of... well, everything.

video to truly capture the feeling of unbridled joy in their music, the Spike Jonze directed Sabotage was lo-fi, cop show pastiche done so well you're left wanting to watch an episode once the song has finished.

6 OK GO – 'HERE IT GOES AGAIN'

OK Go have become synonymous with superb videos, but this is the pick of the bunch. As the track plays, the band perform an unbroken, choreographed dance routine on treadmills that leaves the question, 'How many takes?' on everyone's lips. Seventeen, in case you were wondering.

5 A-HA – 'TAKE ON ME'

With its inventive blending of the real world with an illustrated, comic book narrative as a woman, beckoned by illustrated singer Morten Harket, enters a cartoon strip, this was the result of a clever conceit, a well-worked storyboard and effects that still look great today.

4 THE WHITE STRIPES – 'THE HARDEST BUTTON TO BUTTON'

If Michel Gondry ('Be Kind, Rewind', 'Eternal Sunshine'...) is directing your video, ...) is directing your video, you'd expect something special, but this staccato, stop motion vision of drumkit, guitar amps and band snaking a perfectly-in-time path through a city is simply stunning.

2 PETER GABRIEL – 'SLEDGEHAMMER'

Possibly the most ubiquitous video of its day, this was stop-motion on a grand scale involving, as it did, an actual

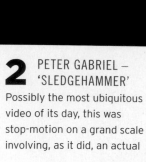

human in among the plasticine chickens and toy trains. Peter Gabriel lay there for 16 hours (!) while animators (including Nick Park) did their bit.

1 MICHAEL JACKSON – 'THRILLER'
With a budget that would put most films of the time to shame, Michael Jackson's horror spectacular boasted amazing effects, dance routines that wouldn't look out of place in a Bollywood spectacular and a high-production gloss that few could match.

	ARTIST	SONG	YEAR
10	Aphex Twin	*Windowlicker*	1999
9	Herbie Hancock	*Rockit*	1983
8	Fatboy Slim	*Praise You*	1999
7	Beastie Boys	*Sabotage*	1994
6	OK Go	*Here it Goes Again*	2006
5	A-ha	*Take On Me*	1985
4	The White Stripes	*The Hardest Button to Button*	2003
3	Dire Straits	*Money For Nothing*	1985
2	Peter Gabriel	*Sledgehammer*	1986
1	Michael Jackson	*Thriller*	1983

TOP 10

Well aware of the power of a controversial video and the sales it can generate (that's real shock value for you), many musicians go to great lengths to provoke and titillate in the hope of getting noticed. Some of the following examples may have softened over the years, but all of them hit hard at the time.

SHOCKING VIDEOS

10 GEORGE *MICHAEL* – 'I WANT YOUR SEX'
While the song itself was the subject of controversy back in 1987 simply because of the title, George's video for the song went one step further and featured shots of full-frontal female nudity. Now that's how you create a buzz for your first solo single!

9 DURAN DURAN – 'GIRLS ON FILM'
Causing consternation in 1981 because of the female flesh on show as women engaged in what appeared to be some sort of erotic It's a Knockout!, the video was promptly banned. Looking back, the most shocking aspect is the rampant sexism.

8 NAS – 'HATE ME NOW'
Despite a massive disclaimer at the beginning of this video saying that Nas isn't depicting Jesus, he carries a cross to a hill where he's then crucified, while – and here's the important bit - wearing a crown of thorns. And lo, there was controversy.

7 M.I.A. – 'BORN FREE'
Depicting a world in which redheads are persecuted, rounded up, beaten, tortured and ultimately killed saw this video banned on YouTube in the UK and US. Despite its undeniably shocking content, it's a powerful and moving piece of work.

6 EMINEM – 'STAN'
The video for Eminem's 2000 hit makes real the rapper's storyboard rhyme. An obsessive fan, possessed by rage and anger ends up killing himself and his pregnant girlfriend (sorry, spoiler alert). Where not banned, it was substantially edited.

5 NINE INCH NAILS – 'CLOSER'
More like a series of unsettling stills, this features a laboratory in which there's a dismembered pig's head, a naked woman and a monkey tied to a cross. Directed by Mark Romanek, it's now in the permanent collection of New York's Museum of Modern Art.

4 THE PRODIGY – 'SMACK MY BITCH UP'

If the title of the song wasn't enough to fuel the fire of righteous outrage, then the video – a point of view document of a debauched night out, including drug taking, sex and violence, was sure to cause nothing short of a national uproar.

3 SERGE & CHARLOTTE GAINSBOURG – 'LEMON INCEST'

It's not a surprise to see Serge Gainsbourg cavorting on a bed with a young woman, but when the 'woman' in question is his 12-year-old daughter and the song is about incest, controversy is bound to follow – and probably start kicking down the door.

2 LADY GAGA – 'TELEPHONE'

Lady Gaga plays a surrealist Madonna with an aversion to clothes, bailed from prison by Beyoncé to go on a killing spree. Despite outrage in some quarters, it's actually pretty funny, like Tarantino-meets-Gaultier. The level of product placement however, is truly shocking.

1 MADONNA – 'LIKE A PRAYER'

So, Madonna witnesses a murder than hides in a church where a statue of a black man starts crying and then comes to life when she kisses his feet. Oh, and Madonna has stigmata. Predictably, middle America was outraged and the single sold by the shedload.

	ARTIST	SONG	YEAR
10	George Michael	'I Want Your Sex'	1987
9	Duran Duran	'Girls on Film'	1981
8	Nas	'Hate Me Now'	1999
7	M.I.A.	'Born Free'	2010
6	Eminem	'Stan'	2000
5	Nine Inch Nails	'Closer'	1994
4	The Prodigy	'Smack My Bitch Up'	1997
3	Serge & Charlotte Gainsbourg	'Lemon Incest'	1985
2	Lady Gaga	'Telephone'	2009
1	Madonna	'Like a Prayer'	1989

CHAPTER 6
ON THE STEREO

TOP 10

Music, like all art, has the potential to be truly transformative. At its most powerful and intoxicating, it can alter the way we perceive the world around us. But can it get us out of bed and into the shower at 6.30am when the clouds are grey and the rain is wet? Mornings can provide some tough crowds – here are 10 to wow us awake.

GOOD MORNINGS

10 KANYE *WEST* – 'GOOD MORNING'
A wake up call in more ways that one, 'Good Morning' introduces Kanye's *Graduation* album. It's a song that waves a dismissive high hand at the rote-learning rat race that he sees education has become, while being simultaneously shot through with self-doubt.

9 YUSEF LATEEF – 'MORNING'
From Lateef's 1957 *Jazz Mood* album, this might not get you out of bed in a hurry, but it's just about the perfect way to ease you into the day. At more than 10 minutes long, this is an exotic blend, full of Eastern influence and incredible dynamics.

8 THE ARCADE FIRE – 'WAKE UP'
From the first, fuzzy blasts of guitar to the soaring choral voices, this is enough to power the windmills of the mind into action. From the band's debut LP *Funeral*, this is so good that instead of getting you out of bed, it'll bring you tea and toast.

7 LEE HAZELWOOD & NANCY SINATRA – 'SOME VELVET MORNING'
This psychedelic pop song is one of the best-known tracks that the duo recorded. A vocal pairing that, at times, echoes that of Serge Gainsbourg and Brigitte Bardot, Hazelwood and Sinatra create a sultry mix of sexual allure and druggy undertones.

6 CCS – 'SUNRISE'
Alexis Korner's Collective Consciousness Society released this jazz-infused, horn-heavy blues number on their first album. Taking the listener through the day, it starts off with a piano and polite percussion before the voices grudgingly herald the dawn of a new day.

5 THE SPECIALS – 'FRIDAY NIGHT, SATURDAY MORNING'
The brilliant, but often ignored, B-side to the band's bleak assessment of Eighties society 'Ghost Town', this song is no less desolate. Terry Hall's matter-of-fact delivery as he talks us through an irony-laden description of a night out on the town is superb.

4 BONNIE DOBSON – 'MORNING DEW'
Canadian folk singer Bonnie wrote this song, which despite a beautiful melody and a lovely lightness of touch, is actually set in a post apocalyptic society and documents the aftermath of a nuclear war. It's chilling and powerful stuff.

3 CHICAGO – '25 OR 6 TO FOUR'
One for the insomniacs among us, the Chicago song is about that time of the day when night becomes morning. Suggestions

that the song was about drug use were dismissed by the band as untrue. Suggestions that it's brilliant, however, have been upheld.

2 VELVET UNDERGROUND – 'SUNDAY MORNING'

As you might imagine, Sunday morning for members of the Velvet Underground involves a hangover of heroic proportions. Perhaps that's why this document of the morning after represents an unusually gentle moment for the band, full of sober reflection.

1 JONI MITCHELL – 'CHELSEA MORNING'

A song positively dripping in optimism and sun-kissed imagery, this should put a spring in even the heaviest of steps, while lyrics such as 'Oh, wont you stay/We'll put on the day/And we'll talk in present tenses,' encourage pure live-in-the-moment abandonment.

	NAME	LISTEN TO	YEAR
10	Kanye West	*Good Morning*	2007
9	Yusef Lateef	*Morning*	1957
8	The Arcade Fire	*Wake Up*	2005
7	Lee Hazelwood & Nancy Sinatra	*Some Velvet Morning*	1967
6	CCS	*Sunrise*	1970
5	The Specials	*Friday Night, Saturday Morning*	1981
4	Bonnie Dobson	*Morning Dew*	1962(live) 1969 (studio)
3	Chicago	*25 or 6 to Four*	1970
2	Velvet Underground	*Sunday Morning*	1967
1	Joni Mitchell	*Chelsea Morning*	1969

Music and fashion has always gone hand in hand. Every new movement brings with it a dress code – from rock'n'roll through mod to punk and beyond. It's an identifier, a way of picking out someone from the same tribe, but it's also a personal statement, a way of saying, 'This is who I am'. Here are 10 that are dressed up to the nines.

DRESS TO IMPRESS

10 PRINCE AND THE REVOLUTION – 'RASPBERRY BERET'

One of the more sober items in his Purpleness's wardrobe, the hat in question was on the head of a woman on whom he had designs. The song's calling card, the signature strings, came courtesy of Prince collaborators Wendy and Lisa.

9 DAVID DUNDAS – 'JEANS ON'

Starting life as an advert for Brutus jeans, David Dundas's 1976 ode to workwear is considered by many to be a guilty pleasure. It's not, it's just a really good song that people aren't sure if they're allowed to like. It's fine, you are. And… relax!

8 SAMMY DAVIS JR – 'HI-HEEL SNEAKERS'

There are thousands of versions of Tommy Tucker's original - including one by Elvis - but we're ignoring those in favour of this funky makeover courtesy of the Rat Pack legend on his Motown-released 1970 LP *Something For Everyone*.

7 RUN DMC – 'MY ADIDAS'

This must have seen Run, DMC and Jam in trainers for the rest of their lives, surely no one has ever displayed their brand loyalty quite as unequivocally as this. That's not to say they've shoehorned it in at the expense of the song, however - this still hit hard.

6 THE CRAMPS – 'SUNGLASSES AFTER DARK'

The best psychobilly band ever to stalk the planet, The Cramps ratcheted up the reverb, fuzz and echo to near-dangerous levels before embarking on this sleazy sartorial onslaught from their 1980 album *Songs the Lord Taught Us*.

5 DAVID BOWIE – 'FASHION'

Musically, this is Golden Years Part II and provides a good indication of the direction in which Bowie was heading after Ashes to Ashes. All dressed up for the disco, the squealing guitar accessories come courtesy of former King Crimson founder Robert Fripp.

4 CARL PERKINS – 'BLUE SUEDE SHOES'

Possibly the most archetypal of all rock'n'roll songs, Carl Perkins' rhythm and blues standard - all boogie rhythm and urgent backbeat - gave birth to a very different kind of rock 'n' roll sound that brought country into the mix - rockabilly.

3 PENTANGLE – 'WEDDING DRESS'

A bowed bassline leaves the picked guitar and banjo to provide the counterpoint rhythms for the funky folk drums on this track from the band's *Reflection* album. There's also a distinctly Celtic feel to this bucolic tale of homespun bridal finery.

2 BRIAN ENO – 'KING'S LEAD HAT'

OK – hands up. This isn't actually about royal headgear – lead or otherwise. One listen to this superb track from Eno's 1977 album (one of his very best) and it all clicks into place when you realise that the title is actually an anagram of Talking Heads.

1 NANCY SINATRA – 'THESE BOOTS ARE MADE FOR WALKIN''

Nancy Sinatra's empowering stomp all over the reputation - and quite possibly body - of her good-for-nothing fella is a joy - right from the descending steps of the opening guitar line to the brassy, celebratory sashay of the finale.

	ARTIST	ALBUM	YEAR
10	Prince and The Revolution	*Raspberry Beret*	1985
9	David Dundas	*Jeans On*	1976
8	Sammy Davis Jr	*Hi-Heel Sneakers*	1970
7	Run DMC	*My Adidas*	1986
6	The Cramps	*Sunglasses After Dark*	1980
5	David Bowie	*Fashion*	1980
4	Carl Perkins	*Blue Suede Shoes*	1956
3	Pentangle	*Wedding Dress*	1971
2	Brian Eno	*King's Lead Hat*	1977
1	Nancy Sinatra	*These Boots are Made For Walkin'*	1966

TOP **10**

'If music be the food of love, play on.' Orsino's plea for more music hoping it would sate his appetite for love in *Twelfth Night* was never likely to work – what he needed was a headache. Or a good book. Having said that, the link between music and food is a strong one and the following 10 all cook up a storm.

SONGS ABOUT FOOD

10 LED ZEPPELIN – 'THE LEMON SONG'
One of the high points of Led Zeppelin II, Robert Plant is having a spot of kitchen trouble - his lemon appears to be dripping all down his leg, a problem that the band can't help him with as they're locked into one of the best grooves of their career.

9 THE JBS – 'PASS THE PEAS'
The spoken word intro to this tune makes an important connection - food makes people happy, music makes people happy. It's a recognition that both are celebratory experiences ideal for sharing - much like this laid back party groove.

8 SQUEEZE – 'PULLING MUSSELS (FROM THE SHELL)'
Chris Difford and Glen Tilbrook are two of the best songwriters to come out of the UK and their gift for conveying

narrative with economy is second to none. This picture of seaside holidays is as detailed as any photo and musically hard to better.

7 NIGHTLIFE UNLIMITED – 'PEACHES AND PRUNES (RON HARDY RE-EDIT)'
The perfect musical dessert, supremely fruity and sugary sweet harmonies layered over a firm bass. This is part disco, part proto house and, thanks to a spectacular re-edit from legendary producer Ron Hardy 100% good for you.

6 THE ROLLING STONES – 'BROWN SUGAR'
This clearly isn't about unrefined sweetner, but no matter - an analogous reference to food is still a reference to food. Possibly written in honour of girlfriend Marsha Hunt (herself a great singer), this upbeat rock dancer maintains a rolling boil.

5 THE BEATLES – 'STRAWBERRY FIELDS'
The Beatles had been spurred into action by the sophistication of The Beach Boys' *Pet Sounds*, but when Brian Wilson heard this masterpiece, legend has it he gave up on the album he was working on, *Smile*, thinking there was no point any more.

4 KELIS – 'MILKSHAKE'
Depending on the thickness, milkshake definitely counts as food, although it may be that Kelis is talking euphemistically here. A defiantly simple track, it gives

246   TOP TEN LISTS MUSIC

Kelis full rein to be at her coquettish best - an opportunity she doesn't waste.

3 JAMES BROWN – 'MOTHER POPCORN'

There were a host of James Brown recordings referencing popcorn (actually a dance) and this is the best of the bunch. It's an opinion shared by the hordes of people who have sampled it, not least Prince for his 1991 hit single 'Get Off'.

2 B-52S – 'ROCK LOBSTER'

There's a surreal sense of fun about this single which takes the energy and experimentation of the new wave scene and adds a concentrated stock straight from Sixties rock'n'roll. The result is an amazing flavour combination unlike anyone else.

1 DR. JOHN – 'GRIS GRIS GUMBO YA YA'

No matter what the problem, Dr John can solve it with his magic ingredient. Gumbo is a traditional one pot stew, which provides a good analogy for the wonderfully thick soup of New Orleans rhythm and blues, psychedelic rock and jazz that the band serves up.

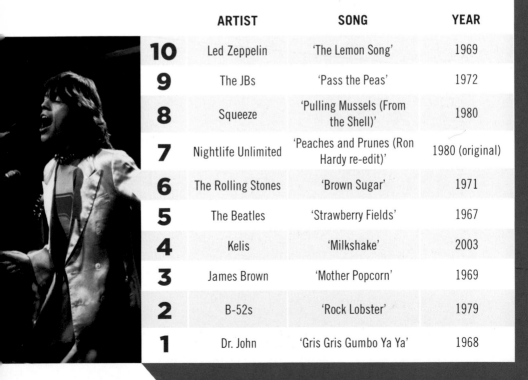

	ARTIST	SONG	YEAR
10	Led Zeppelin	'The Lemon Song'	1969
9	The JBs	'Pass the Peas'	1972
8	Squeeze	'Pulling Mussels (From the Shell)'	1980
7	Nightlife Unlimited	'Peaches and Prunes (Ron Hardy re-edit)'	1980 (original)
6	The Rolling Stones	'Brown Sugar'	1971
5	The Beatles	'Strawberry Fields'	1967
4	Kelis	'Milkshake'	2003
3	James Brown	'Mother Popcorn'	1969
2	B-52s	'Rock Lobster'	1979
1	Dr. John	'Gris Gris Gumbo Ya Ya'	1968

TOP 10

It's the big one. Where themes are concerned, they don't come any bigger. Whether it's literature, music, film or art – everything comes down to love in the end. So, in celebration of the fact, here's a top 10 of songs about love for that special someone – whether mixtape, CD or Spotify playlist, these will get straight to the heart of the matter.

SONGS ABOUT LOVE

8 MADONNA – 'JUSTIFY MY LOVE'

With Public Enemy's 'Security of the First World' as a starting block, it's pretty difficult to go wrong. Taking that beat and laying the Lenny Kravitz-composed song over the top, Madonna was just a risqué video away from the stuff of pop legend.

7 ROY AYRES – 'LOVE WILL BRING US BACK TOGETHER'

When Roy tells you that love's going to bring you back together, you can't help but believe him. This jazz-funk classic oozes class and cool in equal measure, but never breaks into a sweat, such is its sense of laid-back ease.

10 LULU – 'LOVE LOVES TO LOVE'

Managing to use the word 'love' as noun, transitive verb and infinitive in the same sentence deserves some sort of award, as does the bouncy, spiky pop song that has to stand of one of Lulu's best moments, though not as ubiquitous as some.

9 BEYONCÉ – 'CRAZY IN LOVE'

Queen B teamed up with hubby-to-be Jay Z for this absurdly funky tune that defined the Noughties like a dictionary defines words. There's the theme, recurrent in popular music, of love as a crazed state... but mostly there's those DRUMS!

6 TALKING HEADS – 'THIS MUST BE THE PLACE (NAÏVE MELODY)'

Although David Byrne sees this as a love song, it's certainly not in the 'crazy

fireworks' tradition. This could well be its
strength however, as love is presented as a
gradual reveal, a state you find yourself in -
unexpectedly and quite naturally.

5 QUEEN – 'CRAZY LITTLE THING
CALLED LOVE'

Unusually simple for the masters of the pop
opera, this is an old-fashioned love song - even

down to the video, which looks like West Side Story. It works though, and somehow avoids being a novelty record, even though that's sort of what it is.

4 THE GENTRYS – 'I NEED LOVE'
Released on the Sun label in 1969, this may not be quite what you'd expect from Elvis's former home. It's blues-tinged hard rock and, despite being as heavy as metal, it races out of the blocks and doesn't drop the pace for two and a half minutes.

3 MINNIE RIPPERTON – 'LOVIN' YOU'
As well as being Minnie Ripperton's most famous song, it's also the one that made most extravagant use of her incredible vocal range. As well as hitting those high notes though, the former Rotary Connection singer had penned a classic love song.

2 WANDA JACKSON – 'FUNNEL OF LOVE'
This 1961 release features an absolutely stunning vocal performance from Jackson as she details the spiraling madness of head-over-heels love. She does this over a tune that is warmly exotic and instantly absorbing while remaining almost impossible to categorise.

1 NED DOHENY – 'GET IT UP FOR LOVE'
Why this song isn't absolutely massive is a mystery. The opening track on Dohney's 1976 album, *Hard Candy* is highly polished, but in a way that doesn't sacrifice character for sheen. There's a recent reissue on the wonderful American label Numero.

	ARTIST	SONG	YEAR
10	Lulu	'Love Loves to Love'	1967
9	Beyoncé	'Crazy in Love'	2003
8	Madonna	'Justify My Love'	1990
7	Roy Ayres	'Love Will Bring Us Back Together'	1979
6	Talking Heads	'This Must Be the Place (Naïve Melody)'	1983
5	Queen	'Crazy Little Thing Called Love'	1979
4	The Gentrys	'I Need Love'	1970
3	Minnie Ripperton	'Lovin' You'	1975
2	Wanda Jackson	'Funnel of Love'	1961
1	Ned Doheny	'Get it up for Love'	1976

TOP 10

Heartbreak isn't the other side of love's coin – it's knowing that coin's being spent on dinner for someone else while you're sitting at home eating a microwave meal you haven't even bothered to decant onto a plate. We all need to wallow sometimes. Thankfully, music's well aware of this and has given us the best tools for the job...

HEARTBREAK SONGS

10 GLORIA GAYNOR – 'I WILL SURVIVE'

The breakup song for those with an eye on the future, Gloria's done all her crying a long time ago. Now she's empowered and confident, meaning that when her no-good fella turns up, she's simply not interested – she's got a high NRG disco hit to sing.

9 THE STREETS – 'DRY YOUR EYES'

Mike Skinner talks us through the end of a relationship from a devastated ex-boyfriend's point of view. It's a surprisingly touching and direct song that helps to dispel once and for all the idea that men can't talk about their feelings.

8 JIMMY RUFFIN – 'WHAT BECOMES OF THE BROKEN HEARTED?'

Ruffin presents a damning diagnosis for the broken hearted on this wonderful 1966 single, as we're told that, 'All is lost, there's no place for beginning/All that's left is an unhappy ending.' Happily, things pick up and end on a more positive note.

7 ISAAC HAYES – 'BY THE TIME I GET TO PHOENIX'

Jimmy Webb's narrative is just stunning. A man leaves his partner and defines his journey through the events of her day, 'By the time I get to Phoenix, she'll be rising...' At 19 minutes, Hayes's version gives nearly enough time to make the state line.

6 SOFT CELL – 'SAY HELLO, WAVE GOODBYE'

When Marc Almond sings, 'Take your hands off me, I don't belong to you,' it's a proper hairs-on-the-back-of-the-neck moment. Meanwhile, Dave Ball's music is every bit the equal partner to Marc Almond's emotional, but never overly dramatic, delivery.

5 DIONNE WARWICK – 'WALK ON BY'

One of Burt Bacharach and Hal David's most well-known

songs, this plea for quiet dignity and consideration has been recorded by many singers – including a great version by Isaac Hayes – but Dionne Warwick's crystal-clear tone wins hands down.

4 JULIE LONDON – 'CRY ME A RIVER'
Originally written for Ella Fitzgerald, Julie London's version of the song gives very little wriggle room for anyone else to make it theirs. The breathy phrasing and husky timbre of her voice is shot through with emotion and absolutely owns the song.

3 JOE JACKSON – 'DIFFERENT FOR GIRLS'
One for the boys, this. Joe Jackson confounds preconceptions with an

achingly perfect pop song about a boy looking for love from a girlfriend content for a carnal, commitment-free arrangement. His plaintive tone conveys beautifully hurt and confusion.

2 JOY DIVISION – 'LOVE WILL TEAR US APART'

Another stripped back confessional, as Ian Curtis documents the break-up of his marriage in stark terms, completely devoid of any kind of cushioning conceit. Released a month after his death, it took on an even more heart-wrenching significance.

1 CAROLE KING – 'IT'S TOO LATE'

Not a great choice for a wedding waltz, this remarkably honest break-up song is full of resignation and acceptance that makes it seem the saddest thing ever recorded. When King sings 'Still I'm glad for what we had, and how I once loved you', it's heartbreaking.

	ARTIST	SONG	YEAR
10	Gloria Gaynor	'I Will Survive'	1978
9	The Streets	'Dry Your Eyes'	2004
8	Jimmy Ruffin	'What Becomes of the Broken Hearted?'	1966
7	Isaac Hayes	'By The Time I Get To Phoenix'	1967
6	Soft Cell	'Say Hello, Wave Goodbye'	1982
5	Dionne Warwick	'Walk on By'	1964
4	Julie London	'Cry Me a River'	1955
3	Joe Jackson	'Different for Girls'	1979
2	Joy Division	'Love Will Tear Us Apart'	1980
1	Carole King	'It's Too Late'	1971

The tree's up, the stockings are over the fireplace and the house reeks of whatever it is they put in those mulled wine sachets – cinnamon and mould? There's just one thing missing, and it's not Father Christmas, it's music! Where would the season of goodwill be without some good tunes? The following are guaranteed to bring festive cheer.

CHRISTMAS SONGS

10 BOBBY HELMS – 'JINGLE BELL ROCK'

If you take a fairly standard song, add in some casual Christmas references and some bells in the background, you've got yourself a Christmas hit! It's never that easy of course and Helms shows how it's done properly and with consummate skill.

9 THE DRIFTERS – 'WHITE CHRISTMAS'

There's no better misty-eyed look back at Christmas past outside of *A Christmas Carol*. Bing Crosby's recording of the Irving Berlin song is, apparently, the best selling single of all time, but the Drifters' doo wop has got it all wrapped up.

8 BING CROSBY & DAVID BOWIE – 'LITTLE DRUMMER BOY'

Their performance on Bing Crosby's Merrie Olde Christmas TV special added a bit of class to Christmas

(even if their crashingly clumsy scripted intro should have been kept under wraps). Sadly, it doesn't seem to be quite the seasonal staple it once was.

7 BRENDA LEE – 'ROCKIN' AROUND THE CHRISTMAS TREE'

The perfect song for a Christmas party (as proved by Macaulay Kulkin in *Home Alone*), and one Brenda Lee sings with a genuine sense of childish glee. This is understandable as she recorded the country-tinged Christmas pop hit when she was just 13.

6 NAT KING COLE – 'THE BOY THAT SANTA CLAUS FORGOT'

Vera Lyn's recording is better known, but Nat King Cole's delivery brings tears to the eyes almost before he's got to the end of the first line. Reminding us that Christmas is a luxury some can't afford, and focusing our attention on

giving rather than receiving.

5 SLADE – 'MERRY CHRISTMAS EVERYBODY'

Like Father Christmas, Noddy Holder and co's song comes but once a year, but when it does, it screams 'Christmas!' like nothing else (both figuratively and literally). 1973 was a good year for Christmas releases and this held Wizzard's effort off the top spot.

4 PAUL MCCARTNEY – 'WONDERFUL CHRISTMASTIME'

This shares two things with

other songs that stem from the *McCartney II* sessions. Firstly, there's the presence of a massive synthesizer sound and, secondly, quite a lot of people hate it. Which is fine – they're just wrong. It's a brilliant Christmas sing-a-long.

3 WIZZARD – 'I WISH IT COULD BE CHRISTMAS EVERYDAY'

Much has been made of the logistical nightmare of actually having Christmas every day, but leaving aside such concerns for a moment, the sentiment is a fine one. With a nod to Phil Spector, this bold and big production remains a festive favourite.

2 THE POGUES WITH KIRSTY MACCOLL - 'FAIRYTALE OF NEW YORK'

There's not a lot of Christmas spirit in evidence in this curse-filled call and response between two lovers who are arguing on Christmas Eve. That aside, it remains a brilliant, bitter, barbed wonder regardless of the time of year.

1 THE CRYSTALS – 'SANTA CLAUS IS COMING TO TOWN'

It's against several laws to have a Christmas top 10 without including one from Phil Spector's *A Christmas Gift For You* album. The Crystals' hit is such an utter adrenalin rush of pure excitement, galloping along like a magic reindeer, that it leaves all else in its wake.

	ARTIST	SONG	YEAR
10	Bobby Helms	'Jingle Bell Rock'	1958
9	The Drifters	'White Christmas'	1955
8	Bing Crosby & David Bowie	'Little Drummer Boy'	1982
7	Brenda Lee	'Rockin' Around the Christmas Tree'	1958
6	Nat King Cole	'The Boy That Santa Claus Forgot'	1956
5	Slade	'Merry Christmas Everybody'	1973
4	Paul McCartney	'Wonderful Christmastime'	1979
3	Wizzard	'I Wish it Could Be Christmas Everyday'	1973
2	The Pogues with Kirsty MacColl	'Fairytale of New York'	1987
1	The Crystals	'Santa Claus Is Coming to Town'	1963

As well as spreading messages about peace and love around the world, music has also proved popular for those wishing to settle scores or launch an all-out attack. Being able to do so from the relative safety of the recording studio makes it easy, but you still have to make sure that the barbs hit their intended target. Here's a top 10 that really packs a punch.

INSULTING SONGS

10 BILLY BRAGG – 'ACCIDENT WAITING TO HAPPEN'

Addressing the notion that age can see people lose ideals as well as hair, Billy Bragg takes aim at a friend who has grown old disgracefully and manages to squeeze in the superbly worked, Kinks-referencing line, 'You're a dedicated swallower of fascism.'

9 MOSE ALLISON – 'YOUR MIND IS ON VACATION'

Though clearly at the end of his tether with a braying acquaintance, pianist Mose is in no mood to raise his voice. He doesn't have to though, as clever couplets combine to create a perfect put-down, while he gets on and does his thing with incredible class.

8 TUPAC SHAKUR – 'HIT 'EM UP'

This song pulls no punches – in fact it gets as many in as it can. Directed at Tupac's former friend, Biggie Smalls, this casts aspersions on the fidelity of his wife before making direct threats on his life. Three months later, Tupac was murdered.

7 DEAD KENNEDYS – 'HOLIDAY IN CAMBODIA'

The Dead Kennedys get a two-for-one as they attack both brutal totalitarian regimes and the West's sleepwalking complacency when it comes to world events. It also references Dr Suess, using 'star-belly sneech' as an insult - for which double points.

6 SEX PISTOLS – 'GOD SAVE THE QUEEN'

This anger-fuelled attack on the monarchy has been seen as an assault on the very fabric of British society. It's quite clear though that the only fabric on the Pistols' 'to have a pop at' list has ermine trim and costs about a billion quid a square metre.

5 STONE ROSES – 'ELIZABETH MY DEAR'

Poor Liz has to face another angry mob, although this time it's a much quieter affair. To the tune of Scarborough Fair,

Ian Brown sings 'Tear me apart and boil my bones/I'll not rest till She's lost Her throne.' And you can believe every word.

4 JOHN LENNON – 'HOW DO YOU SLEEP?'

After taking umbrage at some speculative pot shots on Paul McCartney's *Ram* album, John Lennon responded with this full-on nuclear assault, which used every lyrical barb and musical hook in his arsenal as well as George Harrison on slide guitar.

3 CEE-LO GREEN – 'FUCK YOU'

Re-titled 'Forget You', to ease the path to worldwide success, Cee Lo Green's song was initially as expletive-laden as Gordon Ramsay's kitchen. The dismissal of a former love and her new, flash boyfriend is a sentiment we can - and did - get on board with.

2 CARLY SIMON – 'YOU'RE SO VAIN'

Thought to be directed, at least in part, in the direction of actor Warren Beatty, this clever, self-referential song is an arch put-down to a boyfriend who has ideas above his station. It's witty and acerbic while also adopting a tone that seems, at times, oddly fond.

1 BOB DYLAN – 'IDIOT WIND '

The raw emotion of Bob's bitter outpourings has led to near endless speculation as to who is the subject of his words. That it ends, 'We're idiots babe/It's a wonder we can even feed ourselves,' suggests a more complex answer than has yet been given.

	ARTIST	SONG	YEAR
10	Billy Bragg	'Accident Waiting to Happen'	1991
9	Mose Allison	'Your Mind is on Vacation'	1956
8	Tupac Shakur	'Hit 'Em Up'	1996
7	Dead Kennedys	'Holiday in Cambodia'	1980
6	Sex Pistols	'God Save the Queen'	1977
5	The Stone Roses	'Elizabeth My Dear'	1989
4	John Lennon	'How Do You Sleep?'	1971
3	Cee-Lo Green	'Fuck You'	2010
2	Carly Simon	'You're So Vain'	1972
1	Bob Dylan	'Idiot Wind'	1975

TOP 10

A musical acknowledgement, a nod of recognition, cover versions are a convenient way for musicians to acknowledge their influences and wear their heart on their sleevenotes. All bands have played someone else's songs at some point in their career, but when someone gets it absolutely right, it's like the song was theirs all along.

COVER VERSIONS

10 THE SPECIALS – 'A MESSAGE TO YOU, RUDY'
Originally by Dandy Livingstone and called 'Rudy, A Message to You', The Specials turned up, turned the title around and... well, that's about it in fact. It's a very good, very faithful cover and there's nothing wrong with that. If it ain't broke, don't fix it.

9 THE LEMONHEADS – 'LUKA'
The Boston-based power-pop punk band's cover of singer/songwriter Suzanne Vega's song reveals some surprising melodic similarities between the two. See also, their cover of Mike Nesmith's 'Different Drum' and Simon and Garfunkel's 'Mrs Robinson'.

8 THE DEIRDRE WILSON TABAC – 'GET BACK'
If you thought The Beatles' original was groovy enough then look out! A driving, funky blues beat gives swing where Ringo would have played a fill and gives the whole thing a loose-limbed flow that allows everything else to fall perfectly into place.

7 BUTTHOLE SURFERS – 'HURDY GURDY MAN'
The Donovan folk-funk original was reasonably far-out as it was, but America's Butthole Surfers managed to tease yet more otherworldly oddness from the song when they decided to record and release it as the title track of an EP in 1990.

6 NIRVANA – 'MOLLY'S LIPS'
A genuine love for the Vaselines' jangly power pop led Nirvana to cover two of their songs (the other, 'Son of a Gun', is great too). Sharing a similar pop sensibility to the Scottish band, they treated the songs with respect – before belting the hell out of them.

5 JESUS AND MARY, CHAIN – 'SURFIN' USA'
Brian Wilson, while familiar with the idea of Phil Spector's 'wall of noise', would never have forseen the treatment meted out to his 1963 ray of sunshine pop by the Reid brothers, who close the curtains for this head-on, no-holds-barred cover.

4 THE JIMI HENDRIX EXPERIENCE – 'ALL ALONG THE WATCHTOWER'

Bob Dylan must be the most covered songwriter on Earth. Jimi Hendrix was among the fans and put his stamp on Dylan's 1968 single so firmly that it's like listening to a completely different song – which is, ideally, what you want.

3 MY BLOODY VALENTINE – 'WE HAVE ALL THE TIME IN THE WORLD'

Known more for drowning vocals – not to mention entire crowds – in waves of distortion and noise, My Bloody Valentine's surprisingly soft and sensitive treatment of the John Barry classic breathes unexpected life into an old standard.

2 JOHNNY CASH – *'HURT'*

A country music legend covering a Nine Inch Nails song just shouldn't work. It's testament to Cash's treatment - and Trent Reznor's songwriting - that it does, superbly well. Reznor, on hearing this version, said, 'That song isn't mine anymore.' Job done.

1 OTIS REDDING – 'TRY A LITTLE TENDERNESS'

The biggest shock here is discovering that Otis's version wasn't the original. That honour went to the Ray Noble Orchestra in 1932. Needless to say, Otis (backed by Booker T and the MGs) gave it a much-needed kick up the chorus.

	ARTIST	LISTEN TO...	YEAR
10	The Specials	'A Message to You, Rudy'	1979
9	The Lemonheads	'Luka'	1989
8	The Deirdre Wilson Tabac	'Get Back'	1969
7	Butthole Surfers	'Hurdy Gurdy Man'	1990
6	Nirvana	'Molly's Lips'	1991
5	Jesus and Mary Chain	'Surfin' USA'	1988
4	The Jimi Hendrix Experience	'All Along the Watchtower'	1968
3	My Bloody Valentine	'We Have All the Time in The World'	1993
2	Johnny Cash	'Hurt'	2002
1	Otis Redding	'Try A Little Tenderness'	1966

TOP 10

Time to put pen to paper and create your own top 10 list of songs to put you in a good mood...

10 ....

9 ....

8 ....

7 ....

6 ....

5 ....

4 ....

3 ....

2 ....

1 ....

TOP 10

There's a special joy to be had in finding new music but, occasionally, the search can mean you overlook artists you think you already know. Most established musicians have tried their hand at different genres over the years, and many of them have great songs squirreled away, out of plain sight. Here's 10 guaranteed to make you look twice...

SONGS YOU'D NEVER EXPECT FROM...

9 PAUL NICHOLAS – 'LAMPLIGHTER'

Although known as an actor, Paul Nicholas started his career as a pop singer. It didn't work out, but he recorded at least two jaw-dropping tunes. One, 'Run Shaker Life', has already been mentioned elsewhere, but this eastern influenced psychedelic effort is a monster.

8 GILBERT O'SULLIVAN – 'TOO MUCH ATTENTION'

Everything about this singer/songwriter gem comes as a surprise, the funky lilt, the instant head-nodding appeal of the drums and bongos, the flute and the scratchy, rhythmic guitar in the background. And on top of all this, everything rhymes!

7 BILL COSBY – 'HOORAY FOR THE SALVATION ARMY BAND'

The comedian is no stranger to the recording studio, but no one surely would have imagined he would produce anything approaching this Hendrix-drenched parody on his 1968 album, which is fun, silly and really rather good. Of course, being backed by the Watts 103rd St. Rhythm Band does help a bit.

6 BEE GEES – 'ON TIME'

No trace of disco boogie or their earlier baroque stylings, this Maurice Gibb-penned folk funk gem begins with the slightly off-kilter strumming of a lone acoustic guitar, by the end though, it's been joined by drums, bass, piano and strings for a rousing finale.

5 HOT CHOCOLATE – 'GO-GO GIRL'

Hidden away on the B-side to 'You'll Always Be a Friend' is this belting bit of poppy garage that sees the rough and ready guitars way up high in the mix

10 BILL WYMAN – 'BEACH CHASE'

Two things spring to mind when one thinks of former Stones bassist Bill Wyman – Mandy Smith and metal detectors (he makes them). He unearthed this treasure in 1981 while composing the score for the film *Green Ice*, and it's a doozy.

and an all-out rock solo. If there's one track that will make you believe in musical miracles, it's this.

4 THE OSMONDS – 'I,I,I'

Well-known for occasionally managing a decent song among the schmaltz, even 'Crazy Horses' couldn't prepare you for this. Bee Gee brother Maurice Gibb, on production duty, coaxes a convincing disco classic out of the boys.

3 JOHN BETJEMAN – 'LATE FLOWERING LUST'

From the *Late Flowering Love* album, John Betjeman reads his poem to a pleasingly offbeat musical accompaniment. It was covered (well, reworked) by the Asphodells – Andrew Weatherall and Timothy J Fairplay – on their 2012 album, *Ruled by Passion, Destroyed by Lust*.

2 APHRODITE'S CHILD – 'MAGIC MIRROR'

Before the kaftan and the film soundtracks, Demis Roussos and Vangelis were two-thirds of Greek psych-rock legends Aphrodite's Child. This track sees the band giving a virtuoso demonstration of exactly how psych-infused rock should be done.

1 CHUBBY CHECKER – 'GYPSY'

Providing something of a twist in the tale of Chubby's career (sorry) is the unexpected experimentalism of his Chequered LP. This, recorded around the same time, sounds like Jimi Hendrix travelling at law-breaking speeds – fast, furious and funky.

	ARTIST	SONG	YEAR
10	Bill Wyman	'Beach Chase'	1981
9	Paul Nicholas	'Lamplighter'	1976
8	Gilbert O'Sullivan	'Too Much Attention'	1971
7	Bill Cosby	'Hooray for the Salvation Army Band'	1970
6	Bee Gees	'On Time'	1972
5	Hot Chocolate	'Go-Go Girl'	1972
4	The Osmonds	'I,I,I'	1979
3	John Betjeman	'Late Flowering Lust'	1974
2	Aphrodite's Child	'Magic Mirror'	1969
1	Chubby Checker	'Gypsy'	1973

TOP 10

Before it was seemely for people in their forties to wear jeans, popular music in all its guises was largely the province of the young. That's all changed now, fifty is the new thirty or something. Pop's preoccupation with youth hasn't shifted however, as the kids look forward to a wide open future and adults gaze wistfully back into the past.

SONGS ABOUT YOUTH

10 THE RAMONES – 'TEENAGE LOBOTOMY'

Not the most straightforward of songs, it's about a boy who, following exposure to the insecticide DDT is in need of a lobotomy. As with all Ramones songs, it has more hooks that a professional boxer and they all land with pin-point accuracy.

9 DION AND THE BELMONTS – 'A TEENAGER IN LOVE'

This touching and sensitive song dealing with the trials and tribulations of the fickle teenage heart was an enormous hit for Dion DiMucci in 1959. It spoke directly to a generation of post-war teenagers who were enjoying freedom like never before.

8 SUPERGRASS – 'ALRIGHT'

Though some people seem to reserve particular disdain for Supergrass's joyful celebration of unfettered teenage abandon, it's difficult to see why they take such offense. It's silly, sure, but it's fun, carefree and utterly lacking in cynicism – like most teenagers.

7 ALICE COOPER – 'SCHOOL'S OUT'

Written specifically to emulate the feeling of breaking up for summer, Alice Cooper knew exactly how big this song could be. Applying the same meticulous thought process to his elaborate stage shows, it was the beginning of his theatrical peak.

6 BIG STAR – 'THIRTEEN'

There's no tantrums, no upsets, no call to arms on this song from Big Star's 1972 #1 Record. It's 'just' a beautiful ballad, written by Alex Chilton and Chris Bell, that perfectly captures adolescence in all its inexpert, fumbling and hopeful innocence.

5 FLAMIN' GROOVIES – 'TEENAGE HEAD'

When it comes to blues-based rock 'n' roll, the Flamin' Groovies' 1971 album, *Teenage Head*, is right up there with the Rolling Stones. The title track sounds not unlike some of the heavier releases on the famous Sun label, which is a definite plus point.

4 THE UNDERTONES – 'TEENAGE KICKS'

Famously one of John Peel's favorite records, 'Teenage Kicks' was played twice in a row by the DJ when he first aired it. It's all perfectly understandable too, as the endearingly naïve adrenaline rush is over almost as soon as it's begun.

3 THE WHO – 'MY GENERATION'

These days, Roger Daltrey presumably sings 'Hope I die before I get *too* old', but back in 1965 The Who's testament to youth drew a line in the sand and marked out two very clear territories - one marked 'the kids' and the other 'everyone else'.

2 NIRVANA – 'SMELLS LIKE TEEN SPIRIT'
The exact meaning of the lyrics is unclear - possibly even to the band themselves - but there's certainly a theme of stretching the elastic of childhood running through much of Kurt Cobain's career, including this unintentional anthem for youth.

1 SONIC YOUTH – 'TEENAGE RIOT'
Daydream Nation remains, for many, Sonic Youth's artistic pinnacle and 'Teenage Riot' is right at the summit, sticking a flag in it. Aaccording to Thurston Moore, the song is about appointing Dinosaur Jr's lethargic guitar hero J Masicis as president.

	ARTIST	SONG	YEAR
10	The Ramones	'Teenage Lobotomy'	1977
9	Dion and the Belmonts	'A Teenager in Love'	1959
8	Supergrass	'Alright'	1995
7	Alice Cooper	'School's Out'	1972
6	Big Star	'Thirteen'	1972
5	Flamin' Groov-ies	'Teenage Head'	1971
4	The Undertones	'Teenage Kicks'	1979
3	The Who	'My Generation'	1965
2	Nirvana	'Smells Like Teen Spirit'	1991
1	Sonic Youth	'Teenage Riot'	1988

TOP 10

There are many things that separate us from the animals we share this planet with – the ability of abstract thought, the scope of our creative compulsion… and mustard. No animal would ever invent mustard. That aside, we love our furry and feathered friends – when we're not eating them – and we're prone to making a song and dance about it too.

SONGS ABOUT ANIMALS

10 ROLLING STONES – 'WILD HORSES'

The Stones are in a reflective, introspective mood on this country-tinged ballad. The authentic sound may have been due to recording it at the legendary Muscle Shoals studio, but there's no doubt that there's a rare sincerity at play here, too.

9 THE CURE – 'THE LOVECATS'

Robert Smith has tried to distance himself from the jazzy chutzpah of 'The Lovecats', and cited alcohol as the driving force behind it. It led to more melodic hooks in three minutes than some bands manage in an entire career, so well done booze!

8 FLEETWOOD MAC – 'ALBATROSS'

Although an instrumental, Albatross manages to convey the sense of the animal it references better than anyone

would have thought possible. The slightly Waikiki slide guitar and crashing cymbals do sound like the sea, but how it so readily suggests flight is a mystery.

7 GEORGE CLINTON – 'ATOMIC DOG'

Although missing out on chart success when it was released in 1982, Atomic Dog didn't go unnoticed - most notably Snoop Dogg was a big fan and sampled the electronic funk beast for his 1993 single, 'Who Am I (What's My Name)?'

6 PRINCE – 'WHEN DOVES CRY'

If Prince has got this right – and he's probably done the research – then an upset dove sounds exactly like an American male pop star's falsetto yelp. Despite the odd allusion to crying birds, this is an enduringly brilliant piece of pop from *Purple Rain*.

5 PIXIES – 'MONKEY GONE TO HEAVEN'

Taken from Pixies' 1989 album *Doolittle*, this track, one of Black Francis's more straightforward lyrical offerings, explores humans' destructive relationship with the environment, referencing the hole in the ozone layer and a great big sludgy mess in the Atlantic.

4 THE BEATLES – 'I AM THE WALRUS'

Taking its cue from Lewis Carroll's *The Walrus and the Carpenter,* I Am the Walrus is absurdist nonsense verse. People have been trying to work out its meaning for years, but they'd be better off enjoying the song rather than struggling to make sense of it.

3 NICK DRAKE – 'BLACK EYED DOG'

In songs, as in literature and painting, animals are often used as symbols and few are

as potent as the black dog of depression. Even at his most harrowing - and this is certainly harrowing - Nick Drake's music was always beautiful and captivating.

2 THIN LIZZY – 'JOHNNY THE FOX MEETS JIMMY THE WEED'

The titular Johnny isn't an actual fox, but rather a man who displays the characteristics we would normally associate with a fox. Namely guile, cunning, a hardwired survival instinct and a penchant for groove-led blues rock and wah wah pedals.

1 AMERICA – 'HORSE WITH NO NAME'

The band's first single and a huge hit, 'A Horse with No Name' has come to be America's signature tune - which is surprising when so many people assumed that it was a Neil Young song. Despite the similarities however, this is very much its own animal.

	ARTIST	SONG	YEAR
10	The Rolling Stones	'Wild Horses'	1971
9	The Cure	'The Lovecats'	1983
8	Fleetwood Mac	'Albatross'	1968
7	George Clinton	'Atomic Dog'	1982
6	Prince	'When Doves Cry'	1984
5	Pixies	'Monkey Gone to Heaven'	1989
4	The Beatles	'I Am the Walrus'	1967
3	Nick Drake	'Black Eyed Dog'	1972
2	Thin Lizzy	'Johnny the Fox Meets Jimmy the Weed'	1976
1	America	'A Horse With No Name'	1972

For many of us, the first time we were confronted with music that enchanted and engaged us was on television or in the cinema. Disney have a special knack for musical alchemy and seem to be able to score films with songs that bury their way into your brain and stay with you forever. Here are 10 that show no sign of moving.

DISNEY FAMILY FAVOURITES

10 'PINK ELEPHANTS ON PARADE'

1941's *Dumbo* was an attempt to get back to the simple art of basic storytelling after the ambitious flop of *Fantasia*. Quite how they thought this song and the trippy visuals that accompanied it would achieve this aim is unclear, but it works.

9 'SUPERCALI-FRAGILISTIC-EXPIALIDOCIOUS'

Another film that could easily have had multiple entries in this top 10, *Mary Poppins* is a fantasy musical that relies as heavily on the music as the fantasy for its success. This song, based around a nonsense word, revels in the joy of language.

8 'UNDER THE SEA'

Disney's 1989 film *The Little Mermaid*, contains this calypso classic during which

Sebastian the crab tries to persuade mermaid Ariel to remain in her watery home. She doesn't, but the Academy Award judges were sufficiently persuaded to give the song an Oscar.

7 'MAN OR MUPPET'
Songs in children's movies need to appeal to kids and their parents. With actor Jason Segel delivering straight-faced lines like 'If I'm a muppet, then I'm a very manly muppet,' meant 2011's *The Muppets* delighted old and young alike – and bagged an Oscar.

6 'YOU'VE GOT A FRIEND IN ME'
Randy Newman's theme tune for 1995's *Toy Story* perfectly captures the special bond between a child and a favourite toy and also manages to sound so familiar that you'd swear it was a classic, dusted off for the film rather than a commissioned piece.

5 'EVERYBODY WANTS TO BE A CAT'
From the 1970 film *The Aristocats*, this is *the* moment of the film. While traveling over the rooftops of Paris, our heroes meet up with a band, who break into this jazzy ditty which soon descends into an unhinged New Orleans-style jam.

4 'HAKUNA MATATA'

Proving that cartoons can be educational, it's good to report that Hakuna Matata actually does mean 'no worries' as the song from *The Lion King* claims. As well as teaching Swahili to pre-schoolers, the tune is also a singalong masterpiece.

3 'BARE NECESSITIES'

1967's *Jungle Book* raised the bar when it came to soundtracks. The voice of Phil Harris (Baloo) is key to the song's success, but the songwriting (Terry Gilkyson) and the arrangement, (by Beach Boys collaborator Van Dyke Parks) is simply stunning.

2 'HE'S A TRAMP'

With Peggy Lee writing the songs, it was a fair bet that 1955's *Lady and the Tramp* was going to be a cut above – and it was. Peggy takes lead vocals on 'He's a Tramp', and turns it into a smoldering jazzy treat – no mean feat for a Pekingese.

1 'I WAN'NA BE LIKE YOU'

Another song from *The Jungle Book*, this one's a joint jumpin' jewel. The 'scat duel' between Baloo and King Louie is a particular high point, but the song's undeniable quality has seen it covered by none other than Kenny Ball and his Jazzmen.

	SONG	FILM	YEAR
10	'Pink Elephants on Parade'	*Dumbo*	1941
9	'Supercalifragilis-ticexpialidocious'	*Mary Poppins*	1964
8	'Under the Sea'	*The Little Mermaid*	1989
7	'Man or Muppet'	*The Muppets*	2011
6	'You've Got a Friend in Me'	*Toy Story*	1995
5	'Everybody Wants to Be a Cat'	*The Aristocats*	1971
4	'Hakuna Matata'	*The Lion King*	1994
3	'Bare Necessities'	*The Jungle Book*	1967
2	'He's a Tramp'	*Lady and the Tramp*	1955
1	'I Wan'na Be Like You'	*The Jungle Book*	1967

TOP 10

The best soundtracks work hand-in-hand with their movie partner, creating tension, heightening emotion and making us laugh, cry and stuff ourselves full of popcorn. The very best can also stand alone without relying on bright lights, flashing colours and huge explosions to make an impact. The following are stars of the screen and the stereo.

MOVIE SOUNDTRACKS

10 BEE GEES – *SATURDAY NIGHT FEVER*

It's not everyone's cup of tea – indeed some disco diehards wouldn't be seen dead dancing to it – but you can't argue with the massive cultural impact this soundtrack had, turning a low-budget film into a worldwide, box-office record breaker.

9 PRINCE – *PURPLE RAIN*

So entwined are the film and the soundtrack, working out which came first can lead to losing oneself in a chicken-and-egg catch-22. That conundrum aside, it remains one of Prince's best albums, whether you factor in the film or not.

8 SPINAL TAP – *THIS IS SPINAL TAP*

Writing an entire album's worth of spoof songs for the 1984 mock 'rockumentary' was an incredible undertaking. Written by the actors themselves, they show an incredible grasp of music alongside the light-hearted lampooning.

7 CHARLEY CUVA – *PUTNEY SWOPE*

The music to Robert Downey Sr's 1969 meditation on the evils of materialism only received a release in 2006, and even then it was a run of 500 copies. Despite its relative obscurity, the songs bring inventive dashes of colour to this largely black-and-white film.

6 ANGELO BADALAMENTI – *THE STRAIGHT STORY*

The score to David Lych's 1999 drama was written by long-time associate Angelo Badalamenti, and manages to emulate the emotion of the sweet, but never cloying, film using subtle folk tones and hints of the Appalachians in the beautiful atmospherics.

5 CURTIS MAYFIELD – *SUPER FLY*

While Cutis Mayfield's score has become a funk staple, revered down the years for its social commentary and deep, heavy grooves, the film itself has blended into the background somewhat, outdone and outperformed by its superior soundtrack.

4 THE BEATLES – *MAGICAL MYSTERY TOUR*

The six-song soundtrack to the 1967 film of the same name was, in some respects, much more of a concept that Sgt Peppers'. The film itself was received poorly (to say the least) but the songs remain standalone successes.

3 ENNIO MORRICONE – *THE GOOD, THE BAD AND THE UGLY*

Morricone is one of the most prolific film composers alive. While there are edgier, more satisfying scores (1970's 'Citta Violenta' for example), this has managed to seep its way into the planet's collective consciousness with a refrain that you can never forget.

2 THE MONKEES – *HEAD*

The Monkees' stream-of-consciousness film may have gone over the heads of many (though some heads regard it as a counter-culture masterpiece), but the brilliant soundtrack shows what happens when ambition - and four young musicians - are allowed to run riot.

1 VANGELIS – *BLADE RUNNER*

Vangelis's trademark synths are all over his 1982 score for Ridley Scott's epic interpretation of Philip K Dick's *Do Androids Dream of Electric Sheep?* and it's hard to imagine this futuristic dystopian film noir without the subtle and satisfying score.

	ARTIST/COMPOSER	FILM	YEAR
10	Bee Gees	*Saturday Night Fever*	1977
9	Prince	*Purple Rain*	1984
8	Spinal Tap	*This Is Spinal Tap*	1984
7	Charley Cuva	*Putney Swope*	1969
6	Angelo Badalamenti	*The Straight Story*	1999
5	Curtis Mayfield	*Super Fly*	1972
4	The Beatles	*Magical Mystery Tour*	1967
3	Ennio Morricone	*The Good the Bad and the Ugly*	1966
2	The Monkees	*Head*	1968
1	Vangelis	*Blade Runner*	1982

TOP 10

Halloween is as good a time as any for a party, but what music to choose for the ideal rave from the grave? You need music good enough to raise the dead and keep the living on their feet, so once you've played 'Thriller' 10 times in a row, what then? Thankfully, popular music is full of horrific hits...

HALLOWEEN

10 BOBBY *PICKETT* – 'MONSTER MASH'
Screaming 'Halloween' in the same way that Noddy Holder signals Christmas is this 1962 novelty hit from Bobby 'Boris' Pickett. And should you ever tire of the overly mannered delivery, there's always the creepy chaos of the B-side, 'Monster Mash Party'.

9 THE RATTLES – 'THE WITCH'
The German group's 1970 worldwide hit, adorned with screaming, cackling overdubs, would fall squarely into the novelty camp were it not for the fact that, hiding underneath the costumed, am-dram ramblings, is a really good song.

8 THE SPECIALS – 'GHOST TOWN'
While the Specials' 1981 single is more party political than party-til-dawn, it's still on the Halloween playlist for the haunting, eerie and downright scary arrangement that begins with the wind whistling through empty streets and continues in the same unsettling vein.

7 OCTOBER COUNTRY – 'MY GIRLFRIEND IS A WITCH'
Boy meets girl, boy falls in love, boy realizes that girl in in fact a witch. This age-old scenario is the jumping-off point for 1968's brilliant bubblegum blast from October Country, a band fronted by West Coast Pop Art Experimental Band prodigy Michael Lloyd.

6 REDBONE – 'WITCH QUEEN OF NEW ORLEANS'
Bringing a touch of R&B boogie to proceedings is Redbone. The distinctive blend of native American voices and chants in the mix certainly helps with the overall feeling of mystery and magic – as do the references to New Orleans staples, zombies and voodoo.

5 THE CRAMPS – 'HUMAN FLY'
If, at any time during your party, the Halloween spirit seems to be flagging, one burst of The Cramps' 1979 song, with incessant buzzsaw guitars and relentless, pounding drums, will be more than enough to re-animate even the deadest of feet.

4 THE VAMPIRES OF DARTMOORE – *DRACULA'S MUSIC CABINET LP*
Believe it or not, this record is a sought-after pseudo soundtrack, full of breaks and beats if not buckets of blood. Played by some of Germany's best session musicians, the jazzy, lounge feel goes better with cocktails than coffins, but is full of exotic charm.

3 SCREAMIN' JAY HAWKINS – *I PUT A SPELL ON YOU*

No stranger shocking dramatics, Hawkins' delivery on this is nothing short of miraculous. It's a combination of music hall exhibitionist schtick, hammy horror acting and absolute anguish that is utterly unsettling and completely compelling.

2 DONOVAN – *SEASON OF THE WITCH*

As a squad of cover versions line up, desperate to be picked, we wave them all away – even the valiant effort by Sam Gopal, with Lemmy on vocals – for the clipped precision and haunting guitar lines of Donovan's original from 1966.

1 RONNIE COOK & THE GAYLADS – *GOO GOO MUCK*

So good The Cramps chose to cover it on their *Psychedelic Jungle* album. It's the Ronnie Cook original however, that gets an invitation to our Halloween hoedown. It fits the bill perfectly with gory grooves, a spellbinding sax line and a sleazy swing.

	ARTIST	SONG	YEAR
10	Bobby Pickett	'Monster Mash'	1962
9	The Rattles	'The Witch'	1970
8	The Specials	'Ghost Town'	1981
7	October Country	'My Girlfriend Is a Witch'	1968
6	Redbone	'Witch Queen of New Orleans'	1971
5	The Cramps	'Human Fly'	1979
4	The Vampires of Dartmoore	'Dracula's Music Cabinet'	1969
3	Screamin' Jay Hawkins	'I Put a Spell on You'	1956
2	Donovan	'Season of the Witch'	1966
1	Ronnie Cook & The Gaylads	'Goo Goo Muck'	1962

TOP 10

The cosmos has long held a singular fascination for musicians. Whether it's exploring the endless sonic possibilities that space suggests or looking to alien life forms as a parallel to the marginalized outsider identities that pepper pop music. And then there's the big rockets and cool space suits of course... The following 10 are all aiming for the stars.

OUT OF THIS WORLD

9 PINK FLOYD – 'INTERSTELLAR OVERDRIVE'

Pink Floyd's *Piper From the Gates of Dawn* album contained a few surprises, but none of them quite as raw and visceral as this improvised journey into unchartered territory. A free-form freak-out, it shows their fearless fondness for experimentation.

8 SPIRITUALISED – 'LADIES AND GENTLEMEN WE ARE FLOATING IN SPACE'

Most people had Spiritualised pinned as space cadets right from the off, but this album manages to float effortlessly while never lacking gravity. Until Elvis' estate complained, this title track incorporated 'Can't Help Falling in Love', to beautiful and thrilling effect.

10 ELTON JOHN – 'ROCKET MAN'

Apparently the inspiration for Elton John's launch into the space was lyricist Bernie Taupin's sighting of a shooting star, and nothing to do with either of them hearing 'Space Oddity'. At all. Not that it really matters, this is a bone fide classic in any case.

7 RAMASES – 'BALLOON'
This lovely, lilting

acoustic rock track comes from the 1971 album *Space Hymns* by Ramases. With the repeated vocal line, 'Balloon - just off the surface of the moon' it's anyone's guess what they were up to, but it sounds amazing.

6 DAVID BOWIE – 'SPACE ODDITY (ORIGINAL VERSION)'

An obvious choice but, just to be different, this is the version from his promotional film, *Love You Til Tuesday*. It's not just to be contrary either, the low-key production gives the song a chance to shine in a different sky. And the drums and bass have more charm.

5 JOHNNY HARRIS – 'ODYSSEY'

This brilliant lunar boogie comes straight from the future - the 25th century in fact. It was composed for an episode of *Buck Rogers* in the 25th Century in which a band, Andromeda, control the minds of their audience through this song.

4 WAR – 'GALAXY'

The best track on the album by light years, the eight-minute space funk of 'Galaxy' sees the band take off into the cosmos at such pace that they are in danger of bending time and landing back on earth before they've actually begun to play.

3 SUN RA – 'SPACE IS THE PLACE'

If you came to Sun Ra with no knowledge of his reputation, one look at the cover would be enough to let you know this wasn't your common-or-garden musician. This serves as a great introduction to Sun Ra's spiritual, unfettered, free-form jazz.

2 ALAN PARSONS – *I ROBOT*

Inspired by the science-fiction tales of Isaac Asimov, Alan Parsons - ably assisted by his Project - set about making a concept LP. The title track is the standout as spacey synth washes give way to a robotic arpeggio that sets the pace for the band to build on.

1 MARVIN GAYE — A FUNKY SPACE REINCARNATION

Gaye walked into the sessions for the *Here, My Dear* album intending to knock something out as quickly as possible as his ex-wife was getting the royalties. One listen to this blissed-out cosmic jam is enough to see that professionalism soon took over.

	ARTIST	SONG	YEAR
10	Elton John	'Rocket Man'	1972
9	Pink Floyd	'Interstellar Overdrive'	1967
8	Spiritualised	'Ladies and Gentlemen we are Floating in Space'	1977
7	Ramases	'Balloon'	1971
6	David Bowie	'Space Oddity (original version)'	1969
5	Johnny Harris	'Odyssey'	1980
4	War	'Galaxy'	1977
3	Sun Ra	'Space Is the Place'	1973
2	Alan Parsons	*I Robot (LP)*	1977
1	Marvin Gaye	'A Funky Space Reincarnation'	1978

TOP 10

Sport's competitive edge is often glimpsed in musical rivalries – hip hop, in particular, is stuffed full of them. The drive to compete fuels our passion for sport and where better to wax lyrical about all of the beautiful games than in song? Like the competitors at a school sports day, these are all winners.

SONGS ABOUT SPORT

10 SURVIVOR – 'EYE OF THE TIGER'
'Eye of the Tiger' - or 'The Theme Tune to Rocky III' as it will always be known - is pretty much like the movie it soundtracks. Full of cloying sentiment and overblown emotion, cheesy as hell, probably not very good for

you, but utterly irresistible.

9 10CC – 'DREADLOCK HOLIDAY'
Based on actual experiences while on holiday in Jamaica, the song documents a man's attempts to deflect potentially tricky subjects by appealing to a shared love of cricket and, in doing so, highlights the power of sport as a universal and unifying bond.

8 YELLO – 'THE RACE'
The Swiss band stepped up a gear with their 1998 ode to motorsports. Snippets of commentary, engine noises and the track's own propulsive rhythms all jostle for pole position and, while the track doesn't quite take the chequered flag, it's a valiant effort.

7 NEW ORDER – 'WORLD IN MOTION'
Despite being generally regarded as a stinker of a world cup, Italia '90 gave England fans much to remember: extra-time victory against Cameroon, Gazza's tears and a devastating penalty defeat against Germany and the best World Cup song ever.

6 ROY HARPER – 'WHEN AN OLD CRICKETER LEAVES THE CREASE'
This 1975 single from the folk legend could make a pretty good case for being his best-known song. There is a real sense of yearning for a time passed, accentuated by the presence of the Grimethorpe Colliery Band, that make this a bittersweet pleasure.

5 SUPER FURRY ANIMALS – 'VENUS AND SERENA'
OK, fair play ref, this is a bit of a foul. Although it takes its title from tennis's Williams sisters, this is actually about a child and his pet tortoises.

That said, the tennis references come quicker than a serve from Sampras.

4 JORGE BEN – 'PONTA DE LANÇA AFRICANO (UMBABARAUMA)'

This football song gets a devastating hat trick, scoring on groove, melody and style. No surprise then, that the architect of this three-point victory is Brazilian - Jorge Ben. From his 1976 album *África Brasil*, David Byrne was also a big fan.

3 INSTANT FUNK – 'WIDE WORLD OF SPORTS'

Getting up a fair old sprint straight out of the blocks is this disco hit from 1979. DJ Q obviously saw this for the winner it undoubtedly is when he used it as the building block for his 1996 house classic 'We Are One'.

2 DON FARDON – 'BELFAST BOY'

If you're going to write a song about a legend, you'd better make sure that song is up to the job. Written to accompany a BBC documentary about George Best is up to the job. A squelchy synth up front , a solid back line and Waddle and Hoddle nowhere in sight.

1 KRAFTWERK – 'TOUR DE FRANCE'

Not content with having 'done' cars and trains, German electronic pioneers Kraftwerk got on their bike and went looking for inspiration for their next release. The result was one of the most celebratory recordings the band ever made.

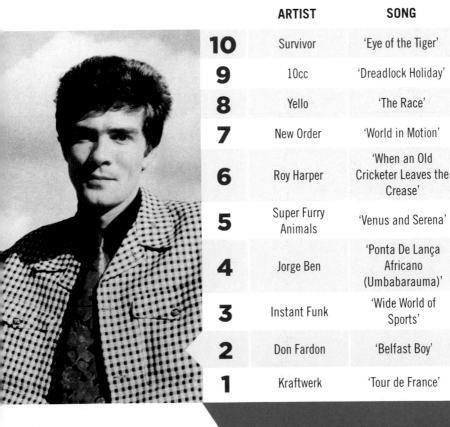

	ARTIST	SONG	YEAR
10	Survivor	'Eye of the Tiger'	1982
9	10cc	'Dreadlock Holiday'	1978
8	Yello	'The Race'	1988
7	New Order	'World in Motion'	1990
6	Roy Harper	'When an Old Cricketer Leaves the Crease'	1975
5	Super Furry Animals	'Venus and Serena'	2004
4	Jorge Ben	'Ponta De Lança Africano (Umbabarauma)'	1976
3	Instant Funk	'Wide World of Sports'	1979
2	Don Fardon	'Belfast Boy'	1970
1	Kraftwerk	'Tour de France'	1983

The passage of time has proved a huge theme for musicians. As the clock ticks down and we all make our way to the same ultimate destination, it provides a truly shared focus, something we can all get on board with. And while philosophers and scientists try to work out the nature of this abstract concept, these songs know what the time is.

TIME

9 BILL HALEY & HIS COMETS – 'ROCK AROUND THE CLOCK'

The most famous time-related song of them all, 1954's 'Rock Around the Clock' let teenagers far and wide know that their time had come. The song's repeated false start is a particular stoke of genius, building tension brilliantly before it all kicks off.

8 THE ROLLING *STONES* – 'TIME IS ON MY SIDE'

Not, as many people think, a Jagger/Richards composition, the Stones version, nonetheless, is the go-to one. Sung as a message to a former lover, assuring them that they won't be able to stay away, it's the classic cocksure confidence of youth.

7 SPARKS – 'BEAT THE CLOCK'

Fans of disco hit 'I Feel Love', Sparks got producer extraordinaire Giorgio Moroder on board to help with the urgent feel of their 1979 track and his fingerprints are all over this. It was an inspired match and this remains one of their best singles.

6 THE CURE – 'SEVENTEEN SECONDS'

A monontonous, metronomic beat sets the pace on this low-key title track from The Cure's second LP. It's a perfect choice for this list, as it's a record that demands time of the listener - it's a song made for reflection, thought and undisturbed attention.

5 ORBITAL – 'TIME BECOMES'

This clever and self-referential 'song' consists of just a voice (that of Star Trek actor Michael Dorn) split through the left and right channels and played with slight delay so that it shifts in and out of time in a manner

10 PWEI – 'DEF CON ONE'

Never shy of a cultural reference or 10 in their musical montages, the Poppies lean heavily on Alan Moore's *Watchmen* graphic novel and the US Armed Forces' DEFCON alert system to tell us that the time is: 'minutes away from nuclear war'.

not dissimilar to work by Steve Reich.

4 THE LEMONHEADS – 'MALLO CUP'
A melodic highpoint from the 1989 album *Lick*, Evan Dando captures time (and place) perfectly with the gorgeous lines, 'Here I am outside your house at 3am/Tryin to think you out of bed/I whistle at your sill/It echoes 'cross the street instead.'

3 DOLLY PARTON – '9 TO 5'
A clockwatching classic! The theme tune to the 1980 comedy film was adopted as an anthem for DJ Sean Rowley's Guilty Pleasures night, but really, what is there to feel guilty about? A good song is a good song and should be an unashamed joy.

2 THE ZOMBIES – 'TIME OF THE SEASON'
Taken from their *Odessey and Oracle* [sic] album, this was an out of time hit, not achieving success until after the band had gone their separate ways, in 1969. It's considered a classic and it's easy to see why as it exudes sophisticated cool.

1 BEASTIE BOYS – 'TIME TO GET ILL'
If there's one track that really sums up the thrill of the Beastie's first album, it's this. With samples from Schooly D, Steve Miller, Creedence Clearwater Revival and Barry White, it perfectly represents their magpie eye when it came to influences.

	ARTIST	SONG	YEAR
10	Pop Will Eat Itself	'Def Con One'	1988
9	Bill Haley	'Rock Around the Clock'	1954
8	The Rolling Stones	'Time Is on my Side'	1964
7	Sparks	'Beat the Clock'	1979
6	The Cure	'Seventeen Seconds'	1980
5	Orbital	'Time Becomes'	1993
4	The Lemonheads	'Mallo Cup'	1989
3	Dolly Parton	'9 to 5'	1980
2	The Zombies	'Time of the Season'	1968
1	Beastie Boys	'Time to Get Ill'	1986

TOP 10

And so we face the final curtain... The only certainty that life has for any of us is that it will end. Some broach the subject with gravitas and grave concern while others take a more lighthearted approach. And that's the key – the destination is fixed, but we decide how we face the journey. These songs are going to the grave in style.

DEATH

10 THE SHANGRI-LAS– 'LEADER OF THE PACK'
This teenage tragedy tells the story of a girl whose relationship with the leader of a motorcycle gang is doomed from the start. After ditching him at her parents request, the girl watches in horror as he speeds off, crashes and dies.

9 MONTY PYTHON – 'ALWAYS LOOK ON THE BRIGHT SIDE OF LIFE'
The hilarious adult-Disney whimsy of Eric Idle's closing moments in *Life of Brian* leaves everyone in stitches. It's also a funeral favourite, possibly because choosing to laugh in the face of death rather than cower in the corner is hugely empowering.

8 BERT JANSCH – 'NEEDLE OF DEATH'
Whether or not this played a part in the inspiration for Neil Young's 'Needle and the Damage Done' (another wonderful song), the two compositions are kindred spirits of a kind. Delicate, fragile compositions lamenting the passing of friends.

7 ELLIOTT SMITH – 'KING'S CROSSING'
Following the singer's suicide, this laid-bare, confessional cry makes for very uncomfortable listening. While the music soars and crashes around him, Smith paints a picture of despair culminating in his plea, 'Give me one good reason not to do it.'

6 BOB DYLAN – 'KNOCKING ON HEAVEN'S DOOR'
Well, it had to be in here somewhere, didn't it? Written for the film *Pat Garrett and Billy the Kid*, the song shows what happens when someone really does shoot the deputy (well, sheriff) and Dylan describes the man's final moments as he slips away.

5 THE FLAMING LIPS – 'DO YOU REALIZE?'
Wayne Coyne's musings on our insignificance in the grand scheme of things never strays too far from the human - or, thankfully from the artfully accomplished and beautifully embellished pop that The Flaming Lips have consistently excelled at over the years.

4 NICK CAVE & THE BAD SEEDS + KYLIE MINOGUE – 'WHERE THE WILD ROSES GROW'

From the Bad Seeds' *Murder Ballads* album, the song is the description of a murder from two intertwined points of view - the killer and his victim. It's simultaneously brutal and beautiful, the hushed voices adding to the unease as the story unfolds.

3 BOBBIE GENTRY – 'ODE TO BILLIE JOE'

Gentry's gift for storytelling outstrips most, but she outdoes even herself on this tale of a local boy who kills himself by jumping off the Tallahatchie Bridge. The casual conversation that follows around the dinner table shows perfectly how life carries on.

2 FRANK SINATRA – 'MY WAY'

If claims that one in seven funerals feature a rendition of 'My Way' are true, it's clearly a hit with both the living and the dead. That's probably because it speaks of a life well lived and (nearly) free of regret and does it with consummate, singalong ease.

1 BLUE ÖYSTER CULT – 'DON'T FEAR THE REAPER'

Thought by some people to be an active endorsement of suicide, there's a far more poetic (and pleasant) reading of the Blue Oyster Cult's touching 1976 single - one that involves the possibility of an afterlife and the certainty of transcendent love.

	ARTIST	SONG	YEAR
10	The Shangri-Las	*'The Leader of the Pack'*	1964
9	Monty Python	*'Always Look on the Bright Side of Life'*	1979
8	Bert Jansch	*'Needle of Death'*	1965
7	Elliott Smith	*'King's Crossing'*	2004
6	Bob Dylan	*'Knocking on Heaven's Door'*	1973
5	The Flaming Lips	*'Do You Realize?'*	2002
4	Nick Cave & The Bad Seeds + Kylie Minogue	*'Where the Wild Roses Grow'*	1995
3	Bobbie Gentry	*'Ode to Billie Joe'*	1967
2	Frank Sinatra	*'My Way'*	1969
1	Blue Öyster Cult	*'Don't Fear the Reaper'*	1976

TOP
10

ACKNOWLEDGEMENTS

Picture Credits

Alamy Globe Photos/ZUMAPRESS.com 218; Pictorial Press Ltd. 29; WENN 35 below. **Amiga** 167. **Delirium Records** 172 centre. Getty Images Alan Singer/NBC/NBCU Photo Bank via **Getty Images** 120; Alice Ochs/Michael Ochs Archives 49; Andrew Maclear 177; Andrew Putler 27, 32; Andrew Whittuck 206; Andy Earl/Photoshot 267; Andy Sheppard 239; Anna Webber 17; Anne Fishbein 256; Bertrand Rindoff Petroff 273 above; BIPS 30; Blank Archives 273 below; Bob Berg 45 above; Brigitte Engl 180; CBS Photo Archive 35 above, 157 below; Charlie Gillett Collection 83; Chris Morphet 20; Dave Hogan 6, 10, 77; Dave M. Benett 215; Dave Tonge 78, 227, 240, 243 below; David Corio 4, 123 above, 140, 277; David Redfern 61 above, 68, 71 above, 75 below, 75 above, 194, 210, 263; David Redfern/Redferns 138; Djamilla Rosa Cochran 146; Dominique Charriau 238; Eamonn McCabe 233; Ebet Roberts 9, 15, 25 below, 34, 133 below, 133 above, 151, 155, 231, 237, 275; Echoes 105; Epsilon 168; Fin Costello 5, 22 below, 87 below, 163, 207; Francois Corbineau 176; Francois Pages 157 above; Frank Hoensch 14; GAB Archive 28, 81, 143, 254, 280, 281; Gabor Scott/Redferns 85; Gareth Cattermole 235; Gary Wolstenholme 19, 89; Gems 71 below, 253; George Wilkes Archive 118; Gijsbert Hanekroot 43, 66, 148, 161 above, 185, 193, 255; Gijsbert Hanekroot/Redferns 159; Gilles Petard 65 above, 250; Gus Stewart 108, 228; Harry Langdon 213; Hulton Archive 261, 269; Ian Dickson 186; Ivan Keeman 182; Jack Robinson 243 above; Jack Vartoogian 52, 141; Jason Kempin 166; Jean-Claude Sauer 175; Jeff J Mitchell 225 below; Jeff Kravitz/FilmMagic 258; Jim Britt 111, 115 below; Jim Dyson 145; Jordi Vidal 276; Jorgen Angel 165; Justin de Villeneuve 41; Kevin Kane 36; KMazur 38; L. Cohen 191 above; Leon Morris 171 above; Lex van Rossen/MAI 279 above; Lindsay Brice/Michael Ochs Archives 283; Luis Davilla 191 below; M. McKeown 82; Mark Metcalfe 284; Mark Weiss 104; Martyn Goodacre 96, 265 below; Michael Caulfield Archive 212; Michael Ochs Archives 8, 33, 37, 42, 51, 59, 63 below, 63 above, 65 below, 67, 69, 72, 99, 107, 109, 113 below, 115 above, 117 above, 150, 152, 153, 178, 181, 183, 189, 203, 234, 236, 245, 265 above, 268, 270, 278, 282; Michael Putland 13 below, 16, 23 above, 40 below, 61 below, 87 above, 95, 97, 106, 113 above, 119, 179, 204, 217, 219, 249, 257; Mick Hutson 90 below, 135, 200, 214; Mike Barnes 50; Mike Cameron 184; Mike Coppola 25 above; Mike Prior/Redferns 251; NBC 192; New York Daily News Archive 154; Nick Cunard/Photoshot 127; Paul Bergen 92, 139;

Paul Natkin Archive 79, 84, 121, 144, 201; Paul Welsh 46; Pedro Gonzalez

Castillo 171 below; Pete Cronin 1; Peter Pakvis 91, 202; Peter Pakvis/Redferns 221; Peter Still 205; Phil Dent 102, 197 above; Phil Dent/Redferns 125; Photoshot 18, 45 below, 100, 259; Ray Avery 197 below; Ray Fisher 285; Richard E. Aaron 279 below; Rob Verhorst 129 below, 161 below, 162, 199, 229, 262; Robert Altman 54, 209 below; Robert Knight Archive 21, 73; Robert R. McElroy 209 above; Ron Galella 101; Ron Howard 247; Samuel Dietz 93; Shaun Curry 225 above; ShowBizIreland 248; Silver Screen Collection 252; Simon King 131; Simon King/Redferns 223; Steve Eichner 147; Steve Jennings 137; Steve Morley 117 below, 187; Steve Rapport/Photoshot 47; Susie Macdonald 230; Suzie Gibbons 13 above, 123 below, 134; Terry O'Neill 56, 98; The AGE 39; Tom Copi 31; V&A Images 211; Virginia Turbett 129 above, 246; Xavi Torrent 90 above. **Squish** 172 below. **Thinkstock** kyoshino/iStock 48-49, 76-77, 124-125, 158-159, 220-221, 260-261. **ZYX Records** 172 above.